A MASS COMMUNICATIONS DICTIONARY

A MASS COMMUNICATIONS DICTIONARY

A Reference Work of Common Terminologies For Press,
Print, Broadcast, Film, Advertising
And Communications Research

Edited by

HOWARD BOONE JACOBSON

Chairman, Department of Journalism
University of Bridgeport

PHILOSOPHICAL LIBRARY

New York

EDITORIAL BOARD

PREFACE

For more than four hundred years the language of communication has been bound up in print technology. It has only been in this century, with the advent of radio, television and film, that the predominance of the graphic arts has dimmed. However, the golden years of print saw the emergence of a huge, special vocabulary, colorful and explicit within its own sphere. True, the rumble of the presses may not be so loud anymore, but many of the mass media are inevitably tied up with its production.

Books, newspapers, magazines and advertising have been great borrowers and users of print terminology. More recently, there has been a healthy cross fertilization of terms and expressions among all the older and newer media. In fact, the vocabulary of mass communication is seething with change and communicators everywhere are sometimes baffled by the new coinage and multiple-meaning words.

Most of them are of the non-technical variety. The same word will often mean a different thing in each medium, and the terms that are likely to give the greatest difficulty are those which serve double and triple duty for two or three media, that is, the borrowed terms.

There seemed to be a practical need for an encyclopedia-type dictionary of terms and expressions commonly used by the workers in the media of mass communication, and of the characteristic vocabularies of each medium, particularly the language of the print shop, the pressroom, the editorial room, the broadcasting studio, the sound stage, the film laboratory and advertising and public relations agencies.

Here are gathered up the current working terminologies in most phases of mass communication. The entries include a smattering of terms from the vast interrelated technical vocabularies of media technology. No claim is made as to the completeness or inclusiveness of the list. Each term has been carefully chosen or newly defined, keeping in mind the needs of the newcomer to mass communication or to a specific mass medium. For this reason, the list tends to be selective and the terms descriptive.

Terms included were taken from a general literature search, standard source and instructional materials, and many of the media journals. In some cases it was necessary to enlist a subject specialist for a particular field.

The book is in a simple alphabetic arrangement in the style of the encyclopedia, with articles and entries ranging from a few words defining a term, and signed monographs on the more important subjects, to a full section dealing with the functions and implications of mass communication.

Each entry has been classified, indicating the medium with which the term is most often associated. In such cases where a term finds different uses in different media, an entry has been made for each medium. Print, Advertising, Film and General Communication terms are individual categories. Books, magazines and newspapers have been grouped under "Press." Radio and television have been classified as "Broadcast." Initials follow all contributor entries. A list of contributors and a key to their initials will be found on page 4.

I wish to express my appreciation to my wife, Dana, whose talent for organization and suggestions concerning procedure were of invaluable assistance.

Finally, in presenting this book an effort has been made

to fill the need for a simple and comprehensive reference tool which would be easy to use and of interest to student, editor, writer, and experienced mass communicators of all kinds. It is hoped to enlarge the scope of entries for the newer media in future editions, always with the constant challenge in mind of reducing the gap between those who talk "shop" and everyman.

Howard Boone Jacobson

University of Bridgeport
Bridgeport, Connecticut

ACKNOWLEDGMENTS

The editor wishes to thank the following individuals, organizations and publications for permission to use material for which they hold the copyright:

American Photo-Engravers Association and *Modern Photoengraving* for excerpts from Glossary of Terms (Copyright, 1952, J. S. Mertle); Audit Bureau of Circulation; American Technical Society for excerpts from *Graphic Arts Procedures* by R. Randolph Karch (Copyright, 1957, by American Technical Society); Chilton Company for excerpts from *Journalism Today* by Thomas Elliott Berry (Copyright, 1958, by Chilton Company); Columbia University Press for excerpts from *The People's Right to Know* by Harold L. Cross (Copyright, 1953, Columbia University Press) and for excerpts from *The Information Film* by Gloria Waldron (Copyright, 1949, Columbia University Press).

Thomas Y. Crowell Company for excerpts from *Amateur Photographer's Handbook* by Aaron Sussman—partially excerpted from *A Glossary for Photography* by Frank Fenner, Little Technical Library (Copyright, 1939, by Ziff-Davis Publishing Company); James J. Donahue; Free Press for excerpts from *Content Analysis in Communication Research* by Bernard Berelson (Copyright, 1952, by Bernard Berelson); Freedom of Information Center, University of Missouri; Houghton Mifflin Company for excerpts from *Radio, The*

INTRODUCTION

Mass Communication

A technical form of communication which permits rapid transmission of information publicly to large, heterogeneous, and impersonal audiences almost simultaneously.

Communication is co-extensive with society, and a precondition of this life is sharing information and meaning with others. Historically, messages were transmitted face-to-face, but in the modern scene the spheres of communication have widened. Creativity and technology have led to new methods of communication, that is, mass communication as distinguished from interpersonal communication.

Regularized mass communication has long attracted the attention of literary historians, political and social scientists, writers and journalists, and social critics in every age. Fear of the established as well as the newer communication forms of each epoch has been a dominant theme of man through the ages. Cultural patterns "mirrored" by the mass media and the influence and social control of and by the major media as they have developed have also been important concerns.

Yet it has only been in the last few decades that the many speculative consequences and uses of the mass media have come under methical research in an attempt to formulate some specific functions of the mass media for people in organized society.

Reflection of Culture. It was Plato who first suggested in his "concept of imitation" that the literary medium expresses

xiii

social behavior,[1] although the assumption that literary content might "reflect" a kind of *Zeitgeist* or cultural pattern had to wait for its first systematic application until 1800 when Madame de Stael wrote *De la Littérature Considérée Dans Ses Rapports Avec les Institutions Sociales* and later *De l'Allemagne* (1813), books which clearly suggest the relationship between the literature of several nations and the culture in which they were nurtured.

Not long afterward Hippolyte Taine wrote *Historie de la Littérature Anglaise* (1863) in which he advanced the theory that literature was the product of race, epoch and era. He inaugurated a trend which stressed social and cultural determinism instead of personal inspiration, explaining literature as a reflection of such things as economics, family relationships, climate and landscapes, political events, morals, war, religion and other aspects of environment and social life.

The reflection theorists, notably social and literary historians, abstracted from literature such all embracing phenomena which they were able to label as "culture mentality," "spiritual principle," "soul," and *Weltanschauung*.

Another version of the same theme is provided by Marxian dialectics. Literature, along with other "ideologies," is seen as "the mode of production in material life," and is sustained by the ideas of the ruling class which are in every epoch the ruling ideas. But in the dialectic process (manifested in the class struggle), Marx says the literature "expresses the tendencies of a rising and therefore revolutionary class." As Engels points out also, the relationship of economic structure and ideological forms is not causally direct and mechanical.[2]

The Marxian approach has been elaborated, interpreted and applied by Veblen, Caldwell, Fox, Calverton, Parrington and Hicks.[3]

Sociological interest in literature, mainly fiction and biography in "popular" forms, seems to center on the question as to what degree these works reproduce faithfully contemporary problems or "reflect" such social facts as divorce, population difficulties, urbanization, sex status, child development, the family, personality stresses, ideological convictions, etc.[4]

Albrecht states that "this hypothesis is perhaps the most mechanistic version of all, since it postulates that literary data somehow correspond to certain types of statistical data . . . (although) the results have been somewhat profitable in that they indicate the direction of the distortion of statistical facts." [5]

Particular attention has been focused not on the writer but on the content of the novel, particularly the fiction of self-criticism and social problems, which flowered at the turn of this century and which continues to this day at a lively pace.

Perhaps the most important sociological analysis of cultural "image" in literature has been Duncan's work. He conceives of the writer consciously manipulating symbols to conjure up both the world of reality and the world of make-believe. The world of fantasy embodies the hopes and fears of the group and becomes a convenient means of escaping the real world. It also provides a means whereby the individual social inhibitions can be released in an approved manner. He believes that literature is a social institution in that "the roles of the characters are the roles of the society, ideally or realistically portrayed." [6]

This interplay between the social forces of a society and the writer's *Weltanschauung* is analyzed by Lowenthal, who finds the major works of the Western literary tradition an expression and measure of the society to which a writer belongs.

Lowenthal claims:

Other sources describe the occupations and preoccupations of the bourgeois at the time of Molière; but only

xv

Molière reveals what it is like to live this experience. Similarly Goethe depicts the social and occupational problems which faced the sensitive bureaucrat or white collar worker of his time. But the writer not only reports how the individual reacts to the pressures of society; he also offers a picture of changing views about the comparative importance of psychic and social forces . . . Precisely because great literature presents the whole man in depth, the artist tends to justify or defy society rather than to be its passive chronicler. All literary materials, including those hitherto considered beyond the province of the sociologist, therefore assume social meanings.[7]

Lowenthal maintains that whether a creative artist wishes to do so or not, he cannot help exhibiting the shaping forms of his society; that is, the very selections of persons and problems which he must make to create dramatic attention reflect the interests and tensions that shape both society and the writer. He further suggests that historians do the same thing, and points out that diaries, memoirs and the like are full of rationalizations and self-justifications which blur the image of society and events.

As for the more formal research, a content study of popular attitudes in magazine articles by Hart (1933) produced evidence that the treatment of religion in the medium reflected a general weakening in the status of religion among the population during this period.[8] Another "pattern" analysis by Barnett (1939) of the American divorce novel revealed that the medium was "surprisingly sensitive" to changes in public interest about divorce.[9] Wolfenstein and Leites (1950) found a great deal of correlation between the content of American feature films and contemporary culture.[10]

Mills, in his broad evaluations about the American middle class, places a good deal of emphasis on the mass media's role as a "mirror" of modern life.[11]

Inglis attempted to compare actual data on employed women with the fictional version in magazines. Although her results were inconclusive, she did find more employed fictional heroines than real life counterparts. She could not compare the two groups occupationally or by economic status because of a ten year time lag of the fictional group behind the actual employment trend with employed women. She concluded that the "reflection" concept between fiction and society was only partially fulfilled, and because it did not operate consistently in her analysis she did not consider the theory valid.[12]

The relevance of employing communication content as an index to diverse cultural norms which most researchers find "mirrored" in the content is strongly questioned by Berelson. He warns of interpretive pitfalls:

> In the first place, it is important to be completely clear about just *what* is being "reflected" in the communication content. Is it the generalized cultural and psychological level of the total adult population which somehow finds expression through the media? Or do the inferences from content refer only to the audience to the particular communications under analysis? If the latter, then the problem of changes in the composition of the audience in trend studies of content must be faced: that is, the changes in content may reflect changes in audience membership rather than changes in psychological properties of constant population groups.[13]

He first attacks the proposition that the nature of the audience determines the content by suggesting that content is created (1) by individuals whose personal conceptions about life and events determine what appears, and (2) by special interest groups with enough power to influence content. He further argues the cause-effect relationship of content to attitudes, suggesting that a one-valued conclusion is meaningless since there is evidence of mutual influence, one upon the other.

Berelson would avoid the "mechanical" application of content analysis to the study of cultural patterns because "It is difficult to know under what conditions inferences can be validly drawn about the total population or only about the particular audiences; to what extent they refer to the audience proper or to the producer's conception of the audience or to the producers themselves as (untypical) members of the audience; whether they legitimately apply to psychological variables in this sense; whether they are correctly based upon a conception of audience characteristics as a source of the content or as an effect of it or both; whether popular values are somehow identifiable, however roughly, as a direct quantitative function of content emphases. In short, the whole relationship between the content and audience characteristics allegedly "reflected" in it is far from clear. At least it is far from a 1-to-1 relationship, and this fact in itself is a cautionary note against the over-interpretation of content data." [14]

The Influence Theory. The influence theory contends that society is "shaped" or "molded" by mass communication. Whether this "influence" is to be considered beneficial or detrimental to society is still a moot point with researchers, but historically, in most cases, it is evident that the people who are concerned about what they believe to be the good or bad effects of the mass media act on their convictions irrespective of any facts that might refute their position.

Again, an early conceptualization of the idea can be traced to Plato, who in defining his "ideal" state feared that the fundamental laws of that state would be altered by the indiscriminate poet, by shifts in modes of music, and by the introduction of more complex stringed instruments other than the *lyre*.[15] The concept found root in the doctrine of the Christian church, where it remained a dominant force throughout the Middle Ages, and where it found its

xviii

strongest expression in 16th century Catholicism and Puritanism.

Historically, the literary medium was said to wield tremendous influence. Milton's *Paradise Lost* was claimed to have had a great effect on Western ideas about *heaven* and *hell;* Rousseau was credited with having brought on the French Revolution or at least hastened its arrival; Dickens was credited with changing the entire school system of Great Britain by writing *David Copperfield, Nicholas Nickleby* and other books; Harriet Beecher Stowe's *Uncle Tom's Cabin* was blamed for the repeal of slavery and for hastening the start of the Civil War.[16]

Albert Guerard in *Literature and Society* persists with the belief that literary works have set fashions such as "fatal pallor," and that Goethe's *Werther* was responsible for a wave of suicides. He also argues that literature has produced the conceptions of national types and beyond that that literary ideas preceded and "guided" political movements and reforms.[17]

Probably the most enthusiastic claim has been made by Downs, who believes that it is a popular delusion that "books are ineffective, peaceful objects, belonging to the cloistered shades and academic quiet of monasteries, universities, and other retreats from a materialistic, evil world. According to this curious misconception, books are full of impractical theory and of slight significance for the hard-headed man of affairs. Yet throughout history the evidence is piled high that books, rather than being futile, harmless and innocent, are frequently dynamic, vital things, capable of changing the entire direction of events—sometimes for good, sometimes for ill." [18]

The last 50 years have seen reprisals, investigations, laws, codes, controls, etc., enacted on historical assumptions of varying degrees of validity about the "influence" of mass communication. The Nazis burned the books. The Russians strictly control the character of all informational and aesthetic

xix

output. In the United States, it takes the form of benevolent national, state and local censorship.

All such measures have been direct efforts to prescribe informational or artistic production or to prevent its circulation, on the assumption that some works extend and perpetuate values antithetical or disruptive to the existent or emerging social order.

Motion pictures, television, comic books and radio have been blamed as a significant factor in the origination of the social stigma: juvenile delinquency. Blumer and Hauser in *Movies, Delinquency and Crime* (1933) concluded that the motion picture may exert adverse effects on the pre-delinquent by the presentation of the criminal pattern and role with which he may identify.[19] A Senate subcommittee investigating juvenile delinquency took the position that negative sequences in films could trigger off antisocial behavior in the emotionally disturbed child.[20] Mortimer J. Adler, whose *Art and Prudence* is a thought provoking critique of the Blumer-Hauser study, raises strong objections concerning the validity of the findings.[21]

Peterson and Thurstone, who tested a series of films on such subjects as race, nationality, capital punishment and war, did succeed in finding that the attitudes of their viewers changed.[22]

There has been much activity by governmental investigation committees and irate citizens' organizations as to the supposedly negative consequences of certain comic books. Psychiatrist Frederic Wertham in his book, *Seduction of the Innocent* (1954), maintained that crime and horror comics were a significant contributing factor to delinquency. Wertham's claims were based on seven years of clinical and non-clinical studies and observations of hundreds of children and adolescents.[23]

Pittman raises his objection to the Wertham findings on the grounds that the psychiatrist ignored scientific rules for research in his attempt to prove the influence of the comic book variable on the personality of the child. He points to the fact that Wertham did not use the usual procedure of having experimental and control groups to ascertain the differential effects on both the normal and maladjusted children. He further claims that Wertham's sample was top heavy with children who already possessed behavior disorders before their addiction to comics. He concludes that there is "nothing in the comic book causation explanation to indicate that it will be more valid than previous particularistic explanations." [24]

As a consequence of the Kefauver subcommittee hearings to investigate the relationship of television programs to delinquency (1955), articles in popular magazines, the public testimony of many psychiatrists on the subject, and concerned lay groups, television has been indicted as failing to promote respect for law and order, suggesting methods for crimes of aggression and violence, disturbing children with programs of violence, terror and aggression, and contributing to the rise in delinquent behavior.[25]

The Senate subcommittee advanced the idea that the viewing of crime and horror programs was a calculated risk and that for delinquency-prone or disturbed children the risk was even greater. As yet researchers in sociology and psychology have produced nothing more conclusive, and Pittman concludes that "no positive correlation can be established between the content of mass media and delinquent behavior. However, scientific information exists neither in quantity nor in depth to dismiss completely assumptions which maintain that mass media involving presentation of crime, sadism or brutality have a negative impact on emotionally imbalanced personalities." [26]

In Erie County during the election of 1940, Lazarsfeld and Katz found that mass communication apparently had very little to do with changing any votes. Later studies helped to confirm another source of "influence" beyond the media. The two researchers found that *personal* influence and interaction are more important, and mass communication influence less important in forming human opinions. The data demonstrated, however, that mass communication enters significantly into personal influence by giving status to people who use the media.[27]

Other research by Lazarsfeld also suggests what he identifies as a detrimental "narcotizing" influence of mass communication. He presupposes that "quite apart from intent, increasing dosages of mass communications may be inadvertently transforming the energies of man from active participation into passive knowledge." [28]

Berelson proposes that "some kinds of communication on some kinds of issues, brought to the attention of some kinds of people under some kinds of conditions, have some kinds of effects." [29] This premise has been operative in much of the "effect" research during the last twenty years. Recent studies of psychological warfare and opinion research in the armed forces,[30] and studies in innovations [31] and advertising [32] indicate quite clearly that mass communication is an "influence" in society, but at the same time the recent research has helped to delineate the limits and conditions of that influence.

Specifically, it suggests that mass communications seem to be selected in every situation according to individual interests and group sanction, and their influence seems to occur primarily in terms of immediate needs and on the basis of the expected maximization of people's values.

The Social Control Theory. Out of the *Gesellschaft* concept of modern society as an aggregation of somewhat semi-autonomous individuals, has developed the idea that the mass media constitute the directive force which guides, for better or worse, countless, otherwise isolated, individuals into paths of conduct which are collective rather than just individualistic. This premise suggests a "social control" theory of communication.

Such a theory presumes that the dominant means of

control over what the masses believe and think and how the masses act are the press, the radio, the film and television, and that the individual must respond and does respond independently of all other individuals to the symbols emanating from the mass media. Thus, this new communications function would necessarily be that of preserving, confirming and strengthening cultural norms, attitudes and ideologies.

Along theoretical lines, Lasswell has proposed three interrelated functions performed in a community by mass communications: surveillance of the environment, adjustment to the environment, and the transmission of traditional and customary patterns.[33] Using Lasswell's categories, mass communicated information acts to strengthen "influence" and "social control" mechanisms.

Lazarsfeld proposes that mass media clearly serve to reaffirm social norms by exposing deviations from these norms to public view.[34] Several studies by Betty Wang prompted the belief that folk songs preserve cultural ideologies.[35] W. Lloyd Warner and associates discovered that the radio serial drama is essentially a minor morality play adopted to a secular society. It does not entertain its listeners, but rather releases their anti-social impulses, anxieties and frustrations, and provides them with a sense of security and instruction for proper social action.[36]

The recent studies of American soldiers during World War II on the effectiveness of the *Why We Fight* film series showed that the motion picture could strengthen attitudes and affect opinions on specific subject matter.[37]

Festinger and associates found instances in their investigation of a contemporary messianic movement of deliberate reliance upon the mass media to control the conduct of and reduce the dissonance among the formerly media-shy proselytized, once it had been revealed that an announced prophecy had failed.[38]

Inglis finds the social control theory only partially justified in her study of the relationship between fiction and society. At the same time, she casts doubt on the theory since it did not operate consistently, and believes that the problem of the kind and extent of control which takes place still remains.[39]

Even though there seems to be some concurrence in the contemporary literature that the mass media are agents of social control,[40] few scientific studies exist which show the nature and extent of the control which Inglis suggests.

Sociologist Richard T. LaPiere deprecates the current concern over the effects on contemporary society of the mass media. Although he acknowledges that much of the literature seems quantitatively impressive, he insists that most of it is "about as meaningful as the small child's excited prattle over the new puppy." [41]

He states his case with these words:

> The new means of communication certainly have, each in its turn, enabled men to enlarge their social organizations; many of the activities of contemporary societies are directly dependent upon one or more of these new devices; and most activities are at least indirectly influenced by them. But it does not follow that these new forms of communication and the new social organizations they have fostered have changed the laws governing human conduct, including those that determine the processes of social control.[42]

LaPiere would have one believe that a person's knowledge and understanding of events past and present are primarily a function of the group norms with which he identifies or which he holds. Furthermore, he possesses strong doubts about the idea that such sources of vicarious experience as novels, magazines, comic books, motion picture, radio and television make for good or bad conduct solely because of the inherent goodness or badness of the stories. He points out that this view completely overlooks the interpretive role of status groups. And if there is any "influence" or "control" demonstrated, it is probably "status-group mediated." [43]

He expresses his exasperation at the heavy reliance by American propagandists on the so-called "magic powers" of the mass media, reminding that although in the past "mass" procedures have produced marvelous results elsewhere, "men are not automobiles; and the conduct of men cannot be determined by anything analogous to mass production means." [44]

Schramm disapproves of LaPiere's "underestimate" of the function of mass communication in society in the face of the mounting evidence produced by communication researchers of the last twenty years. He charges it is as unrealistic and as belittling as the earlier overestimates of the 1930's, when the images of mass manipulation and persuasion were the popular notion. He believes that any current estimate of the social functions of mass communication cannot and should not ignore all this investigative effort, and persists that there is "everything to be gained by trying to say accurately and specifically what are the limits of the influence." [45]

As has been seen, most of this early communications research attempted to ascertain the influence of the media on attitudes and behavior. Study after study confirmed that the media do less to people than was supposed, and that there are very specific conditions when the media are likely to be persuasive or have more than short run effects.[46] Only surveillance, re-inforcement and supportive functions of the mass media were re-affirmed.

When the disenchantment with the mass influence concept set in, many of the researchers turned to the greener fields suggested by some of the early studies of the uses to which people put the mass media, and particularly with the social and psychological variables in people which are associated with specific media use.

Katz believes that "classifying the audience in terms of some meaningful criterion—as recent studies tend to do—makes possible a powerful connection between the book-keeping tradition of audience research, on the one hand, and the concerns of social and psychological theory, on the other." [47]

This new interdisciplinary approach to mass communication study seems likely to create a new interest in and a greater depth of understanding about mass media effects.

Howard Boone Jacobson

A MASS COMMUNICATIONS DICTIONARY

A

A.A.A.A.

American Association of Advertising Agencies. (Generally known as the 4-A's.) The national organization of the advertising agency business.

A.A.N.R.

American Association of Newspaper Representatives, Inc.

A.A.W.

Advertising Association of the West. A regional association covering advertising clubs in western states and British Columbia.

A.B.C.

Audit Bureau of Circulations. Sponsored by publishers, agencies, and advertisers to audit publisher's circulation statements.

A.B.P.

Associated Business Publications. An organization of trade, industrial and technical publications.

A.C.I.

The Advertising Council, Inc. A non-profit organization dedicated to public service advertising supported by advertisers, agencies and media.

1

A.F.A.

Advertising Federation of America. A national organization composed of local advertising clubs, national advertising associations and sustaining members.

A.F.M.

American Federation of Musicians. The national musicians union.

A.F.T.R.A.

American Federation of Television and Radio Artists. A labor union encompassing actors, announcers, singers.

A.N.A.

Association of National Advertisers.

A.N.G.

American Newspaper Guild.

A.N.P.A.

American Newspaper Publishers Association.

A.P.A.

Agricultural Publishers Association.

A.R.F.

Advertising Research Foundation, Inc. An organization supported by advertisers, agencies and media which promotes greater effectiveness in advertising and marketing through objective and impartial research.

ASA

These letters, which stand for the American Standards Association, are now used (with a number) to indicate the emulsion speed of film. All American film and meter manufacturers, and most of the European ones, now use ASA figures. These film speeds have replaced the Weston, GE, Din, and BSI (British) film speed designations. (F)   A.S.

A.S.C.A.P.

American Society of Composers, Authors and Publishers.

Organization which protects the rights and copyrights of its members and collects royalties on their behalf.

Aberration
Any of several optical errors contained in photographic lenses, and which prevent the instrument from giving perfect definition. (F) **J.S.M.**

Abstraction
A composition or creation suggested by a real object or organic figure which is transformed by the artist into a non-representational design with recognizable elements. (A) **H.V.G.**

Acid Resist
Any coating that does not allow the etching away of a portion of a plate by acid. (PR) **R.R.K.**

Account
The advertiser employing the services of an advertising agency. A term often interchanged with "client." (A) **H.V.G.**

Account Executive
Member of an advertising agency staff who directs and services a client's advertising. Acts as principal contact between agency and advertiser. (A) **H.V.G.**

Acetate
A slow-burning transparent chemical substance used as a film base (F) **G.W.**

Acetate
A type of disc used for recording in the studio; a platter. (B) **N.A.B.**

Achromatic
Free from color. A photographic lens corrected for chromatic aberration, or one bringing visual and actinic rays to the same focus. (F) **J.S.M.**

Acid Bath

The solution in which metal gets its "bite" during an etch. (PR)   H.V.G.

Across Mike

Talking almost parallel to face of mike. (B)   N.A.B.

Across the Board

A radio or TV program broadcast on a Monday through Friday schedule at the same time each day. (B)   H.V.G.

Actinometer

An instrument for measuring the actinicity or chemical power of light. (PR)   J.S.M.

Action

Movement before the camera or on the film. (F)   G.W.

Acutance

The measure of sharpness of a photographic image. It is not the same as "resolving power." The resolution of a photographic image depends as much on the resolving power of the lens as on the acutance of the emulsion. Both are necessary to produce a sharp image. (F)   A.S.

Ad

Abbreviation for advertisement; generally, display advertisements. (A)   B.C.B.

Ad Copy

Copy for an advertisement. It consists of all matter to be printed, with appropriate directions for setting and arranging. (A)   T.E.B.

Adapter

A frame or attachment permitting small plates to be used in plateholders for large process cameras. (PR)   J.S.M.

Add

Additional parts of a story. When the first page of a story

4

is sent to the composing room, it is marked "number 1" or "page 1." The next page is marked "add 1" or "page 2", according to the system used by the particular newspaper. The term "add" is employed similarly by the wire services to identify the consecutive parts of the stories filed. (P) T.E.B.

Additive Exposure System

A proposed system of exposure nomenclature offered by the American Standards Association which would replace conventional f-stops and shutter speeds with a set of Aperture Values (AV) and Time Values (TV). Scene brightness would be indicated by a sequence of Brightness Value (BV) and film speed by a set of Speed Values (SV) which would replace the conventional ASA exposure index numbers. The equation for the system is $AV + TV = EV$ (Exposure Value) $= BV + SV$. (F)

Additive Synthesis

Pertaining to those three-color processes wherein colored lights are blended (added) together to form the sensation of white. (PR)   J.S.M.

Adjacencies

The programs sandwiched, or on either side of a show, all broadcast over the same station. (B)   H.V.G.

Ad Lib

To improvise lines not included in the original script; to talk extemporaneously. (B)   H.V.G.

Ad-Side

That part of the newspaper composing room devoted to the setting in type of advertisements. (P)   B.C.B.

Advance

A story about something not yet happened, hence often to be held for a specified release date. (P)   B.C.B.

Advertisers' Copies

Copies of a publication given free to advertisers in the

5

publication (one copy to each advertiser) for checking their advertisements. (P) A.B.C.

Advertised Price
The price set by the publisher as the cost of a single copy or subscription of a newspaper or magazine. (A) H.V.G.

Advertising Agency
An organization which plans, creates and executes advertising campaigns for its clients. The agency is not legally "agent" but contracts with media in its own name, as an independent contractor. (A) H.V.G.

Advertising Agencies' Copies
Free copies of a publication given to advertising agencies for the purpose of checking advertisements placed by such agencies. (P) A.B.C.

Advertising Impressions
The total number of times a given outdoor display message is observed. (A) R.D.L.

Aerial Image
An image existing in space which can be captured on a ground glass, film, or any other suitable surface. It can also be caught by another lens system. (F) A.S.

Aerial Perspective
An impression of depth or distance in a photograph that depends upon the effect of the atmospheric haze in suppressing distant detail. (F) A.S.

Affiliate
A radio or TV station belonging to or affiliated with a specific network. (B) H.V.G.

Afghanistanism
A criticism leveled against newspaper editors for avoiding community causes and issues and for advocating causes and

6

issues far enough away to remain unchallenged by un-oriented readers. (P)

Against the Grain
Applied to paper folding when fold is made at right angles to the grain of the paper. (PR)   R.A.F.

Agate
Type 5½ or 6 points in depth; smallest used by modern newspaper. Column lengths and advertising space are generally measured in agate lines. (P)   B.C.B.

Agate Line
A unit by which advertising space is sold, measuring 5½ points deep by one column wide. There are 14 agate lines to the inch. (PR)   H.V.G.

Ag. b.f.
Agate boldface type; black-faced agate. (P)   B.C.B.

Aged Developers
Certain classes of developers, employed for suppressing grain in miniature negatives, give much better grain suppression after they have been held or aged for several months after mixing. (F)   A.S.

Agence France-Presse (AFP)
The French national and world news agency which operates as a public establishment of the government and whose revenues are derived from subscription payments. AFP serves France and its territories and maintains news exchange agreements abroad. (P), (B)

Agency
This term in radio and TV usually refers to a talent or program agency which serves advertisers in supplying talent and complete productions for broadcast use. (B)   H.V.G.

Agency Commission
See 15 and 2.

Agent
An individual representing radio and/or TV talent in the sale of their services on various shows. (B)　　H.V.G.

Agitation
Stirring or motion of solutions during mixing and use, such as agitation of developers and etching baths. (PR) J.S.M.

Agony Column
The personal want-ad column. (P)　　　　B.C.B.

Aided Recall
An interview technique used in trying to determine a respondent's level of perception of an advertisement. The respondent usually gets some information or a second look at the ad in context in order to refocus his attention on the initial exposure to the ad. (A)

Airbells
Small bubbles of air occurring in glass and film supports, also those forming on photographic surfaces during development. (F)　　　　　　　　　　J.S.M.

Air Brush
A type of sprayer operating on compressed air capable of producing a very fine spray which gives subtle gradations of tone. Used principally in the retouching of photographs and for smooth backgrounds in posters, etc. (A)　　H.V.G.

Air Brushing
A method used in art studios to add shading to drawings by mechanical means. Air brush work requires the use of halftones for reproduction. (PR)　　　　　　B.B.

Air Check
The recording made of an actual broadcast or any part thereof, either by direct line to the recording studio or by regular radio reception. (B)　　　　　　　N.A.B.

Albumen
White of egg.

Albumenizing
Application of albumen substratum to glass plates for wet collodion photography. (PR)　　　　　J.S.M.

Albumen Plate
A lithographic press plate used for short runs on less exacting work, for runs under 50,000. (PR)　　R.R.K.

Albumen Process
A method of sensitizing metal plates with an aqueous mixture of bichromated albumen, the exposed image rolled up with etching ink before development. (PR)　　J.S.M.

Alcohol Streaks
Longitudinal depositions of alcohol on the surface of wet collodion plates, causing disagreeable blemishes or differences of tone, and due to excess alcohol in the silver bath. (PR)　　　　　J.S.M.

A Lift
The maximum number of sheets of paper placed at one time under the knife of the cutting machine to be cut. (PR)　　　　　R.A.F.

Alive
A microphone that is turned on and "hot." (B) N.A.B.

Alive
Type after it has been set, before it is ready for distribution. (PR)　　　　　R.R.K.

Alley
An aisle in a print shop, as ad-alley, linotype alley, Sunday alley. (PR)　　　　　B.C.B.

All in Hand
Denoting the fact that all copy has been given to the linotype operators. (P)　　　　　T.E.B.

9

All Other

A self-explanatory phrase used specifically in newspaper reports to designate all circulation not included in city and retail trading zones. (P)   A.B.C.

Allotment

See Showing.

Alltone Process

A method of newspaper platemaking involving etching of type matter and halftone illustrations as a single unit on zinc plates, the ordinary non-printing areas of the plate bearing a formation of small halftone dots, which serve as bearers for the inking rollers when printing direct from the plates on rotary newspaper presses. (PR)   J.S.M.

All Up

Term used as a synonym for the sentence, "The copy has all been set in type." It is also used by the various departments of the newspaper to indicate that their work has been completed. (P)   T.E.B.

Alphabet

A set of distinct sign-types from which messages may be generated by selection. (C)   C.C.

Alterations

Changes from original copy, or author's corrections. Expensive—and the printer's bugaboo. (PR)   R.A.F.

A.M.

A morning newspaper. (P)

Ampersand

The old name for the character "&." (PR)   R.A.F.

Amplitude Modulation

The standard method of radio transmission, better known as AM. (B)   H.V.G.

Anaglyph

An illustration giving a stereoscopic or relief effect when viewed through proper color filters or spectacles. (PR) J.S.M.

Anastigmat

A photographic lens corrected for astigmatism. Process lenses are anastigmats. (F)   J.S.M.

Anchoring

Mounting of metal printing plates on wooden blocks by means of screws and columns of solder poured through holes in the blocks. (PR)   J.S.M.

Angle

Viewpoint or premise from which a story is to be written or the slant taken. Hence, the angle may be humorous, serious, etc. (P)   T.E.B.

Angle Bars

Printing press attachments that turn paper into folder or in new direction. (PR)   B.C.B.

Angle, Camera

The viewpoint from which the camera photographs the scene. (F)   G.W.

Angled

The position of an outdoor advertising display, usually in relation to a road or street. The display panel is angled if one end is six (6) or more feet farther removed from the line of travel than the other end. (A)   R.D.L.

Angle Shot

A shot taken after the master scene with the camera in a different position. (F)   G.W.

Angle Tint Tools

Certain tools employed by finishers and engravers and made in sizes ranging from 1 to 12. (PR)   J.S.M.

Angstrom Unit
A minute unit for measuring wavelengths of light; equal to the ten-millionth part of a millimeter, or the 1/254,000,000th part of an inch. (PR)　　　　J.S.M.

Aniline Dyes
Those made from aniline, or products of coal tar. (PR)
　　　　J.S.M.

Aniline Print
An insolubilized image of glue or cold enamel that has been stained with an aniline dye either during or after development, the dyed print promoting greater visibility. (PR)　　　　J.S.M.

Animation
A series of stationary drawings or models photographed one frame at a time. Slight changes in each drawing produce the effect of continuous movement when projected on the screen. (F)　　　　G.W.

Animation
Moving parts of an embellished painted bulletin or spectacular. (A)　　　　R.D.L.

Animation Board
The desk on which the individual drawings are made. (F)　　　　G.W.

Animator
The artist who draws the pictures or makes the models for the animation. (F)　　　　G.W.

Ann.
In a script, indicates announcer's part either on or off camera. (B)　　　　N.A.B.

Answer Print
The print presented by the producer to the sponsor for his final okay. (F)　　　　G.W.

Antique

A rough-surfaced paper stock. (PR)   R.R.K.

Antique Finish

Refers to rough-textured printing paper, which may be had in various grades and weights, both in book paper and cover stock. It is suitable for printing type and line engravings, but it won't take halftones in letterpress printing. Antique finish paper may be had "sized" for offset, and halftones can be printed on it by that process. (PR)   B.B.

Aperture

The opening in camera, projector, sound recorder or positive printer at which each frame stops during exposure, projection, or printing. The diaphragm or opening of a lens which permits the passage of light rays. (F)   G.W.

'A' Picture

The main feature in a movie house showing. (F)

Aplanatic

A lens corrected for spherical aberration. (F)   J.S.M.

Apochromatic

Lenses corrected for chromatic and spherical aberration, and especially designed for three-color photography. (PR)
J.S.M.

Approach

The distance measured along the line of travel from the point where the outdoor advertising panel first becomes fully visible to a point opposite the panel, or where the copy ceases to be readable. (A)   R.D.L.

Arbitron

An automated scoring system for TV shows that employs an electro-mechanical device attached to home TV receivers which records and sends out through telephone lines information on audience size and program switching. (B)

13

Arc Lamp
A powerful illuminant in which an electric current is passed through a pair of slightly separated electrodes or carbons, causing combustion (vaporization) of the carbons and emission of intensely bright light. (PR)   J.S.M.

Argentometer
Hydrometer used for testing silver nitrate solutions, and indicating the strength in grains per ounce of solution. (PR)   J.S.M.

Arrears
Subscribers whose names are retained on active subscription list after period for which they are paid has expired. (P)   A.B.C.

Art
General term for art work, comprising any hand drawn elements of an advertisement. This classification would include illustration, spot drawings, diagrams, lettering, decoration, etc. (A)   H.V.G.

Art
General term for all newspaper illustrations. (P) B.C.B.

Art Buyer
The person in an advertising agency who keeps a file of artists and photographers and arranges for the purchase of art material. (A)   H.V.G.

Art Director
The person in an agency who designs the graphic form of the finished advertisement and who selects the artists to execute the finished art. (A)   H.V.G.

Art Film
A film which explores its subject in a consciously artistic or experimental manner. (F)   G.W.

Art Gum

A soft gum eraser used by artists for cleaning surfaces. (A)   H.V.G.

Artist

1. Layout man—one who specializes in the arrangement of the elements (the headline, illustration, copy, logotype, etc.) of an advertisement or printed matter.

2. Illustrator—one who makes illustrations for reproduction, either product or situation illustrations.

3. Lettering man—one who does hand lettering for reproduction. (A)   H.V.G.

Art Representative

A salesman or agent for a studio, a group, or an individual artist or photographer. (A)   H.V.G.

Ascenders

With reference to type, ascenders are the longer lines extending above the body in some letters, as in the lower case b, d or t. (PR)   B.B.

Aspect Ratio

Aspect ratio is the relationship of the width of the TV picture to the height, which is four units wide by three units high. (B)   H.V.G.

Assignment

Any news-gathering task allotted to a reporter. He may be assigned to obtain a newsstory, or one angle of such a story, or pictures, etc. (P)   B.C.B.

Assignment Book

The city editor's record of assignments given out to reporters. Usually there are "day" and "night" books. (P)
                                                                    B.C.B.

Associated Press (AP)

A nationwide cooperative news agency owned by its

American newspaper members. AP distributes local, national and international news and has exchange agreements with the major world wire services. (P), (B)

Association Subscription
Subscription received because of membership in an association. (P)   A.B.C.

Astigmatism
Inability of a photographic lens to sharply focus both vertical and horizontal lines, especially near the margin of the field or image. (F)   J.S.M.

Astonisher
(1) Name applied by some newspapers to a banner line; (2) name applied by some newspapers to a startling lead; (3) newspaper slang for an exclamation point. (P)   T.E.B.

Attribute
Any property of a phenomenon, thing, event . . . as-sumed, by the observer, to be of significance. (C)   C.C.

Attribution
A characteristic of the standard news story which gives it an objective flavor, wherein the reporter indicates the specific source or authority for statements of fact and opinion as part of the story. (P)

Audience Composition
The makeup or type of people represented in an audience listening to a program with respect to income group, age, sex, etc. (A)   H.V.G.

Audience Duplication
A measure of the number of listeners or viewers reached by more than one program by the same sponsor, or a measure of the potential duplication of exposure to different issues of the same magazine or among different magazines. (A)

Audience Flow

The movement of a specific program audience to or from a station or channel as well as the length of time before switching or turning a station or channel off. (A)

Audience Turnover

The process of change or "turnover" in audiences during the broadcast of a specific program or series of programs over a period of time. (A)   H.V.G.

Audimeter

An electro-mechanical device attached to home receivers which accurately records the pattern of listening. (A) H.V.G.

Audio

The sound portion of a film or television program. (B)   N.A.B.

Audit

Examination of a publisher's records and corroborative data in order to check for correctness the Publisher's Statements covering the period audited. (P)   A.B.C.

Audit Report

Official document issued by the Audit Bureau of Circulations, detailing its findings as the result of audit. (On white paper to differentiate it from Publisher's Statements.) (P)
                                                                A.B.C.

Audit, Traffic

A traffic audit of all potential views of a showing or group of advertising panels in individual plants or entire market areas. Traffic Audit Bureau, Inc. (T.A.B.) verifies or audits the circulation and space position value claimed by plants for their bulletins or poster showings. Audit figures are expressed in terms of: "average daily effective circulation per #100 showing" and "average space position value of the plant."
(A)   R.D.L.

Audition

Trying out or testing a performer or program; usually done before the microphone or camera. (B)　　　H.V.G.

Author's Alterations

Changes from the original copy made after type has been set. Commonly called "A.A.'s." (PR)　　　H.V.G.

Autochrome

The first successful tricolor screen-plate for producing full-color transparencies by a single exposure of objects. (PR)　　　J.S.M.

Autofocal

A term describing enlargers having a link mechanism which keeps the image in focus on the easel as the enlarger head is moved up or down to secure the necessary degree of enlargement. (F)　　　A.S.

Automatic Engraving

Direct production of relief line and halftone printing plates from photographic images by means of automatically operated engraving machines; Scan-a-Graver (PR)　　　J.S.M.

Autotype

German name for halftone photo-engravings. (PR)　　　J.S.M.

Available Light

A system of photography which uses whatever light happens to be available, without resorting to additional artificial light. This requires fast films such as Tri-X and Royal X Pan, or medium speed films such as Plus X with speed-increase developers like Promicrol. (F)　　　A.S.

Availabilities

A listing of time periods available for purchase on a station or stations. (B)　　　H.V.G.

Average Net Paid

Average circulation of all the issues arrived at by dividing the total of all the issues during the period by the total number of issues. (P)   A.B.C.

Avoirdupois

System of weights by which photographic chemicals are sold and formulae compounded in English-speaking countries. It has the grain as a basis and involves a pound containing 16 ounces or 7,000 grains. (PR)   J.S.M.

Axe-Grinder

(1) Editorial that purports to be news; (2) person who has a personal motive (usually publicity for a cause) in supplying news to a paper. (PR)   T.E.B.

19

B

B.M.I.
Broadcast Music, Incorporated. The competitive organization of A.S.C.A.P. subsidized by the broadcasting industry.

B.N.F.
Brand Names Foundation. An organization supported by leading brand manufacturers, agencies and media.

B. of A.
Bureau of Advertising of the A.N.P.A. The promotion arm of the American Newspaper Publishers Association.

B.P.A.
Business Publications Audit. An organization which audits the circulation statements of publications which are sent free to selected lists.

Back Cloth, Back Drop
Any drapery used as a background in photographic work (F)   A.S.

Back Combination
The half of a doublet lens nearest the film. (F)   A.S.

Back Copies
Copies of periodicals of date prior to current issue (P)
A.B.C.

Back Lining
A paper cemented to the backbone of sewed books to bind the signatures and allow space between the backbone of the book and the backbone of the cover. (PR)   R.A.F.

Back Up
Printing on paper of which the reverse side has been printed. (PR)   H.V.G.

Backbone
The bound end of a book. (PR)   R.A.F.

Background
Music or sound effects used as accompaniment to a radio or TV program. Also, the set or scene in a television program (B)   H.V.G.

Backgrounding the News (explanatory writing)
Denotes the kind of newspaper writing designed to give meaning to raw facts by providing historical setting and sequence. Not to be confused with interpretative writing which speculates about the significance of bare facts as well. (P)

Backing, Antihalation
A colored coating applied to the back of photographic plates and films to prevent halation or blurred images. (F)
                                                         J.S.M.

Backing Up
A metal backing soldered to plates generally to make them 11-points thick for printing or making pattern plates. (PR)   R.A.F.

Backlighting
A style of photographic lighting which illuminates the side of subject opposite the camera. Such lighting results in pictures with a "halo effect" around the edges of the subject. (F)   A.S.

Backroom

The mechanical section of a small newspaper plant, as distinguished from the *front office*. (P)   B.C.B.

Bad Break

Term used when body type begins new column with scant line, or quad line, causing awkward appearance. Also when long story finishes a column on end of paragraph, giving reader erroneous impression story is at an end. (P)   B.C.B.

Bait Advertising

An insincere method used to advertise a product at an irresistible price or on some other alluring basis in order to get customers into a store where they may be sold a higher priced item by one means or another. Sometimes called "bait and switch." (A)

Balance

A pleasing arrangement of type masses. (PR)   R.R.K.

Balance

The relationship between various sounds in a studio as they are heard through the microphone. Usually refers to the volume intensity of various instruments in an orchestra. (B)   H.V.G.

Balloon

Lines drawn from mouths of characters in advertisements. Within the area of the lines are words spoken by characters. (A)   P.W.B.

Balop

Abbreviation of balopticon. A projection machine or mechanism used in television to project objects, photographs, still pictures. (B)   H.V.G.

Band

A range of radio frequencies extending from 550 to 1600 kilocycles. (B)   P.W.B.

22

Band Saw

A machine with a continuous saw in the form of a narrow circulating blade, designed for accurate cutting of mounted printing plates to inch or pica measurements; PicaMaster. (PR)   J.S.M.

Bank

Table on which type is kept; also lower portion of headline. (PR)   B.C.B.

Banner

A headline stretching over the top of a page. Also called "streamer," "line," or "ribbon." (P)   B.C.B.

Bare Bulb Flash

The use of flash without a reflector. The effect is a mixture of bounce and available light, less harsh and directional than reflected flash, not as soft as bounce light. *Caution:* Should not be used too close to the face of the photographer, to avoid injuring the eyes in case the bulb accidentally shatters. (F)   A.S.

Barrel Marks

The lettering on a camera barrel that indicates the focal length, F-number, maker's name, and the serial number. (F)   A.S.

Barter Broadcast Time

Spot time for free mentions from stations in exchange for operating capital or merchandise. (A)

Base

Support for a printing plate; synonymous with block or mount. (PR)   J.S.M.

Base

The transparent celluloid film which supports the photographic image in a photosensitive emulsion. (F)   G.W.

Basic Network
A radio or television group made up of a so-called basic or minimum number of stations which an advertiser may buy under contract. (A)   H.V.G.

Basic Price
The price at which the publication may be purchased by anyone, without limitation, for a definite duration, as opposed to a special price for a limited period or to a limited class or under limited conditions. (P)   A.B.C.

Basis Weight
The name given to a sheet of paper in terms of the weight of 500 sheets in a certain size. (PR)   R.R.K.

Bassani Process
Method of highlight halftone photography, involving slight rotation of halftone screen during a portion of the exposure. (PR)   J.S.M.

Bastard Type
Type that does not conform to the standard system of "one point equals 1/72 inch." (PR)   T.E.B.

Bath
Chemical solutions in which film is processed (F)   G.W.

Bath
Embracive term for chemical solutions employed in photoengraving, but specifically applied to silver nitrate, developing, fixing and etching solutions. (PR)   J.S.M.

Bath Holder
Vertical container for chemical solutions. (PR)   J.S.M.

Batten
A pipe suspended above the television studio and used for hanging lights or scenery. (B)   P.W.B.

Baumé Hydrometer
An instrument for determining the relative density and

strength of liquids, particularly those heavier than water.
(PR)   J.S.M.

Bayonet Mount
A device used on some cameras to facilitate the exchange of lenses. Lens has prongs fitting into camera, and a lever locks them in place from within. (F)   A.S.

Beard
The beveled space below the face of a type. (PR) R.R.K.

Bearer
A lead rule, type high, usually 2 picas wide, placed on the four sides of a type form. Also the margin of metal around an engraving. Used to evenly distribute the pressure of molding. (PR)   H.V.G.

Beat
(1) Story printed by one newspaper before its rivals have been able to obtain it; (2) story that is the exclusive property of one newspaper; (3) district or special news source (courts, city hall, etc.) assigned to a reporter. In the first two uses listed, the term "beat" is synonymous with the terms "scoop" or "exclusive." (P)   T.E.B.

Bed
If a printer says he has twenty beds in his shop it doesn't necessarily mean that he runs a hospital on the side, or that his help sleeps on the premises. He is probably referring to press beds; the expression is frequently used in describing pressroom equipment.

The flat surface on which a printing form lies on a press during printing is called a "bed." (PR)   B.B.

Bed
The foundation structure of a bellows camera including bottom plate and the focusing slide rails. (F)   A.S.

25

Bellows

The folding portions which unite the front and back sections of process cameras. (PR)   J.S.M.

Ben Day

Undoubtedly there once was an engraver by the name of Benjamin Day, who gave his name to a very useful process. A Ben Day is now a tint or screen effect for the reproduction of shaded copy in line engravings. Whereas zinc etchings, as such, can only be used for the reproduction of line drawings, type matter, hand lettering, and so on—that is, either lines or solids—the engraver is enabled to achieve shaded effects by the use of Ben Day screens. If copy for line engravings submitted to the engraver carries shaded areas as well as lines and solids, it will automatically be charged for at the Ben Day scale of prices, which is higher than that for straight zincs. There may also be a charge for "tint laying," depending on the copy submitted. (PR)   B.B.

Benday Process

A mechanical method of transferring line and dot patterns to metal, paper and other surfaces by local pressure on inked relief films; bendaying is the operation and art of using such films to achieve illustrative effects. (PR)   J.S.M.

Bendayed Plates

Relief etchings on zinc or copper, on which various tints or patterns were introduced through the medium of benday films. (PR)   J.S.M.

Beveler

A machine for cutting a narrow rabbet or bevel around the edges of square and rectangular printing plates, so as to provide a channel or flange for nailing plates on wooden blocks. The flange is the "bevel" of the plate, and the operation of the machine is known as "beveling." (PR)   J.S.M.

26

Beveling Plane
Shoot board. (PR)   J.S.M.

B.f.
Abbreviation for bold face or black face type. (P)

B.G.
Background. (B)

Bibliotherapy
The notion that the semantic interaction between the reader and print media can precipitate such vicarious experiences as identification, projection, introjection, transference of emotion from early experience, catharsis, or insight which may provide a new frame of reference that permits the reader to understand and to alter reality. (C)

Bichromated Colloids
Various substances (albumen, glue, gum arabic, shellac) used as vehicles in photoengraving, and rendered sensitive in solution by the addition of ammonium bichromate. (PR)
J.S.M.

Billboard
Popular name for what the outdoor advertising industry prefers to call an outdoor poster. (A)

Billboard
The opening announcement or portion of the program that tells what and who may be heard during the broadcast. (B)   N.A.B.

Billing
Total billing of an agency to its clients for gross space, time and talent, production, fees and all other legitimate charges. (A)   H.V.G.

Binary Code
A code which employs two distinguishable signs only (binary digits). (C)   C.C.

Binder
A cover for sheets; one who does bindery work. (PR)
                                                     R.R.K.

Binding
The process of folding, trimming and assembling various elements of a printed folder, brochure or book. (PR)
                                                     H.V.G.

Bindery
A shop where books are assembled. (PR)   R.R.K.

Bit (abbreviation of Binary Digit)
The unit of measurement of quantities of selected information as used in communication theory (C)   C.C.

Bit
A small part in a dramatic program. A performer who plays a "bit" part is referred to as a "bit player." (B) J.C.W.

Bite
The etching action of acid on metal in making an engraving (PR)   H.V.G.

Black and White
Reproduction in one color only, as distinguished from two or more colors. (PR)   B.C.B.

Black and White Line Finish
A narrow black finish line, separated from the edge of a halftone plate by a white line of suitable width. The effect can be mechanically introduced with a lining beveler. (PR)
                                                     J.S.M.

Blade Coating
A finishing process which produces a much more level

sheet for the coated paper (magazine) field. Less coating is required than with the standard roll coated paper. (PR)

Blanket
In offset lithography, the rubber-surfaced roller upon which the image is first printed and from which it is "offset" onto the paper. (PR)   B.B.

Blanket Contract
An agreement between the advertiser and the broadcast station or stations, covering all of the advertiser's products, regardless of the assignment of these products among various advertising agencies. (A)   H.V.G.

Blanket Head
A headline topping all the columns occupied by a given story of newspaper department. It may *blanket* both text and pictures. (P)   B.C.B.

Blanking
The matting of white paper between the sheets of copy and the molding of a poster panel. It adds to the attractiveness of a poster as a mat adds to the attractiveness of a picture. (A)   R.D.L.

Blasting
Placing sound too close to the microphone so that it causes too much volume. (B)   N.A.B.

Bleaching
Whitening of photographic images during intensification, or for purpose of removing the image entirely. (P)   J.S.M.

Bleachout Process
Method of making line drawings on photographs and silverprints with waterproof inks, the image serving as a guide to the artist and afterwards removed by bleaching, leaving only the drawing on the surface of the paper. (PR)
                                                    J.S.M.

29

Bleed

A cut *bleeds* when it runs to the edge of a sheet. Cuts often bleed in magazines, seldom in newspapers (PR) B.C.B.

Bleed Page

An advertisement which is not confined to the editorial margins of the publication, but printed to the very edge of the page. Sold at a premium rate. (A) H.V.G.

Blind Emboss

An impression made by a steel die without ink, resulting in a design in low relief. (PR) H.V.G.

Blind Interviews

An interview story in which the interviewed person is not revealed, *e.g.*, "a highly placed official" or "a spokesman for—." Also called a *lamp-post interview*. (P) B.C.B.

Blisters

Small bubbles formed under the emulsion due to the detachment of the emulsion from the paper or film. (F) A.S.

Block

A series of similar type programs scheduled one after another. (B) H.V.G.

Block

The wood backing under a printing plate to make it the same height as type. (PR) H.V.G.

Block Booking

The practice of requiring an exhibitor to book films other than the ones he wants. Illegal in the U.S. (F)

Blocking

Operation of mounting or nailing printing plates on permanent wood supports. (PR) J.S.M.

Block Flush

To anchor a cut from which the nailing edge has been removed. Usually done by a two-sided adhesive. (PR) H.V.G.

Block Letter
"Gothic" or sans serif type faces. (PR)   R.R.K.

Block Leveler
A machine for milling (planing) wooden and metal mounts of relief printing plates to perfect planity or evenness. (PR)   J.S.M.

Block Paragraphing
The conventional English paragraph includes a complete thought or idea. Newspaper paragraphing breaks a complete thought into subtopic units of that thought to facilitate the insertion of later story matter and the deletion of dated material. (P)

Blocked Up
Highlights in a photograph that are so over-exposed that no definition or detail is to be seen are said to be "blocked up." (F)   A.S.

Blocking Lumber
Specially prepared lumber or wooden panels of good quality, used as a base or support for printing plates to bring them type high. (PR)   J.S.M.

Blocking Nails
Small flat-headed steel wire nails for fastening plates to blocks. (PR)   J.S.M.

Blocking-Out
Painting over portions of a negative with opaque paint (usually an uninteresting background) so that the portions so covered will not print. (F)   A.S.

Blocking Slab
Cast iron or type metal plate about one inch thick, which provides a solid bed or surface on which blocking of plates can be performed. (PR)   J.S.M.

Blockout
An outline or silhouetted halftone plate from which the background has been eliminated by etching or routing: cutout. (PR)   J.S.M.

Bloop
Sound caused by a splice across the sound track. (F) G.W.

Blooping
Patching the sound track on the print to eliminate the bloop. (F)   G.W.

Blooper
Irritating or egregious error. (P)   B.C.B.

Blotter
Office record or orders for carriers, distributors, etc., from which charges are made. (P)

Blowout
Highlight halftone, especially one made from highlight negative. (PR)   J.S.M.

Blowup
An enlarged reproduction of photographs, artwork or other advertising matter for display purposes. (A)   H.V.G.

Blueprint
A photo print made from the lithographer's negative and used as a proof. (PR)   R.A.F.

Blurb
A statement handed out for publicity purposes. (B)
                                                             J.C.W.

Blurred Negatives
Any negative showing indistinct outlines of the image or double outlines is "blurred." This may be due to: (1) A poor lens, (2) Camera out of focus, (3) Holding the camera

32

in the hands with a shutter speed of less than 1/25 second, (4) Object moving too rapidly for the shutter speed, and (5) Underexposure or underdevelopment. (F) A.S.

Blurred Prints
The loss of sharp detail and confused outlines on the print (when the negative is good) may be due to (1) Imperfect contact between the paper and negative, (2) The paper may be against the glass or celluloid back of the negative instead of against the emulsion (3) Loose paper slipping over the negative, (4) The lamphouse or holder of the enlarger may vibrate during the exposure, and (5) The enlarger lens may be out of focus. (F) A.S.

Board
A control panel through which a program passes from the studio control board to the master control or the transmitter. (Broadcast media). (B) P.W.B.

Board Fade
A fade accomplished on the control panel. (B) N.A.B.

Body
The size of type from the bottom of the descenders to the top of the ascenders, excluding leading. (PR) R.R.K.

Body Type
Type used for straight matter composition; regular paragraph type for newspapers and books. (PR) R.R.K.

Boilerplate
Name applied to news matter and features purchased from syndicates in the form of thin metal plates which are attached to metal bases when it is desired to print them. (P) B.C.B.

Boil it Down
A copydesk expression for reducing wordage of a story. (P) P.C.B.

Bold Face

A characteristic of type face which gives the overall effect of blackness, heaviness, boldness. Ex. Bold face. (PR)
H.V.G.

Bond

A type of paper made of rag or sulphite used primarily for stationery and business forms. (PR)   H.V.G.

Book End

Paper used for covering inside of book covers. (PR)
R.A.F.

Bookholder

Special copyholder accommodating open books during photography of pages or matter therein. (PR)   J.S.M.

Booking

Reserving a film to be used at a definite time. (F) G.W.

Booklet

An advertising medium in small book form. Usually made of paper and folded or bound by saddle wire stitching. (A)   H.V.G.

Book Papers

A class of paper used for books, catalogs, periodicals, booklets, and general advertising literature (antique, laid, wove, vellum, eggshell, machine finish, English finish, super-calendered, process coated, and coated). (PR)   R.A.F.

Bookplate

A label placed inside the cover of a book to designate ownership; printing plate for such labels. (PR)   J.S.M.

Boom

A traveling crane used to hold the microphone or camera in a television studio. (B)   H.V.G.

Boom Light

Light on a long arm or spar that is easily adjusted over model or set up at a height of several feet from floor. (F) A.S.

Boom Microphone

A microphone suspended from a boom which can be lowered or raised and otherwise moved about in order to keep the microphone near actors as they move about in broadcast studios. (B)   P.W.B.

Border

Finishing line or design on the printing edges of plate. (PR)   J.S.M.

Border

Strips of type metal used to form boxes about headline or story. These borders come in many forms—stars, dots, wavy lines, double lines, etc. (P)   B.C.B.

Bounce Light

A softer light than regular flash or flood, produced by reflecting the light from a ceiling, wall, or other surface. If color film is being used, make sure the reflecting surface is white or neutral, otherwise there will be an over-all tint to the light. The additional exposure required depends on the color and distance of the reflecting surface, usually from 3 to 5 times the regular exposure. (F)   A.S.

Bourges

Trade name for colored transparent sheets used as overlays on black and white layouts or finished art. (A)   H.V.G.

Box

A rectangle of type rules set around a single item or a part of a page, generally for emphasis or for the sake of balance in arrangement. An "Obit Box" is made up of four point rules or heavier, giving it a very black appearance, and is used for death announcements. If you specify the use of a box, be sure to have the type within it set in at least one and one-half picas narrower measure than your columns; otherwise it won't fit. (PR) **B.B.**

Box Head
A heading inclosed by the strips of metal forming a box. (P) **B.C.B.**

Box Office
Generally used to denote a film's profit potential with the public; its box office results. (F)

Box Set
An almost full-wall construction in a TV or stage setting of a scene or room. (B) **H.V.G.**

Box Story
A newsstory or feature inclosed by a "box." (P) **B.C.B.**

Boy Sales
Sales of single copies of a periodical by boys acting as independent agents. This is no longer a large part of circulation sales of major publications. (P) **H.V.G.**

'B' Picture
The second feature in a movie house showing. (F)

Brand Image
The association of thoughts or atmosphere aroused in the public by the mention of an advertised brand product. (A) **H.V.G.**

Brand Manager
The person in the advertiser's firm responsible for the marketing and advertising of one specific brand. (A) **H.V.G.**

Brand X
The much badgered term employed by some advertising copywriters to refer to the competitive product. (A) (B)

Break

Station identification. (B)   N.A.B.

Break

The point at which a story turns from one column to another; a story *breaks* when it becomes available for publication; news is said to *break* when it happens. (P) B.C.B.

Break for Color

In composition, to separate the parts to be printed in different colors. (PR)   R.A.F.

Break-Off Rule

A line printed clear across a column, or two columns, or a page, intended to indicate that the text above the line has nothing to do with that printed below it. (PR)   B.B.

Bridge

A short phrase of transitional music or sound effects used to connect two dramatic sequences in a program. (B) H.V.G.

Brilliant

A term used to describe a print or negative with fairly strong contrast and sharp detail. In other words, a print with plenty of "snap." (F)   A.S.

Brilliant

The name formerly used to denote the size of type now known as 4 point. (PR)   H.V.G.

Bristol Board

A paper available in several types of surfaces, finishes, and weights, generally used for pen and ink drawing. (A)
                                                            H.V.G.

Broadcaster

An individual who owns and/or operates a radio or TV station. (B)   H.V.G.

Broadside
A promotion piece consisting of one large sheet of paper, generally printed on one side only. (A)   H.V.G.

Brochure
An elaborate type of booklet usually bound with a special cover. (A)   H.V.G.

Bromide
Overused expression such as "hall of fame," "quick as a deer," "fleecy clouds," etc. Also termed a "cliché," a "trite expression," a "stereotype." (P)   T.E.B.

Bromide Print
A photograph, usually an enlargement, made on bromide paper. (F)   J.S.M.

Bronzing
Brushing a fine bronze powder over a freshly printed sheet. The powder adheres to the wet print. (PR)   H.V.G.

Buckeye
An advertisement crude in design, overcrowded, using large, bold type. (A)   H.V.G.

Buffered
A developer so compounded as to retain its power and chemical balance while in use. Usually applied to a solution containing an acid and one of its salts. This increases the stability of the developer since the extra acid is brought into action only as it is needed. (F)   A.S.

Bug
Any type ornament used in a fancy headline or by the side of a cut or layout; also a Morse telegrapher's sending apparatus. (P)   B.C.B.

Build-Up
Method used to promote the popularity of a personality, product or program. (A)   H.V.G.

38

Builds Up

A term applied to the gradual increase in density as metallic silver is set free in print or negative during development. (F) A.S.

Bulk

The degree of thickness of paper. (PR) R.A.F.

Bulk Sales

Single copy sales in bulk—sales of copies of a single issue of a publication in quantity to one purchaser. Subscriptions: Bulk (term subscriptions in bulk)—subscriptions for two or more consecutive issues of a publication sold in quantity to one purchaser. (P) A.B.C.

Bull Pen

The section of an agency art department where comprehensive layouts are rendered from the art director's visual or rough. (A) H.V.G.

Bulldog

Name given an early edition or one printed out of regular hours. (P) B.C.B.

Bullet

A heavy dot, available in various sizes, used to draw attention to phrases in the text. (PR) H.V.G.

Bulletin

Last minute news regarding some important development in a story; it is generally set in heavier type than the body of the story and precedes it. The headline on it reads simply "Bulletin." Each newspaper has its own typography for bulletins. (P) B.C.B.

Bulletin

A large, standardized outdoor advertising panel usually larger than a poster panel. It is painted rather than posted. (A) R.D.L.

Bulletin Types

Deluxe urban—A standard painted display structure with overall dimensions of 13′4″ by 46′10″ and using a conventional base.

Painted wall—A painted display with the copy painted directly upon the wall surface.

Standard Highway—A standard painted display structure with overall size 13′ by 41′8″ and using a contemporary style base.

Standard Streamliner—A standard painted display structure with overall dimensions 15′ by 46½′. (A)　　R.D.L.

Bulletin, Embellished

Any painted bulletin also carrying animation, letters and/or lighting that may extend beyond the normal outlined edge of the bulletin. (A)　　R.D.L.

Bullpup

Name given first mail-edition of Sunday newspapers. (P)　　B.C.B.

Bull's Eye

A magnifying lens mounted on a stand and used by finishers for concentrating light on any area of the printing plate. (PR)　　J.S.M.

Bump-Up Process

Method of etching and treating halftone plates to introduce premakeready in the printing surface. (PR)　　J.S.M.

Bun

Wire symbol for bulletin. (P)　　B.C.B.

Bundling

The tying up of signatures of a book. (PR)　　R.A.F

Buried Advertisement

An ad sandwiched into a page layout so that it is surrounded on all sides by other ads. (A)

Burin

A steel graver or cutting tool with a lozenge-shaped point, used for line engraving on metal. (PR)   J.S.M.

Burned Up

Badly overexposed. (F)   A.S.

Burning-In

A process used in enlarging. It means to give excessive exposure to certain portions of the print while other parts are held back by dodging. Used to darken light areas which detract, or to bring up detail in very dense portions of the negative without overexposing other portions. (F)   A.S.

Burning-In

Heating a developed glue print on copper or zinc to bake the enamel image and impart resistance to acids or mordants; in etching, application of heat to a plate dusted with etching powder, so as to fuse or melt the applied powder. (PR)
J.S.M.

Burnish

A "last resort" engraving technique, rarely used in one-color halftones, by which the dark portions of an illustration are made darker and more "contrasty." The theory of the process is that the halftone dots are rubbed down an infinitesimal degree, thus decreasing the area of white space that shows between them. In nine out of ten cases it would probably be cheaper and more satisfactory to make a plate over than to attempt burnishing, but it is sometimes resorted to in the case of complicated engravings where time is a factor. Strictly a "headache," to be avoided if at all possible. (PR)   B.B.

Burr

Thin ridge or shoulder of metal left on surface of printing plate by graver, saw, router or cutter. (PR)   J.S.M.

41

Business

Visual action indicated by the TV writer or developed by the director or performer to clarify the character or situation. (B)   N.A.B.

Business Publication

A business publication is one dealing with management, manufacturing, sales or operation of industries or some specific industry, occupation or profession, and is published to interest and assist persons actively engaged in the field it covers. (P)   A.B.C.

Butt

Refers to separate engravings that are to be printed flush against one another. The position of the shoulders on the engravings determines how closely together they can be printed. If you plan to use pictures in this way, discuss the possibility of having them made together, or mounted together, with your engraver. If neither is practicable, be sure the shoulders are placed on the sides that do not butt.

The expression is also used occasionally in connection with linotype slugs. Most linotype machines cannot set lines longer than 30 picas; it is necessary therefore, to butt the slugs together if longer lines are required. (PR)   B.B.

By-Line

Reporter's name placed over the story. Thus we read, "By Joseph K. Preston." (P)   T.E.B.

By-line Story

Any signed story in the newspaper. (P)   B.C.B.

C

C.lc.
Abbreviation used for capital and lower case letters. (P)

C-Print
An inexpensive color reproduction of color art, without
the high fidelity of a dye transfer print. (A)   H.V.G.

Cab
The carriage or negative carrier used in the three-point
bar system of color composing; the line negative or photographic image employed in color composing for accurate
                                                      J.S.M.

C.U.
Television term referring to close-up, or close shot. (B)
positioning of continuous tone separation positives. (PR)
                                                      P.W.B.

Cabinet
An enclosed chest used to hold type cases. (PR)   R.R.K.

Cablese
Abbreviated or coded copy sent by code. (P)   B.C.B.

California Job Case
The shallow wooden drawers in a print shop divided
into many compartments to which each letter of the alpha-

bet is assigned. Capital letters occupy the right end and lower case letters occupy the left end of the drawer. The type case got its name because it was designed by a resident of California. (PR)

Calender
A paper-making machine which gives the finish to paper. (PR)   R.R.K.

Calendered
A term descriptive of a high-surfaced paper procured by passing paper between calender rolls. (PR)   R.A.F.

Call
The offer of a job on a show received by an actor, singer, or musician. The time that a rehearsal starts. (B)   H.V.G.

Call-At-Office Subscribers
Subscribers who obtain their copies at office of publication. (P)   A.B.C.

Calligraphy
Lettering or type style derived from writing with a broad tipped pen. (A)   H.V.G.

Call Letters
Letters assigned by the F.C.C. to each station. (B) H.V.G.

Call Reports
Agency man's reports of contacts with clients, or prospective clients. (A)   P.W.B.

Camera
Light-tight apparatus or box with lens for photographing subjects and originals. (F)   J.S.M.

Camera
A unit which converts a visual image into electrical impulses by means of an optical system and light-sensitive pickup tubes. (B)   H.V.G.

44

Camera Angle

The point of view from which the subject is photographed. (F)   A.S.

Camera Extension

Strictly, the distance between the exit node of the lens and the focal plane in which the film lies. When focused on infinity the camera extension equals the focal length of the lens. (F)   A.S.

Camera Lucida ("Lucy")

A series of lenses by which a drawing may be enlarged or reduced to any desired size. (A)   H.V.G.

Camera Mixing

The television control room operation by which pictures from the various studio cameras are selected for transmission. (B)   H.V.G.

Camera Rehearsal

A dress rehearsal where all the cast is in costume and the complete production is shot by a cameraman for final check-up before telecasting. (B)   H.V.G.

Camera Reporting

Televising a program not specifically planned and arranged for television; for example, putting a legitimate stage play before the cameras without adaptation. (B)   H.V.G.

Camera Scaling

Equipping a process camera with scales or other devices which permit bringing images to correct size without measurement on a focusing screen. (PR)   J.S.M.

Camera Shots

The angle and distance relationship of the subject to the camera. The composition of the picture as "seen" by the camera. (B)   H.V.G.

Camera Stand
Heavy frame or support for process cameras, designed to absorb or prevent vibration of the camera proper. (PR)

J.S.M.

Campaign
A series of coordinated advertisements using a definite theme or appeal planned to accomplish a specific task. May be local or national in scope and last from a few weeks to several years. (A)

H.V.G.

Campbell's Soup Position
The traditionally requested right-hand page opposite a magazine's editorial page by this soup company. (A)

Can
A metal container for shelving or shipping films; also, the mixer's earphone. (F)

G.W.

Canned Copy
Copy released by press agents. (P)

B.C.B.

Canned Music
Recorded music or transcriptions. (B)

J.C.W.

Canon 35
Section 35 of the Canons of Judicial Ethics of the American Bar Association denies photographers the right to take pictures in the courtroom during sessions. The argument is that picture-taking, broadcasting or televising detracts from the dignity of the court and creates misconceptions in the public mind about court proceedings. (P), (B)

Capacity (of an Information Store)
The maximum number of independent binary digits which may be stored unambiguously. See limiting capacity. (C)

C.C.

Caps
Abbreviation for capital letters. (PR)

H.V.G.

Caps and Small Caps
Two sizes of capitals made on one side of type body, commonly used in most forms of roman letters. (PR) R.A.F.

Caption
Text matter describing an illustration. Also called "title." (A) H.V.G.

Caption
Literally, any heading, but used specifically in regard to picture headings and accompanying text. Usually over a picture, whereas a *cutline* goes under a picture. (P) B.C.B.

Carbon Print
A photograph made on carbon tissue. (PR) J.S.M.

Carbons
Long cylindrical rods of baked carbon, used as electrodes or light sources for arc lamps. (PR) J.S.M.

Carbon Tissue
A light-sensitive, gelatin-coated paper stock used in gravure plate-making. (PR) R.R.K.

Carboy
A large glass bottle encased in a protective wooden box, and serving as a container for acids and corrosive liquids. (PR) J.S.M.

Carbro
A photographic print in color, usually made from three separate negatives. (A) H.V.G.

Car Card
A small card generally with poster-like design placed in buses, street cars and subways. (A) H.V.G.

Cardboard Engineer
A specialist in the mechanics of designing display and packaging material. (A) H.V.G.

Carrier
The adjustable bars in a plate-holder for process cameras. (PR)   J.S.M.

Carrier
Individual engaged in delivery of papers as independent contractor, or appointed; not a U.S. mail carrier. (P) A.B.C.

Carrier Delivery by Independent Carriers Filing Lists.
System of newspaper operation by which accounts with subscribers are kept and collections are made by the carrier on his own account, who furnishes a list of such subscribers to publisher periodically. (P)   A.B.C.

Carrier Delivery Office Collect System
System of newspaper operation by which accounts with subscribers are kept in office of the paper and collections are made by the paper's own employes. (P)   A.B.C.

Carrier, Independent
On who carries or delivers newspapers to subscribers but who keeps his own account, the publisher having no record of these subscribers. (P)   A.B.C.

Carry Over
A continuation of a story or article farther back in the book, generally with the notation "Continued on page—."
(P)   B.B.

Cartridge Film
A roll of sensitized film wound on a metal spool, the roll being encased in a metal casing (cassette) for protection against light and dampness. Film feeds out through slit in casing. Used mostly with 35 mm films. (F)   A.S.

Cartouche
An ornamental design or frame generally in an oval shape. (A)   H.V.G.

Case

(1) Cabinet at which the printer works; (2) terminology used for capital and small letters. Thus, a printer speaks of "upper case" and "lower case" letters. (PR)   T.E.B.

Case Bound

A book with a stiff cover, which is made separately, the sewed book being inserted. (PR)   R.A.F.

Case Stand

A framework used to hold type cases. (PR)   R.R.K.

Casein

An opaque water-based pigment which has been mixed with casein to give a more permanent pigment and color. (A)   H.V.G.

Cash Discount

A deduction allowed by media (usually 2% of the net) for prompt payment, passed along by the agency to the advertiser so as to be able to collect and pay media promptly. (A)   H.V.G.

Cassette

A container for roll film which may be loaded in the darkroom and used subsequently for daylight loading of the camera. (F)   A.S.

Cast

To force metal into a mold and against matrices, as in line-casting machines. (PR)   R.R.K.

Casting Box

A device for casting flat stereotypes. (PR)   R.A.F.

Casting Director

The agency or station executive responsible for auditioning and selecting talent for parts in radio or TV programs. (B)   H.V.G.

Catch Lights
Reflections, generally in the subject's eyes when portraits are being made, from the light sources used for illumination. (F)   A.S.

Catchline
Guideline or slugline used to identify a story before the type is set in page form. Thus, a story slugged "kill" will bear that catchline at the top of the type until the type is set in the page. (P)   T.E.B.

Cells
The individual frames used in animation. (F)   G.W.

Celluloid Proof
Ink impressions made on celluloid, heavy cellophane or other transparent material; used as an aid in registering colorplates, and sometimes as artificial positives in photography. (PR)   J.S.M.

Cellulose
A fibrous substance used to make paper obtained from cotton, linen, hemp, and wood. (PR)   R.R.K.

Cellulose Acetate
A transparent sheet, insoluble in water, used for films, reproduction proofs of type, and a base for deep etch stripping in offset-lithography. (PR)   R.R.K.

Cement
Adhesive used to join together two pieces of film. (F)   G.W.

Center Spread
An advertisement appearing on the two facing center pages of a publication, printed as a single sheet. (A)   H.V.G.

Centered
Placed in the center of a sheet or line. (PR)   H.V.G.

Chain Break

A live or transcribed commercial announcement between two network programs. Usual length is 15 to 20 seconds transcribed, or 50 words live. (B)   H.V.G.

Chain Marks

The parallel lines on laid paper parallel with grain usually about one inch apart. (PR)   R.A.F.

Chairman

Printers' union title for head of office branch, or chapel. (PR)   B.C.B.

Chalking

Application of magnesium carbonate to etched halftone plates, the material (chalk) filling the etched areas and imparting good visibility to the halftone image for study of tone values and progress of etching. (PR)   J.S.M.

Chalk Overlay

An overlay mechanically made; used in making ready halftone plates in letterpress printing. (PR)   R.R.K.

Chalky

Applied to negatives or prints which show excessive contrasts. (F)   A.S.

Change-Over

A change from one projector to another without interruption of picture or sound. (F)   G.W.

Channel

A group of wave lengths or operating frequencies assigned to radio and television stations. (B)   H.V.G.

Chapel

A very old term in the printing unions. It is believed that the term is derived from the fact that Caxton set up his first printing press in a chapel adjoining Westminster Abbey.

The chairman and spokesman of the chapel is known as the father of the chapel. Union members in a town and usually the surrounding area form a branch, and the branch is represented on a district council.

The chapel deals with internal office affairs, the branch with the wider concerns of the members. General questions of union policy are considered, contributions are collected, and applications for benefits are made by the branch. (PR)

Charcoal
A piece or pencil of fine charcoal used for drawing. Also refers to an illustration done in charcoal. (A)　　　H.V.G.

Charcoaling
Polishing a metal plate by rubbing with wet charcoal. (PR)　　　J.S.M.

Charter Subscription
Subscription taken with guaranty to subscriber that subscription price will never be raised to charter subscriber, provided he renews regularly on expiration. (P)　　A.B.C.

Chase
Frame in which all the metal (type, cuts, etc.) for a given page is placed. In large print shops, the stereotype mat is cut from the chase; in small print shops, the chase is used on the press. (PR)　　　T.E.B.

Chase
Frame or negative carrier used on photocomposing machines. (PR)　　　J.S.M.

Chaser
An extra edition, usually following the final home edition. (P)　　　B.C.B.

Check Binding
A book side-stitched with board sides, covered with marble paper, cloth back, cut flush. (PR)　　　R.A.F.

Checking
Process of recording and verifying actual appearance, reproduction, and position of advertisement in magazine, newspaper, or use on radio station, television station, billboards, etc. (A)   H.V.G.

Checking Copy
A copy of a publication sent to an advertiser and his agency as proof that the advertisement appeared as ordered. (A)   H.V.G.

Check Up
A copyeditor may check up or verify a story (P) B.C.B.

Cheesecake
The slang news photographers commonly use for pictures generous in revelation of female legs. (P)   B.C.B.

Chemical Development
Development by chemical action in a solution, in distinction to physical development. (F)   A.S.

Chemical Focus
The point at which the actinic rays of light are brought together when focused by a lens that is not corrected. (F)
                                                          A.S.

Chemical Fog
Fog produced on paper or films by chemical means, such as a too energetic or contaminated developer. (F)   A.S.

Chemical Reversal
Converting a negative to a positive (or vice versa) by chemically treating the photographic image. (PR)   J.S.M.

Chewed Plate
Imperfect etching, in which the lines or dots have been attacked and rendered ragged or broken by untoward action of the mordant, or failure of the acid resist. (PR) J.S.M.

Chiaroscuro

The effect of the distribution of light and shadow in a picture. (F)   A.S.

Chinese Brushes

Oriental writing brushes used for application of ferric chloride solution in re-etching copper halftones. (PR) J.S.M.

Chinese White

An intense white used for cleaning up lettering, silhouetting photographs, etc. (A)   H.V.G.

Chisel

Tool used by finishers to remove burrs and excrescences from surfaces of printing plates. (PR)   J.S.M.

Chisel Point

A type of pencil point used to give a crisp, clean lettering indication for rough layouts. (A)   H.V.G.

Choreographer

The director or arranger of original specialty dance or ballet numbers. (B)   H.V.G.

Chroma

The degree of intensity from black to white. (PR) R.R.K.

Chroma Key

A camera which is made "blind" to a certain color and which can produce optical tricks during a color television production. (B)

Chromatic Aberration

Inability of a photographic lens to bring yellow and red rays to the same focus of blue and violet; lack of color correction. (PR)   J.S.M.

Chromatone

Photographic colorprint process. (PR)   J.S.M.

Chromium Dermatitis

A recognized occupational disease in photoengraving, causing sores, ulcers and various afflictions by absorption of bichromates or chromium compounds through the skin, or by wounds on the hands or bodies of workers. Also known as bichromate or chromic poisoning. (PR)   J.S.M.

Cinching

Tightening loosely-wound film by pulling on the free end of it. Invariably causes scratches on the surface of the film which reproduce as black lines on the print or enlargement. (F)   A.S.

Cinematographer

The cameraman in charge. (F)   G.W.

Cinematography

Film-making. (F)   G.W.

Circle of Confusion

The diameter of the circle created by a lens photographing a true point. The smaller the circle of confusion, the sharper the print will be when the negative is enlarged. (F)   A.S.

Circle of Illumination

The circular area on the focusing screen illuminated by light passing through the lens. There is no sharp boundary, as the amount of illumination decreases gradually at the edge of the circle. (F)   A.S.

Circulars

Advertising matter in the form of letters and handbills. (A)   R.R.K.

Circus Makeup

A method of making up a newspaper's pages in which the columns are broken up by many headlines of various sizes and many kinds, with no thought to regularity, symmetry or apparent order. (P)   B.C.B.

City Editor
The editor in charge of the city room; one who handles local news. (P)   B.C.B.

City Mail Subscription
Subscription served by mail in the established city zone of the publication. (P)   A.B.C.

City Room
The room in which local news is handled. (P)   B.C.B.

City Zone
City Zone is the corporate limits of the city in which the newspaper is published. Contiguous areas may be included in the zone to the extent they have substantially the built-up characteristics of the city and thus cannot readily be distinguished from the city itself. (P)   A.B.C.

City Zone Circulation
The sales of newspapers within the corporate limits of the city of publication, or, in some cases, including territory beyond the corporate limits. In the latter cases the Audit Bureau of Circulations determines the "city zone." (P)
    H.V.G.

Clasp
An envelope whose flap is secured by a small metal fastener. (PR)   H.V.G.

Class Magazines
Publications with sophisticated or serious story matter which are usually read by middle and higher income or status conscious people. (A)

Claw
A mechanism in camera and projector that pulls the film into place as it unwinds. (F)   G.W.

Clayboard
Drawing paper bearing a thick coating of baryta white (barium oxide). It is removable with a needle or knife. (PR) J.S.M.

Clean Proof
Proof needing few corrections. (P) B.C.B.

Clear
Term used to indicate completed action. Thus, a story "clears" the copy desk when it leaves for the composing room. When a department completes its work, it is said to be "all clear." Thus, the city room is "all clear" when all stories for an edition have been written and sent to the copy desk. (P) T.E.B.

Clear a Number
Receiving permission from the publisher or composer of a musical composition to perform it on the air. (B) H.V.G.

Clearing
Removal of veil, fog, scum or stains from photographic negatives, especially wet collodion images. (PR) J.S.M.

Client
The advertiser employing the services of an advertising agency. (A) H.V.G.

Clipping Bureau
A firm which checks publicity or develops advertiser leads and name lists. (A)

Clips
Abbreviation for clippings from current newspapers or from files in morgue. (P) B.C.B.

Clipsheet
A sheet, usually printed, containing several publicity stories which can be clipped. (P) B.C.B.

Clogged

Term used in reference to shadow parts of a print or highlights (dense portions) of a negative when they are one heavy tone instead of showing differences in tone in the subject. (F)   A.S.

Closed Circuit

For radio or television—a program designed for a special group, not for general broadcast. May be limited to a number of rooms in one building, to a number of buildings in one city, or to a certain number of cities. (B)   P.W.B.

Close-Up

A close view, so that the photographed image fills nearly all the screen. (F)   G.W.

Closing Date

The day when all copy and plates must arrive at the publication if advertisement is to appear in a particular issue. Also known as "deadline." Closing dates are specified in advance by the publisher. (A)   H.V.G.

Cloze Procedure

Derived from the term "closure" which refers to the notion that humans tend to perceive a familiar pattern as a whole even when parts of it are missing or distorted, the concept has been used to predict communication success by contrasting the "readabilities" of printed materials. Mutilated passages are used which have had deleted words replaced by blank spaces. Subjects are asked to guess the missing words and the "cloze score" for any passage is the total number or percentage of its missing words filled in correctly. The passage that scores the largest total of correct fill-ins is considered "most readable" for the individuals tested. (C)

Club Bundle

Three or more mail subscriptions, which are wrapped

together in one package to facilitate handling by the post office, going to the same post office. (P) T.C.M.A.

Club Raiser

Person who takes subscriptions in clubs. Differs from "group organizer" in that the club raiser may sell subscriptions at any price between the full basic price and 50 per cent thereof. See group organizer. (P) A.B.C.

Clubbing

A magazine subscription practice which allows potential subscribers to choose several magazines from an inclusive list at reduced rates. (P)

Clubs

Two or more subscriptions to the same publication obtained by solicitors, not part of publisher's organization, under plan of offering specified reward for sending in a specified number of subscriptions. (P) A.B.C.

Coated Paper

A paper which has been chemically treated to provide a very smooth surface suitable for printing fine screen halftones. (PR) H.V.G.

Coaxial Cable

A specially designed cable in television to carry the picture signals from the camera to the transmitter or from station to station on a TV network. (See Micro-wave.) (B) H.V.G.

Code

An agreed transformation, or set of unambiguous rules, whereby messages are converted from one representation to another. (C) C.C.

Cognitive Dissonance-Consonance Theory

A theory of human behavior which suggests that individuals acquire new information via social communication, mass media, etc., in order to increase the existing consonance (the internal state of reduced physiological tension), and thus cause the total dissonance (tension, uncertainty, ambiguity, etc.) to be reduced. The cognitive theory of dissonance suggests that communication has "consummatory" and "instrumental" purposes, that is, it has become an instrument to elicit immediate or delayed responses from other people to achieve dissonance or consonance ends. (C)

Coincidental Survey
A telephone survey to determine listening, viewing or reading activity at the time of the phone call. (A)

Coincidental
A program rating method which involves the sampling of its radio or TV audiences by telephone call during the time the program is on the air. (A)   H.V.G.

Col.
Abbreviation for column. (P)   B.C.B.

Cold
Starting a program without a theme; going into a program without rehearsal. (B)   N.A.B.

Cold Enamel
Photoengraving sensitizer for metal plates consisting of a solution of bichromated shellac, the image being ready for etching after development and drying of the print. (PR)
J.S.M.

Collage
A term used to designate a montage effect made by pasting up a composite photograph from portions cut from other photographs. The paste-up is usually copied on a new negative. (F)   A.S.

Collating
Assembling all ages or elements of a publication after they have been printed. (PR)   H.V.G.

Collodion
Mixture of pyroxylin in a solution of alcohol and ether. (PR)   J.S.M.

Collodion Base
Plain (or weakly iodized) negative collodion. (PR) J.S.M.

Collodion Emulsion
Negative collodion emulsified with silver bromide, with or without the addition of color sensitizing dyes. (PR) J.S.M.

Collodionizing
Act of coating glass plates with negative collodion. (PR)   J.S.M.

Collodion, Negative
Special photographic collodion salted or impregnated with iodides and other salts, and intended for production of images on glass plates by wet collodion procedure. (PR)   J.S.M.

Collodion Process
Wet collodion photography. (PR)   J.S.M.

Collodion, Stripping
Plain collodion containing castor oil, applied to rubber-coated wet collodion images to increase their strength before transfer (stripping) to final glass support. (PR)   J.S.M.

Colloid
Water-soluble non-crystalline substances of gelatinous nature (albumen, gelatin, glue, gum arabic, dextrin) employed as vehicles in photomechanical sensitizers and rendered light sensitive by addition of a bichromate. (PR)   J.S.M.

Colophon
An inscription at the end of a book with facts about its production, such as the kind of type used. The word is also used to describe a publisher's emblem on the title page or spine of a book. (PR)

Color
Representation of hues other than black or white, a phenomenon manifested only in the presence of light, and due to differences in the length and vibration-rapidity of light waves. (F)   J.S.M.

Color Analyst
An apparatus operating on the principle of additive synthesis and designed to show a full-color picture from monochrome color separation prints or halftone proofs as an aid in judging the results of color photography and plate-making. (PR)   J.S.M.

Color Artist
Benday artist. (PR)   J.S.M.

Color Chart
Colors in various hues printed or painted on a chart, and used for testing the specific sensitivity of photographic plates, as well as the effect of color filters. (PR)   J.S.M.

Color Composing
The accurate assembly and exposure of two or more continuous tone positives on a single photographic plate, the positives made from different separation negatives and correctly positioned according to the requirements of the particular color job. (PR)   J.S.M.

Color Correction
Improvement of color rendition by masking of separation negatives, or by treatment of printing plates; eliminating chromatic aberration in a lens. (PR)   J.S.M.

Colorfilm

Modern multilayer photographic film (Kodachrome, Ansco) capable of producing colored positives by exposure and processing of the image. (F)   J.S.M.

Color Filter

Sheet of colored gelatin, glass or plastic used on lenses to absorb (filter) certain colors for better rendition of others while photographing subjects or originals; tricolor filters are those used to "separate" primary colors in three-color photography. (PR)   J.S.M.

Color Form

Type and printing plates comprising the elements which are to print in a given color on a printing job of two or more colors. There is a separate form for each color to be printed. (PR)   H.V.G.

Color Guide

Scheme, instructions or supplementary originals to facilitate accurate color reproduction by indicating hues desired. (PR)   J.S.M.

Coloroto

Rotogravure in colors. (P)   B.C.B.

Color Overlay

A transparent paper overlay on a black and white drawing on which colors are indicated as a guide for reproduction. (A)   H.V.G.

Color Photography

Photographic reproduction of a subject or original in its natural colors; photography of any colored original to record one or more colors. (F)   J.S.M.

Color Process Plates

Halftone colorplates, particularly those made from separation negatives. (PR)   J.S.M.

Color Proof
Proof of combined and registered plates printed in proper colors. (PR)   J.S.M.

Color Scale
Gray scale. (PR)   J.S.M.

Color Scanner
Any of various photoelectrical or electronic devices for production and automatic color correction of continuous tone separation negatives made from multi-color originals, the devices intended for more accurate balancing of a set of four-color images and the elimination of undercolors therefrom. (PR)   J.S.M.

Color Separation
When making black and white plates from colored copy, or when making plates for color reproduction, it is necessary for the camera operator to subtract, as it were, the unwanted colors. This is done photographically by the use of a color filter which absorbs the other colors. Necessarily, there is an extra charge for this operation.

The term is also used in the composing room to designate the operation of physically separating the different typographical elements which are to appear in another color. Also referred to as "breakup for color." (PR)   B.B.

Color Temperature
Means of measuring and indicating the spectral quality of visible light by determining the relative amounts of blue and red rays in sources of illumination. Measurement is done with specially designed meters and is expressed in degrees Kelvin ($^\circ$K), which are equivalent to the actual temperature of the light source, plus 273 degrees Centigrade. (PR) J.S.M.

Color Toning
A method for coloring a black and white photograph by the use of bleaches and dyes. (A)   H.V.G.

Color Transparency
A full-color positive image on screenplates or colorfilms; a positive image on a transparent support and rendered in natural colors. (PR)   J.S.M.

Color Sensitizing
Increasing the color sensitivity of emulsions on photographic plates and films by addition of certain rare dyes or "color sensitizers." (PR)   J.S.M.

Color Screen
Color filter. (PR)   J.S.M.

Colorwork
Production of any type of photoengraving in two or more colors. (PR)   J.S.M.

Colotone
Special form of shading sheet intended for color correction and as an aid in color reproduction. (PR)   J.S.M.

Colotype
See Photogelatin. (PR)

Column
One of two or more sections of type composition separated by a rule or a blank space; e.g., newspaper column. Also a regular feature article written by a special editor or columnist. (P)   H.V.G.

Column Rules
Strips of rule used between columns. (PR)   R.R.K.

Comb
A rake-like tool matching the ruling of halftone screens and used by finishers as a multiple graver. (PR)   J.S.M.

Combination Plates
Printing plates in which both line and halftone images

are combined on one surface, either for monochrome or multicolor effects. (PR)   J.S.M.

Combination Printing
Combining parts of several negatives in one print; a method by which a sky can be printed into a landscape, etc. (F)   A.S.

Combination Rate
Reduced rate for advertising which appears in both morning and evening newspapers published by the same firm. Many publishers of morning and evening newspapers sell their space only in combination. (A)   H.V.G.

Combination Sale
Subscriptions to two or more different publications sold at a special combination price. (P)   A.B.C.

Combined Bath
A mixture which both tones and fixes the prints. (F)
                                                         A.S.

Comets
Peculiar tail-like blemishes occurring in wet collodion images. (PR)   J.S.M.

Comic Strip
Continuity style art work with pictures and balloon captions, similar to newspaper comic strips. (A)   H.V.G.

Commercial
The sponsorship of a program by an advertiser. Also, the advertiser's message presented during the program as a separate announcement. (B)   H.V.G.

Commercial Film
A sponsored industrial film or a film for theaters. (F)
                                                         G.W.

Commercial Signs
Usually recognized as signs other than standardized out-

door advertising displays, but which also advertise products and services for sale. (A)   R.D.L.

Commission

Compensation allowed by individual advertising media to the advertising agencies which they "recognize," in payment for the service and development of advertising; usually 15% of the gross cost of space or time. (A)   H.V.G.

Communication

Broadly: The establishment of a social unit from individuals, by the use of language or signs. The sharing of common sets of rules, for various goal-seeking activities. (There are many *shades of opinion*.) (C)   C.C.

Communication Arts

The many arts which are used in the exchange of messages, ideas, attitudes or feelings, e.g. the art of journalism, of film, of television, of dance, of theater, of folk and popular music, of literature, of public forum, and of graphic and fine arts. (C)

Communication (in linguistic analysis)

The substitution of one segment for another, in a context. (C)   C.C.

Company Publication

A newspaper or magazine produced by management for employees, either production or management personnel, or for an audience outside the immediate company. (P)

Complementary Colors

Those having the property of producing the sensation of white when superposed optically in proper proportion in the form of colored lights; the hues or colors which, combined with others, complete the spectrum. (F)   J.S.M.

Comprehensive

A drawing, complete in detail, with component parts

accurately proportioned, copy scaled and measured, photostats of artwork and illustrations pasted in position—in short, a "working model" of any piece of printed material. See layout. (PR)   B.B.

Comp.
A compositor or typesetter. (P)   B.C.B.

Complimentary Copies
Free copies given as a courtesy. (P)   A.B.C.

Composing Machine
Device used to produce single types and lines of type on one slug; the Intertype, Linotype, and Monotype machines. (PR)   R.R.K.

Composing Stick
A device held in the compositor's hand into which all single type is placed, As the stick is filled the type is then transferred to the galley. (PR)   H.V.G.

Composition
Setting type according to a layout and assembling it with cuts, ready for a complete proof. (PR)   H.V.G.

Compositor
One who sets type. (PR)   R.R.K.

Concavo-Convex Lens
A lens, one surface of which is a concave spherical surface and the other a convex spherical surface. Such a lens may be either convergent or divergent, depending on the radius of curvature of the surfaces. If the middle of the lens is thinner than the edges, it is divergent; if thicker, it is convergent. (F)   A.S.

Condensed Type
Narrow type, as opposed to that of standard width. (PR)   B.C.B.

Congruity Theory of Communication

A theory of attitude change which suggests that when a message is received which relates two or more objects of judgment, via an assertion in a particular communication situation, evaluative behavior is always in the direction of increased congruity with the existing frame of reference. Application of the principle of congruity to prediction of attitudes requires the use of a set of evaluative, polarized scales to rate the objects of judgment. See Semantic Differential. (C)

Conjugate Foci

On a process camera, the perspective distances from the lens to the copyboard and from the lens to the image or focal plane at any scale of reproduction. (PR)   J.S.M.

Connected Dot

In negatives and plates, those halftone dots joined together by a bridge. (PR)   J.S.M.

Console

Control panel in the control room. (B)   N.A.B.

Consumer Advertising

Advertising placed in publications, radio, television, billboards or other media reaching the general public. (A)   H.V.G.

Consumer Panel

A representative cross-section of people in different professions, income brackets, and so forth, used as a pilot group to test products, advertising appeals, etc., or to record purchases. (A)   H.V.G.

Consumer Product

One that is sold and advertised for use by the general public. (A)   H.V.G.

Contact Print (or Sheets)

A quick and economical way of seeing pictures from a single negative or roll of film. The negative or positive is put directly on a sheet of photographic paper and the image is printed same size as the film itself. (F)

Contempt of Court by Publication

Legal action by a presiding judge in a court case against any publication for comments relating to court litigation.

It is the claim of the court that any public discussion of judicial questions while a case is pending or until the time limit for appeal has expired endangers or obstructs the administration of justice. Such publication constitutes contempt of court. Truth and good intent are inadmissible in defense of contempt citations. Trial by jury, impartial hearing and provisions for change of venue are not provided for in contempt cases.

The constitutional guarantees of freedom of press and a fair trial clash on this court practice. Newspapers have maintained that they have the right of editorial criticism of a position taken by a court in its ruling or decision in a case, and have cited judicial abuse and arbitrary use of the contempt power. American judges continue to place emphasis on striking an arbitrary balance between the rights of an individual to a fair trial and free reporting of court trials. See Canon 35 and Trial by Newspaper. (P) (B)

Content Analysis

What is meant by the term "content analysis"? Review of several definitions which have appeared in the technical literature will serve to identify the major characteristics of content analysis.

"Systematic content analysis attempts to define more casual descriptions of the content, so as to show objectively the nature and relative strength of the stimuli applied to the reader or listener" (Waples & Berelson).

"A social science sentence may be called one of 'content

70

analysis' if it satisfies all of the following requirements: 1) it must refer either to syntactic characteristics of symbols . . . or to semantic characteristics. . . . 2) it must indicate frequencies of occurrence of such characteristics with a high degree of precision. One could perhaps define more narrowly: it must assign numerical values to such frequencies. 3) it must refer to these characteristics by terms which are general. . . . 4) it must refer to these characteristics by terms which occur . . . in universal propositions of social science. One may consider adding to this definition another requirement: 5) a high precision of the terms used to refer to the symbol characteristics studied" (Leites & Pool).

"The content analyst aims at a quantitative classification of a given body of content, in terms of a system of categories devised to yield data relevant to specific hypotheses concerning that content" (Kaplan & Goldsen).

" 'Content analysis' may be defined as referring to any technique for the *classification* of *sign-vehicles;* which relies solely upon the *judgments*—which, theoretically, may range from perceptual discriminations to sheer guesses—of an analyst or group of analysts as to which sign-vehicles fall into which categories, on the basis of *explicitly formulated rules;* provided that the analyst's judgments are regarded as the reports of a *scientific observer.* The results of a content analysis state the frequency of occurrence of signs—or groups of signs—for each category in a classification scheme" (Janis, his emphasis).

". . . The technique known as content analysis . . . attempts to characterize the meanings in a given body of discourse in a systematic and quantitative fashion" (Kaplan).

This group of definitions provides six distinguishing characteristics of content analysis:

1) it applies only to social science generalizations: Leites & Pool

2) it applies only, or primarily, to the determination of the effects of communications: Waples & Berelson

3) it applies only to the syntactic and semantic dimensions of language: Leites & Pool

4) it must be "objective": Waples & Berelson, Leites & Pool, Janis, Kaplan

5) it must be "systematic": Leites & Pool, Kaplan & Goldsen, Kaplan

6) it must be quantitative: Waples & Berelson, Leites & Pool, Kaplan & Goldsen, Janis, Kaplan

As we shall see, the first and second of these characteristics define the field of content analysis too narrowly. The review of the literature will show that it has been applied successfully in other fields than the social sciences and for other purposes than the description of the effects of communications upon readers and listeners. But the other four characteristics are required for a proper definition of content analysis.

The *syntactic-and-semantic requirement* is meant to rule out the analysis of communication content for the pragmatic dimension of language (the third branch of semiotic, the general science of signs, as developed by Charles Morris). That is, content analysis is ordinarily limited to the manifest content of the communication and is not normally done directly in terms of the latent intentions which the content may express nor the latent responses which it may elicit. Strictly speaking, content analysis proceeds in terms of what-is-said, and not in terms of why-the-content-is-like-that (e.g., "motives") or how-people-react (e.g., "appeals" or "responses"). Three reasons have been given for this delimitation: 1) the low validity of the analysis, since there can be little or no assurance that the assigned intentions and responses actually occurred, in the absence of direct data on them; 2) the low reliability of such analysis, since different coders are unlikely to assign material to the same categories of intention and response with sufficient agreement; and 3) the possible circularity involved in establishing relationships between intent and effect on the one hand, and content on the other, when the latter is analyzed in terms referring to the former.

The *requirement of objectivity* stipulates that the categories of analysis should be defined so precisely that different analysts can apply them to the same body of content and secure the same results. Like the first requirement, this ordinarily limits content analysis to the manifest content. This requirement, of course, is necessary in order to give some scientific standing to content analysis.

The *requirement of system* contains two different meanings. In the first place, it states that *all* of the relevant content is to be analyzed in terms of *all* the relevant categories, for the problem at hand. This requirement is meant to eliminate partial or biased analyses in which only those elements in the content are selected which fit the analyst's thesis. Thus "system" means that if some occurrences of the category are taken into consideration, within a specified body of content, then all occurrences must be—or the definition of the problem changed.

The second meaning of "system" is that analyses must be designed to secure data relevant to a scientific problem or hypothesis. The results of a content analysis must have a measure of general application. Thus a tabulation simply reporting the number of books of different kinds acquired by a particular library in a given year would not represent a content analysis study (unless the results were used for a trend or comparative analysis, or for some other generalization). By this requirement, content analysis is designed for the establishment of scientific propositions.

The *requirement of quantification,* the single characteristic on which all the definitions agree, is perhaps the most distinctive feature of content analysis. It is this characteristic of content analysis which goes farthest toward distinguishing the procedure from ordinary reading. Of primary importance in content analysis is the *extent to* which the analytic categories appear in the content, that is, the relative emphases

73

and omissions. Now this requirement of quantification does not necessarily demand the assignment of *numerical* values to the analytic categories. Sometimes it takes the form of quantitative words like "more" or "always" or "increases" or "often." Although results of this kind may be appropriate for certain studies, it should be recognized that such terms are just as "quantitative" as the terms 37 or 52%; they are only less exact and precise. In most applications of content analysis, numerical frequencies have been assigned to occurrence of the analytic categories.

This review of the distinguishing characteristics of content analysis, then, results in the following definition: *Content analysis is a research technique for the objective, systematic, and quantitative description of the manifest content of communication.* (C)   B.Ber.

Contest
Competition among subscription solicitors or among carriers and dealers or among readers or prospective readers of a publication for a prize of money or other valuable consideration.

Context
The linguistic environment. (Broadly: the words or other segments which precede or follow a particular word or segment and which bear upon the meaning.) (C)   C.C.

Continuing Action of Light
The peculiar property of bichromated colloids to become increasingly insoluble (tanned) after exposure to light, the action continuing even in darkness. (PR)   J.S.M.

Continuity
Script written to include all spoken lines and cues. (B)
H.V.G.

Continuity

The actual relationships of scenes and sequences in a film; a written script. (F)   G.W.

Continuity-Impact Discount Rate (CID)

A newspaper space discount rate for national advertisers which combines the standard continuity and volume discounts. Discount percentages on space size and line contracts vary with the needs of each paper. (P)

Continuous-Tone Negative

A negative made in a camera without the use of a screen; has no dot formation. (PR)   R.R.K.

Contract Year

Designated duration of a media contract, beginning with the first advertisement which usually must appear within thirty days of signing a contract. (A)   H.V.G.

Contrast

The degree of difference in tone between the lightest and darkest areas in a television picture (B)   H.V.G.

Contrast Factors

The amount of contrast in a finished photograph may be attributed to several factors. These are: the exposure given the negative, the filter used, the kind of film, the duration of development, the duration of exposure and development in printing, the paper used in printing, and the developer used both for the negative and the print. (F)   A.S.

Contrasty

Applied to prints with very dark shadows and white highlights, due to underexposure or overdevelopment of the negative, or where the paper used is of the wrong contrast (too hard). (F)   A.S.

Control Processes

Photographic processes in which the operator exercises a

considerable amount of control over the tone values. Not only can the tonal key be controlled, but the relative value of tones can be altered. Gum bichromate, oil, and bromoil processes are examples. (F)   A.S.

Control Room
The booth adjoining a radio or TV studio from which the program is electronically controlled and balanced by engineers and directors. (B)   H.V.G.

Conversions
The making of offset plates with reproductions pulled from letterpress plates. (PR)

Cooked
Overdeveloped film. (F)   G.W.

Cooperative Advertising
A method for delivering the retail sales message by which both the manufacturer and the dealer handling his product coordinate their advertising and sales activities at supposedly lower costs. (A)

Cooperative Program
A program broadcast by a network and designed for sponsorship by local advertisers. (B)   H.V.G.

Coordinated Advertising
The technique of designing all advertising and promotional material around a central copy theme and art motif to increase total impact by constant repetition of related mental impressions. (A)   H.V.G.

Copper Colorimeter
Device for determining the concentration or content of dissolved copper (cupric chloride) in used ferric chloride etching baths. (PR)   J.S.M.

Copper Etching
Act of etching line and halftone images in relief on copper; a copper plate so etched. (PR)   J.S.M.

Copperplate Engraving
Work done from either copper or steel engraved dies, engraved intaglio. The ink on the completed job appears intense in color, and stands out from the surface of the paper or card. (PR)   R.R.K.

Copy
In general, any type of material (words, pictures, designs) used in the production of printing. (PR)   R.A.F.

Copy
(1) Material to be set in type, as news copy, ad copy, etc.; (2) person about whom a story is to be written. Colorful public figures, for instance, sometimes are referred to as "good copy." (P)   T.E.B.

Copy Approach
The method used in presenting the advertiser's message; the "theme" of an advertisement. (A)   H.V.G.

Copy Casting
Counting the characters in a piece of copy and estimating the space it will require when set in specified type. (PR)   H.V.G.

Copy Chief
Creative head of an advertising agency's copy department. (A)   H.V.G.

Copy-Cutter
One who divides copy into "takes," or small sections, which are given to compositors to set in newspaper shops. (P)   R.R.K.

Copy Negative
Very often it is necessary to re-photograph a photograph

for purposes of reproduction, either to prevent soiling or destroying the original, or sometimes for the sake of economy in making engravings. In such cases, of course, a photographic negative is made, from which prints, enlarged, reduced, or same size may be ordered. (PR)   B.B.

Copy Platform (Policy)

The presentation of the basic ideas for advertising campaign as well as the major selling points to be used to carry it out. (A)

Copy Print

A photographic print obtained by photographing the original artwork or photograph. (PR)   H.V.G.

Copy Scaling (Or Fitting Copy)

The important job of determining how much space a given amount of typewritten copy will fill when set in type—which, of course, depends not only on the size of the type to be used but also upon what style or "face" of type has been decided upon, as the same size type in various faces does not measure the same. All sorts of systems for this purpose are in use, some quite accurate and some that are often regarded as "close enough."

It's only fair to say, though, that no system that depends upon word count—so many words to the square inch—is going to be very reliable in dealing with a language that contains a lot of one and two-letter words and any number of much longer ones, like "industrial" and "journalism." The only really dependable way to fit copy is by character counting—but that's not as tough as it sounds.

You know, of course, the style and size of the type you propose to use, and the width of your column, in picas. Take a sample of anything printed in the same type, measure off the width of the columns in your own publication, and count the number of characters set within that measure, counting all punctuation marks and each space between

78

words as characters. Do this with six lines of the printed sample, and strike an average. If your publication were to be printed in 10-point Bodoni Book, for instance, and if your columns were 13½ picas in width, you would find that the average number in characters set in that space was 38.

Now count off 38 characters on your typewriter, or on the typewritten copy, and draw parallel vertical lines that distance apart. By typing your copy within these lines, you will know exactly how many lines in type you are filling. Or, if you're measuring copy already typewritten, it will be easy to estimate the number of lines it will require in type. Once you know the number of lines you are going to need, the rest is simple mathematics. As there are 72 points in an inch, 10-point type, set solid, will run about seven (plus) lines to the inch; 10 on 11 about six and one-half lines, 12-point solid six lines to the inch, and so on. (PR)   B.B.

Copy Testing

Experimenting with various types of copy appeals in test campaigns in order to determine which is most effective. (A)   H.V.G.

Copyboard

Variously constructed boards, frames and other devices for holding originals in position on process cameras during photo-reproduction. (PR)   J.S.M.

Copyboard Chart

A card bearing solid patches of tricolor inks, together with a gray scale and register marks as an aid in three-and four-color photography. (PR)   J.S.M.

Copyboy

Boy who carries copy from one department or person to another. He also does errands and performs other minor duties in the news room. Frequently, he is termed an "office boy." (P)   T.E.B.

Copycutter

Composing room employee who assigns copy to linotype operators. His name arises from the fact that he frequently cuts copy apart, especially on long stories, to speed the copy into print. (P)   T.E.B.

Copyholder

In proofroom practice one proofreader holds the proof of the type matter and makes corrections and a second one holds the copy and reads it aloud for comparison purposes. (P)   B.C.B.

Copyholder

Glass-covered copyboard. (PR)   J.S.M.

Copying Camera

Special camera for copying; a process camera. (PR) J.S.M.

Copyright

Legal right to the sole use of original writing or art work. To copyright a publication requires, first of all, a request to the U.S. Patent Office, Copyright Division, Washington, for the proper application forms, and as there are a number of different types, the request should be specific as to the kind of publication in question. When the application has been executed it is sent to Washington with the proper fee, and two copies of the publication. No publication may be copyrighted before it is printed, and every different issue requires a separate copyright and a separate application with fee. The names of publications cannot be copyrighted, although the distinctive style or lettering in which the name appears may be patented—subject, of course, to a rather laborious patent search and a substantial charge. (P)
                               B.B., H.V.G.

Copywriter

One who writes headlines and text for advertisements

and promotional material. Usually creates advertising ideas and campaign themes. (A) H.V.G.

Corner Bullet
A small dot placed in the 4 corners of an ad to guarantee its proper position on the page. (PR) H.V.G.

Corner Card
The printed name and address in the upper left-hand corner of envelopes. (PR) H.V.G.

Correspondent
(1) Person who submits news from his home town or area, usually on a space basis, to a newspaper; (2) reporter assigned by his newspaper to a distant news source. Most large newspapers in the United States, for instance, maintain correspondents in their own state capitals and in Washington, D.C. (P) T.E.B.

Correspondents' Copies
Copies of a publication given free to correspondents of the paper, reporters and editorial writers. (P) A.B.C.

Co-Sponsorship
The participation of several sponsors in a single program where each advertiser pays a proportionate share of its cost. (A) H.V.G.

Cost-Per-Thousand
A figure obtained by dividing the rate of the publication by the circulation or number of readers in thousands. Also, the figure derived from dividing the cost of a program by the number of listeners in thousands. (A) H.V.G.

Counter Card
A point-of-sale device—a small card describing the product and giving the price. Generally placed in store where product is sold. (PR) H.V.G.

Counter Sales

Newspapers sold over publisher's counter to individual purchasers. If sold in quantities of 11 or more, such copies are allocated to bulk sales. (P)   A.B.C.

Cover

Cover space for advertisements, sold at extra cost. The front cover is generally not sold. Inside front cover is called "second cover," inside of back cover is "third cover," and the outside of back cover is "fourth cover." (A)   H.V.G.

Cover

To handle an assignment. Hence, a reporter "covers" a story by getting the facts and a photographer "covers" the story by getting the pictures. (P)   T.E.B.

Cover Papers

Heavy, decorative papers used for pamphlet covers, etc. (PR)   H.V.G.

Cover Positions

The premium priced outside front cover, inside front cover, inside back cover and outside back cover of a publication. (A)

Coverage

The circulation and penetration of an advertising medium in its particular market. (A)   H.V.G.

Covering Power

The capacity of a lens to give a sharply defined image to the edges of the plate it is designed to cover, when focused with the largest stop opening. (F)   A.S.

Cowcatcher

A spot announcement preceding a commercial program, but within the sponsor's allotted time, used to promote another of the same sponsor's products. (B)   H.V.G.

Craftint
Modern form of shading sheet. (PR)   J.S.M.

Crash Finish
A paper finished with a surface similar to coarse linen.
(PR)   R.A.F.

Crayoning
Application of greasy litho crayon to halftone etchings
as a delicate and blendable acid resist. (PR)   J.S.M.

Creative Director
The person in charge of the creative departments responsible for an agency's total output of advertising. (A)
                                                     H.V.G.

Credit Line
A line giving source of copy or illustration. (P) B.C.B.

Credits
Names of those connected with show. (B)   N.A.B.

Credit Subscription
One upon which no payment is made at time of order.
(P)   A.B.C.

Crimping
Creasing the binding-edge of ledger sheets so that book
will open freely. (PR)   R.A.F.

Crop
To trim or cut away a part of a print to eliminate some
undesirable portion or to improve the composition. (F)
                                                     A.S.

Crop Marks
Markings placed at edges of original or on guide sheet to
indicate area desired in reproduction, with negative or
plate trimmed (cropped) at the markings. (PR)   J.S.M.

Crossbars
Printing press attachments for guiding or turning the print paper. (PR) B.C.B.

Cross-Fade
To fade in one sound from one source while sound from another is faded out. (B) J.C.W.

Cross-Hatching
Drawing or tooling parallel lines to cross each other at certain angles for effect of tone or texture. (PR) J.S.M.

Crossline
A line of the headline centered, separating decks or banks. (P) B.C.B.

Crossline Screen
Halftone screen of standard ruling. (PR) J.S.M.

Crusade
A newspaper campaign for a reform. (P) B.C.B.

Cub
A beginning reporter. (P) B.C.B.

Cue
Signal used in a radio or television program to guide some action of a performer—may be verbal or printed. (B) P.W.B.

Cue Card
Large card bearing a sentence, or several names or facts, to prompt the actor or speaker. (B) H.V.G.

Cue Sheet
An outline of all the elements in a program, giving the timing and musical or spoken cues. (B) H.V.G.

Curved Plate

In letterpress printing, one which is backed up and curved to fit a rotary press. (PR)   R.A.F.

Cushion

A section of a radio or TV program which can be lengthened or shortened in the event the performers vary from the rehearsed speed of their roles. (B)   H.V.G.

Cut

An engraving or electrotype. Usually refers to a single illustration or design. (See Plate.) (PR)   H.V.G.

"Cut," "Stop the Camera"

Signal that the shot is finished. (F)   G.W.

Cut

The change or transition from one scene to another. (F)
G.W.

Cut

To cut a story is to eliminate some of its type. Thus a copy-editor may be directed to "cut ten agate lines out of the fire story," meaning that the story must be shortened by space equal to ten agate lines in order to confine it to the room available in the page. To *cut in* a story is to reduce it to a certain space. (P)   B.C.B.

Cut-back

Repetition of or continuation of a previous scene shown earlier in the film. (F)   G.W.

Cut-In Letter

Large initial letter beginning a paragraph. See *Stick-up initial.* (PR)   B.C.B.

Cut Line

Term used synonymously with "caption for a cut." Sometimes called "underline." The term "cut lines" usually means the lines under the cut, but it may also include the lines over a cut. (P) T.E.B.

Cut-Out
A blockout; a highlight halftone negative; a color separation negative. (PR) J.S.M.

Cut-Outs
Printed pieces cut into irregular shapes by steel dies. (PR) R.A.F.

Cutter
The technician who carries out the actual separating and joining of shots and scenes until the finished picture is assembled. (F) G.W.

Cutting
Clearing and treating line and halftone negatives on wet collodion plates; reduction of density or dot size. (PR) J.S.M.

Cutting
Selection and arrangement of scenes into a completed film (see editing). (F) G.W.

Cutoff
A *rule* placed across one or more columns to separate boxes, cuts, layouts, page datelines and advertisements from the rest of the page. The cutoff rule is intended to guide the reader and avoid confusion. A double cutoff consists of two rules together, in some cases a light one and a heavy one. (P) B.C.B.

Cyanotype
Blueprint on paper sensitized with iron salts. (PR) J.S.M.

Cylinder Press
The type of printing press in which the paper is carried

over and around a cylinder, which impresses it on the type form. The Miehle Horizontal, the No. 2 Kelly and the Miller Simplex are presses of this type. (PR)   B.B.

Cylindrical Casting

Stereotype cast into a curved mat to produce a casting suitable for rotary press. (PR)   R.A.F.

D

D.M.A.A.
Direct Mail Advertising Association.

Dagger
A reference mark. (PR)   B.C.B.

Daguerreotype
First practical photographic process, comprising an image
on a silvered copper plate. (PR)   J.S.M.

Dailies
Rush prints of each day's shooting. (F)   G.W.

Dandy Roller
A wire cylinder used on papermaking machines that
make wove or laid effects on the texture, as well as the
watermark, as in bond, ledger, and antique book paper.
(PR)   R.R.K.

Dark Slide
The removable panel covering photographic surfaces in
a plateholder; the British term for plateholder. (PR) J.S.M.

Darkroom
Chamber free from actinic light, in which photographic
operations are carried out with light-sensitive materials.
(F)   J.S.M.

Darkroom Camera
Type of process camera having the rear section of the apparatus permanently built into the wall of a darkroom. (PR)   J.S.M.

Dash
A short line separating parts of head, stories, etc.; a punctuation mark. (P)   B.C.B.

Dateline
The line at the top of each page, giving the date on which the newspaper is published; also the line giving the point of origin of a telegraph, cable or radio story. (P)   B.C.B.

Dawn Patrol
Announcers and engineers who put on early-morning programs in broadcast studios. (B)   P.W.B.

Day-Glo
The commercial trade name for an ink or paint with a fluorescent quality which greatly intensifies the brilliance of color on signs, posters, car cards and outdoor bulletins. (PR)   H.V.G.

Day-Glo Posters
Standardized outdoor posters using activated color. (A)
R.D.L.

Day Side
A newspaper employe working days is on the day side. (P)   B.C.B.

Daytime Station
One which broadcasts only during daylight hours. (B)
H.V.G.

Dead
(1) Part of the newspaper already in type in which no further changes will be made (the classified ad section, for instance, is "dead" several hours before the presses begin);

(2) metal page already used that will not be used again. Generally, a pressroom employee strikes the type page with a hammer to deface it and then returns it to the stereotype department for remelting. (*Note*—the terms "killed" and "dead" must not be confused.) (P) · T.E.B.

Dead Bank
Composing room term applied to the *rack* on which is placed type no longer available for use, whether in the form of stories, parts of stories, or headlines. (P) B.C.B.

Deadline
Time at which all the work of a given department must be completed. Thus, there are deadlines for the news department, the copy desk, and the various departments of the composing room and the pressroom. (P) T.E.B.

Dead Metal
Metal left or inserted in blank areas of an engraving or type form to evenly distribute the pressure of molding. (PR) H.V.G.

Dead Mike
One not working or disconnected. (B) N.A.B.

Deal
The head of a copydesk passes out or *deals* copy to his copyeditors. (P) B.C.B.

Dealer
A person who sells and rents films and/or projection equipment. (F) G.W.

Dealer Imprint
A 20-inch strip across the bottom of the outdoor poster, used to identify the local retailer handling the product advertised. Normally, the dealer imprint represents 20 percent of the poster area. (A) R.D.L.

90

Decalcomania

A process of transferring pictures and designs from specially prepared paper to china, glass, etc. (A)   H.V.G.

Deck Head

A secondary, minor, heading for a story that appears between the main head and the body of the article. Not to be confused with a sub-head, or topical head which appears as an interruption between sections of the story itself. (P)   B.B.

Deckle

A torn effect along the edge of a sheet of paper; the natural, untrimmed edge of paper. (PR)   H.V.G.

Deductible from Dues

Association subscriptions of members of an association which allows its members to deduct the subscription price from their dues if they do not wish to receive the publication. (P)   A.B.C.

Deep Etch

In photoengraving, to re-etch parts of a halftone for the purpose of making the light areas lighter. For instance, white letters or numerals in the darker portions of an illustration would have to be deep-etched to provide the necessary "printing depth," as well as to eliminate the halftone dot. Otherwise they'd fill up with ink when printed. (PR)   B.B.

Deep Etch (Offset Lithography)

One of the two methods of offset plate-making; the other is the albumen or surface method. Deep etch offset plates are coming into ever-wider use, and are thought by many to be "better" than the surface type, although excellent results are obtainable by either method if the copy is properly prepared and the camera and platemaking operations are skillfully done. (PR)   B.B.

Deferred Subscriptions
Subscriptions served a month or more late, usually from copies unsold from initial distribution and returned by distributor. (P)   A.B.C.

Definition
The defining power of a lens, or its property to project sharp images. (F)   J.S.M.

Delayed Action
An adjustment on a camera shutter by means of which the photographer may set the shutter and then take his place in a group or view so that he is included in the picture. (F)   A.S.

Delayed Broadcast
Recording made of a program to be broadcast at a later time or date. (B)   H.V.G.

Deliquescence
Tendency of certain chemicals to absorb atmospheric moisture. (PR)   J.S.M.

Denotation
The imputed non-causal relationship between a sign and its referent, especially when the latter is a physical thing, event, or property (a "denotatum"). (C)   C.C.

Densitometer
Photoelectric instrument for measuring the density of photographic negatives and positives. (F)   J.S.M.

Density
The quality or degree of opaqueness of the negative or positive print. (F)   G.W.

Depth
In relief plates, the vertical distance from the actual printing surface to the bottom of any low (etched) area. (PR)   J.S.M.

Depth Microscope
A specially designed optical instrument for measuring the depth of relief printing plates by ocular focusing. (PR)
J.S.M.

Depth of Field
The range of a camera. (F)

Depth of Focus
The camera range, after focus, in which everything before the camera registers in sharp focus. (F) G.W.

Depthometer
Calibrated gauge for micrometrically measuring the depth of printing plates; halftonometer. (PR) J.S.M.

Descenders
Used in connection with type, descenders are the longer lines extending below the body in some letters, as in lower case g or p. (PR) B.B.

Descriptive Syntax
The syntax of historical, ordinary, languages. (C) C.C.

Desensitizer
An agent applied to films or plates in the dark after which development can be conducted in comparatively bright yellow light. (F) A.S.

Designatum (of a sign)
"That which is referred to." Any attribute of the outside (non-linguistic) world with which a sign-event is associated in thought. (There are many *shades of opinion*.) (C) C.C.

Desk
A copydesk. (P) B.C.B.

Desk Editor
An editor directing reporters or copyeditors. (P) B.C.B.

93

Detail
   In originals and reproductions, the minute subdivisions of an image. Good detail indicates accurate portrayal of all subdivisions in their proper tonal value or strength. (PR)
J.S.M.

Detail
   In pictorial photography, detail includes everything which does not contribute to the motif of the photograph. In commercial photography, detail is desirable; in pictorial photography it detracts. (F)   A.S.

Detail Stop
   The particular aperture in halftone photography employed to render middletones, as differentiated from shadows and highlights. (PR)   J.S.M.

Developer
   The chemical used to bring out the image on exposed film. (F)   G.W.

Developing
   Treating the film chemically to bring out the image. (F)
G.W.

Development
   Act of rendering visible exposed or latent (invisible) images through action of a reducing agent or developer; in platemaking, the removal of soluble (unexposed) particles of bichromated colloid from the image proper. (PR) J.S.M.

Devil
   The printer's apprentice. (PR)   B.C.B.

Diaphragm
   A camera mechanism for masking the lens to control the amount of light reaching the film; also a vibrating disk in a microphone or loud speaker that transforms sound waves to electricity or electricity back to sound waves. (F)   G.W.

94

Diaphragm Control
Various devices for process cameras, designed to coordinate all optical factors of line and halftone photography, and to indicate correct apertures for any camera extension and screen ruling. (PR)   J.S.M.

Diaphragm Indicator
A pointer or device attached to the iris diaphragm of process lenses for ascertaining the exact diameter of the aperture. (PR)   J.S.M.

Diapositive
A photographic transparency or image intended for viewing and reproduction by transmitted light. Common descriptive terms—"transparent positive," "negative-positive" —for this type of image are erroneous. (PR)   J.S.M.

Diary Method
A method of measuring the listening or viewing audience, in which the listener keeps a record of stations and programs heard over a period of time (a week or more). (A)   H.V.G.

Die Cut
A sheet of paper cut to any shape other than rectangular; a cut-out of any shape in a promotion piece. (PR) H.V.G.

Die Stamping
Intaglio printing done by means of a die and counter die. (PR)   H.V.G.

Dichroic Fog
A condition in a negative where the film or plate looks red when seen by light coming through, and green by light reflected from it. Due to defects in the emulsion, hypo in the developer, etc. (F)   A.S.

Dick Strip
A continuous roll of subscriber labels used in mailing operations. A newer electronic approach to subscription ful-

95

fillment will see the use of magnetic tape which will produce a dick strip which is both a label and the punched tape. (P)

Differential
The difference in newspaper rates for local and national advertising space. (A)   H.V.G.

Diffraction
Deviation of light rays from a straight course when partially cut off by an obstacle, or in passage near the edges of a small opening or through a small hole. (F)   J.S.M.

Diffraction Theory
A theory of halftone photography in which dot formations are assumed to be due to the action of diffracted light. (PR)   J.S.M.

Diffuser
A screen used to soften the light. (F)   G.W.

Diffusion of Focus
Also called "soft focus" or "soft definition." Lack of sharpness in the picture image due to a defective lens, imperfect focusing, or a special lens made to give soft effects. (F)   A.S.

Digging Out
Removing small surface areas of metal in relief plates by manual effort with tools. (PR)   J.S.M.

Dimensions
In speaking of the dimension of a piece of printed material, it's generally presumed that the horizontal measurement is named first, as "eight and one-half by eleven." This is a firmly established practice; if you were to speak of a magazine as being "eleven by eight and a half" any printer would be sure you were talking about a book bound on the 8½" side, and opening the long way. (PR)   B.B.

Dimension Marks
Points indicated on an original outside image area to be reproduced, between which size of reproduction is marked and focusing performed. (PR)   J.S.M.

Diminishing Glass
Reducing glass. (PR)   J.S.M.

Din
A system of rating plate and film speeds generally accepted in Germany and other places on the Continent. (F)   A.S.

Dingbat
Printer's terms for ornaments used in headline or with cuts. Also a boxed story, generally one spread over a number of columns. (P)   B.C.B.

Dinky Dash
A special form of dash used in lieu of subheads, or to separate a number of short items. (P)   B.C.B.

Diorama
Miniature setting used to give illusion of large locations which are impossible to construct in TV studios. (B) H.V.G.

Dip
Each single intensification of a wet collodion image. (PR)   J.S.M.

Dipper
Long supporting holder for lowering collodionized plates into silver baths and cold enamel prints into developer. (PR)   J.S.M.

Dipping
Immersing photographic plates or images in chemical solutions. (PR)   J.S.M.

Direct Advertising
Advertising material reproduced in quantity and distributed directly to prospects, either by mail, house-to-house delivery, bag stuffers, etc. (A)   H.V.G.

Direct Halftone
A halftone for which the screen negative was made directly from the article to be reproduced (PR)   R.A.F.

Direct Halftone Process
Production of color separation negatives from originals directly through color filters and halftone screen. (PR)
                                                                            J.S.M.

Direct Mail Advertising
Letters, folders, reprints or other material sent through the mails directly to prospective purchasers. (A)   H.V.G.

Direct Positive
The positive image obtained by exposure in the camera with subsequent chemical treatment to develop and "reverse" the image. (F)   A.S.

Direct Take (or cut)
An immediate change from one picture or scene to another without a transition. (B)

Director
The person in complete charge of the filming of a picture. (F)   G.W.

Director
The supervisor of the production of a radio or TV program. In most cases he auditions and chooses the performers, conducts rehearsals and directs the program on the air. (B)   H.V.G.

Disc
A transcription or recording. (B)   N.A.B.

Disc Jockey

A radio entertainer whose program consists of popular records, glib chatter, time checks and both live and recorded commercials. (B)   H.V.G.

Discount

A discount is the per cent of reduction in rate earned proportionate to the number of total broadcast periods purchased from the station or network. (A)   H.V.G.

Display

Material used, usually in retail outlets, to influence the sale of a product or service, e.g., window display, floor display, etc. (A)   H.V.G.

Display

Type composition in the larger sizes; that type matter which first attracts the eye. (PR)   R.R.K.

Display Order

A pre-publication proof of a retail advertisement. (A)

Display Surface

The surface made available by the outdoor structure, either for the direct mounting of letters or decoration, for the direct pasting of posters or for painted copy carrying the entire advertising message. (A)   R.D.L.

Display Type

The largest and specially designed type faces used to attract attention. (PR)   R.R.K.

Dissolve

A television control technique by which a picture on the air is gradually faded out as a picture from another camera is simultaneously brought into full view. In a "lap" (overlap) dissolve, one picture appears to be wiped off, leaving another in its place. (B)   H.V.G.

99

Dissolve

The fading-in or -out of one scene to another, so that they overlap. (F)   G.W.

Distinctive Features (in linguistic analysis)

A minimal set of binary attributes (oppositions) by superposition of which phonemes may be presented. The attributes may be defined by spectral or articulatory criteria (after Jakobson). (C)   C.C.

Distortion

In lenses, any departure from the proper perspective of an image; in photography and platemaking, departure in size or change of shape of negative or reproduction as compared to the original, due to lack of parallelism in camera equipment, or errors in stripping and handling of negatives and printing plates. (P)   J.S.M.

Distribution

The placing of type and materials back into type cases and racks. (PR)   R.R.K.

Distributor

A general term applied to carriers, dealers, street vendors and all others who sell publications as a vocation or part of their business. (P)   H.V.G.

Distributor

One who sells, rents, lends, deposits, or leases films. (F)
                                                                G.W.

District Man

Reporter assigned to cover a definite section of the city. He maintains a vigilance over hospitals, police stations, morgues, and other places likely to be news sources. He is known also as a "legman." (P)   T.E.B.

Documentary

A form of dramatic program characterized by the fact

that its main purpose is to inform and to instruct, with entertainment an important but definitely secondary consideration. It is chiefly factual and usually deals with political, economic, and social problems. (B)   J.C.W.

Documentary
A film based on real life made in the actual setting without professional actors. (F)   G.W.

Dodging
The process of shading a part of the negative while printing or enlarging. (F)   A.S.

Dog-Watch
After the newspaper has finished issuing its regular editions for the day, and staff and deskmen have gone home, one copyeditor generally is kept on duty to watch for stories suitable for replates and extra editions. He is sometimes called the dog-watch man, or the lobster-trick man, and will have working under him one or two reporters and the necessary mechanical force. (P)   B.C.B.

Dolly
A truck or movable platform on which the camera and the microphone are carried while shooting a scene. (F)   G.W.

Dolly
A truck with silent rollers used to move the TV camera about the studio. Also the act of moving the camera up to or away from the subject being televised. (B)   H.V.G.

Dope
Slang term for advanced news story material, background material for a story, actual facts of a story. (P)   T.E.B.

Dope
A varnish used on a negative to facilitate retouching, by

giving a surface on which the pencil marks will "hold."
(F)   A.S.

Dope Story
Forecast or "think piece." (P)   B.C.B.

Dot
The individual element of a halftone printing plate.
(PR)   J.S.M.

Dot Etching
The process by which a color retoucher changes the
tone values on a halftone negative or positive. (PR) R.R.K.

Dot Formation
The arrangement and proper size of dots in halftone
negatives and printing plates; proper dot formations are
necessary for accurate translation of detail and tone values.
(PR)   J.S.M.

Double Coating
Many films, particularly those prepared for amateur use
and X-ray photography, are coated with two emulsions,
either one on top of the other, or one on each side of the
base. One coating is a slow-speed and the other a high-speed
emulsion. The slow emulsion provides correct exposure of
the highlights and the fast emulsion provides detail in the
shadows. The effect is to increase both the latitude and
the tone scale of the film. (F)   A.S.

Double Exposure
Two scenes photographed one on top of the other on
the same film. (F)   G.W.

Double Extension
A term applied to a camera or bellows which allows a
distance between the lens and focusing screen about double
the focal length of the lens. (F)   A.S.

102

Double Feature

A typical movie house fare, made up of an 'A' picture and a 'B' picture.

Double Frame

Some miniature cameras using standard motion-picture film make a negative of double-frame size—i.e., 8 pictures to each foot of film. In single-frame negatives the long dimension lies across the film; in double-frame negatives it lies along the film. (F)   A.S.

Double Image

A duplication of the outlines of a photograph is due to a movement of the camera or subject during exposure. Also used in reference to a print where the paper has been moved during printing. (F)   A.S.

Double Image

A television picture impaired by a weaker, secondary image. Usually caused by an echo signal—one picture is received while the other is reflected in transmission. Commonly called "ghost." (B)   H.V.G.

Double Leading

If a story does not fill the required space, it is *leaded* (leded) *out,* by placing thin strips of metal, from one to three points thick, between the linotype slugs. If one lead between lines is not enough, two leads are used; this is *double leading*. First-page articles and editorials often are double leaded. (P)   B.C.B.

Double Printing

The act of printing different negatives (both line and halftone) in succession and register on the same sheet of sensitized metal. A double print is a plate or reproduction produced in such manner. (PR)   J.S.M.

Double Spotting
Station practice of occasionally placing one spot announcement immediately after another. (B)　　　H.V.G.

Double Truck
A two-page advertisement or editorial layout made up as a single unit. Also, known as *double spread*. (P)　　B.C.B.

Doublet
Item, word or passage accidentally set twice and repeated in same paper. Same as *dupe*. (P)　　　B.C.B.

Doubletone
A drawing material or surface originally intended for the preparation of comic cartoons; Craftint; Multicolor Board. (PR)　　　J.S.M.

Doubling-Up
The emergency measure of having two craftsmen simultaneously engaged on the same plate or set of plates. (PR)　　　J.S.M.

Down-and-Under
Instruction to soften sound in order that dialogue may be heard; usually given musician or sound effects man in radio or television. (B)　　　P.W.B.

Down Style
The newspaper style in which a minimum of capital letters is used. (P)　　　B.C.B.

Dragon's Blood Process
A method of relief etching in which the sides of lines and dots are protected against undercutting by dusting the plate on all four sides with dragon's blood or etching powder, then heating the dusted plate to melt the powder and cause it to form an acid-resisting coating on the top and sides of the relief formations. (PR)　　　J.S.M.

Draw

The number of copies of a publication charged to dealer, carrier or other distributor. (P)　　　　　A.B.C.

Draw

The draw of a camera is the extent to which the bellows will permit the lens board to be racked forward. (F)　A.S.

Draw Tool

A finisher's tool in the form of a hooked steel blade, used for cutting white lines and borders into relief plates. (PR)　　　　　J.S.M.

Dress

A program rehearsed for the last time exactly as it is to be broadcast. (B)　　　　　J.C.W.

Drop Dot

A highlight halftone process akin to Kemart, but employing different artist materials and involving the use of blue-colored light for the highlight exposure. (PR)　　J.S.M.

Drop Head

Headline accompanying a streamer line and based on the same story; also called a *read out*. (P)　　　　B.C.B.

Droplines

Stepped lines, such those that make up the top part of a headline (P)　　　　　B.C.B.

Dropout

A highlight halftone negative or printing plate; "dropping-out" is the elimination of highlight dot formations in halftone negatives by photographic procedure, and of obliterating such dot formations in halftone plates by continued etching. (PR)　　　　　J.S.M.

Drybrush Drawing

A drawing made on a textured board or paper with

a brush, using the color or ink semi-dry so that a texture of dark and light appears in the stroke. (A)   H.V.G.

Dry Effect
A defect in the form of a peculiar relief appearance occurring in wet collodion negatives after drying; frequently due to excessive intensification. (PR)   J.S.M.

Drying Cabinet
A heated metal cabinet for drying negatives and other surfaces. (PR)   J.S.M.

Drying Net
A sheet of thin, fluffless material such as mercerized lawn stretched out flat. Used for drying matte prints. The prints are laid on the net face down which prevents the formation of blobs of water as well as undue curling. (F)   A.S.

Dryplate
A photographic material in the form of a glass plate sensitized with a film of gelatino-silver emulsion, the plate exposed in a dry condition. (PR)   J.S.M.

Dry Run Rehearsal
The initial rehearsal without cameras, in or outside the TV studio. (B)   N.A.B.

Dubbing
Putting new sound onto a sound track; mixing several sound tracks and re-recording into the finished combined track. (F)   G.W.

Dub-In
Introduction of sound in a recording or film which does not originate in the studio at the time of broadcast. (B)   H.V.G.

Dud
A copy of a previously transcribed program. (B)   N.A.B.

106

Dufaycolor

A colorfilm of the screen-plate type for producing direct color transparencies from colored objects. (PR)   J.S.M.

Dummy

Blank paper cut and folded to form a model of a proposed booklet or folder, showing the shape, size, weight of paper and suggested layout. (A)   H.V.G.

Dummy

Preliminary "mock-up" layout for a publication, made up in correct size and number of pages, showing the position each story and picture is to have. (P)   B.B.

Dump

Type is always dumped, e.g., into galleys. (PR) B.C.B.

Duograph

A type of engraving designed to give an effect of color from a one-color picture or "copy." Duograph plates consist of two halftones, which are, of course, printed one on top of the other in two different colors, or different shades of the same color. Two separate press impressions are required, the same as in any other two-color printing. In duographs, only one of the halftones is etched for detail; the second may be little more than a tint block. They are much less expensive than duotones. (PR)   B.B.

Duotone

Used for the reproduction of a one-color picture in two colors, or different shades of the same color. In duotones, both of the halftones are etched for detail, and carefully balanced with one another, which involves much time-consuming hand work. They are expensive, and in many cases much the same effect can be obtained by using the far less costly duograph process. (PR)   B.B.

Duotype

Two-color halftone reproduction made from a single halftone negative taken from a monochrome original, one of the printing plates (keyplate) being etched for detail, the other etched in low contrast to print in light-colored ink. Good register is required on printing press to prevent moiré in the final result. (PR)   J.S.M.

Dupe
Contraction of duplicate. News items identical as to facts, printed by mistake in the same copy of a newspaper, are *dupes*. Same as *doublet*. Also, carbon copies of news stories. (P)   B.C.B.

Dupe
Duplicate negative. (F)

Duplex Paper
Paper having different colors or finishes on opposite sides. (PR)   R.A.F.

Duplex Screen
Special type of halftone screen for production of high-light effects and combination line-halftone negatives. (PR)   J.S.M.

Duplicate Plate
Extra printing plate made from the same negative, etched and finished in the same manner. Used in lieu of electrotype or stereotype. (P)   J.S.M.

Dusting Box
A revolving cabinet containing resinous dust, occasionally used for depositing a dust grain on metal plates as a medium of tone translation; the cabinet or box containing the etching powder used in relief etching. (PR)   J.S.M.

Dye Retouching
Retouching of continuous tone, line or halftone negatives with solutions of red or black dyes. (PR)   J.S.M.

Dye Toning

The process of toning a photograph with a dye which will replace the silver image. (F)   A.S.

Dye Transfer

An opaque photographic print in color. (A)   H.V.G.

E

Ears

Little boxes on either side of the newspaper title plate on first page; generally they carry weather prediction, circulation figures, edition name or some like feature as text. (P)   B.C.B.

"Eat" Papers

To accept and pay for more copies than one has customers for. (P)   A.B.C.

Eau de Javelle

A reducer for negatives the active ingredient of which is sodium hypochlorite. It is also used to remove the last traces of hypo from film, and as a stain remover. (F)   A.S.

Eberhard Effect

The name given to the phenomenon which darkens the edges of developed film, though the entire area has been uniformly exposed. (F)   A.S.

Ebonite

Hardened rubber of black color and horny substance, used as acid-proof material for photographic receptacles. (PR)   J.S.M.

Echo Chamber

Device consisting of tunnel containing a microphone and

speaker which produces echo-like or distant-sounding reverberations. (B)   H.V.G.

Ecology in Communication
An organizing concept for the study of communication which attempts to give overt symbol systems some semblance of structure, order and relations; the interrelationships of one symbol system to another, and of man with his total symbol environment.

E.D.
Abbreviated instructions for inserting a newspaper advertisement every day. (A)

Edge Fog
The fog on film that is due to the leakage of light between the flanges of the spool on which the film is wound. (F)   A.S.

Edge Light
In portraiture, a light placed behind the subject to give a halo effect and illuminate the edges of the head and shoulders. (F)   A.S.

Editing
Selecting, arranging, and combining scenes and sound tracks to make the final film. (F)   G.W.

Editor
Name given loosely to an editorial department employee who is in charge of a department. Thus, one finds the sports editor, the city editor, the radio editor, etc. The simple title, "editor," is usually given the highest-ranking person on the newspaper, excepting the publisher. (P)   T.E.B.

Editor
The person who supervises the selection, arrangement, and combination of scenes and sound to make the final film. (F)   G.W.

111

E. & P.

Editor and Publisher magazine, the definitive trade journal in the newspaper field.

Editorialize

To express an opinion in a newsstory or headline. (P)
B.C.B.

Educational Film

A classroom film or a film designed to inform or to educate. (F)
G.W.

Effective Aperture

The diameter of the diaphragm of a lens measured through the front lens element. Sometimes this may be larger than the actual opening in the lens diaphragm because of the converging action of the front element of the lens. (F)
A.S.

Eggshell

A paper having a surface similar to that of an eggshell. (PR)
R.A.F.

Ektachrome

Color transparency manufactured by the Eastman Kodak Company. (A)
H.V.G.

Ektacolor

A color negative film (Kodak) processed by the user and forming a set of corrected tricolor separation negatives in a single film. (PR)
J.S.M.

Ektar

An apochromatic process lens (Kodak) fitted with a shutter and a built-in aperture control. (PR)
J.S.M.

Electrical Etching

Etching of relief printing plates by means of electrolysis —really an inversion of electroplating. (PR)
J.S.M.

Electro

Short for electrotype, it's a facsimile of a block of type, or an engraving, or a combination of both. It consists of a thin shell of either copper or nickel which has been deposited by electrolytic action in a wax or lead mold of the original, then backed with a lead alloy. They have lots of uses, perhaps the principal one of which is that they are less costly than the original plates, and hence can be worn out, discarded and replaced more readily in long press runs. Then, too, any number of electros can be made from one original for use in printing several copies simultaneously. Most small publications are said to "run from type and originals," meaning that they are printed from the type cast by the linotype or monotype machines, and from engravings as produced by the photoengraving process. This is the most practicable and inexpensive procedure if the press run is less than about 30,000 impressions on paper of ordinary character, and if there is small likelihood that reprinting will ever be required. Otherwise, electros are called for. When a printer uses the expression "printing plates" he generally means electros or nickeltypes, not original engravings. (PR)   B.B.

Electron Metal

Various magnesium alloys suggested as substitutes for zinc, copper and brass in photoengraving. (PR)   J.S.M.

Electronic Flash

High speed light source used in photography as a substitute for flash bulbs. (F)   H.V.G.

Electronic Scanner

Color scanner. (PR)   J.S.M.

Electrolyte

The solution of bath in electric etching machines. (PR)
                                                                  J.S.M.

113

Eleven Point Metal
Photoengraving zinc rolled to .152 inch thickness; heavy metal. (PR)   J.S.M.

Ellipsograph
A machine or trammel for drawing or cutting ellipses and circles on originals, masks, negatives and printing plates. The term "oval" is popularly but erroneously used in photo-engraving to designate an ellipse, but an oval is a figure having the lengthwise outline of an egg, with one end larger than the other. (Abiding with the common trade usage, ellipses are called "ovals" in the present work.) (PR)
J.S.M.

Em
The square of any given size of type; formerly it was the space occupied by the letter M. An *en* is one half the width of an em. Ems pica (12 point) are used by the printer in measuring column width and the length of type lines. (PR)   B.C.B.

Emboss
The ordinary meaning refers to raised impressions, on the order of Braille, but it also means the result of too heavy a printing impression, so that type and rules can be seen on the reverse side of the paper. It can be the fault of poor makeready or of inferior paper. (PR)   B.B.

Embossed Mount
A mount whose center portion is depressed with a die (plate-sunk) or an embossing tool (embossed), leaving a raised margin to frame the print. (F)   A.S.

Embossing Plate
A plate etched or engraved below its surface (intaglio), into which paper is forced for the production of a raised (embossed) design on surface of sheet. (PR)   J.S.M.

114

Emcee

A slang term for master of ceremonies. (B)   H.V.G.

Empathy in Communication

A perceptual and experiential process by which the communicator develops expectations or predictions about the personality of the communicatee; to acquire a sense of audience.

Employes' Copies

Copies given free to employes of a publication. (P)
                                                        A.B.C.

Emulsion

The light sensitive coating on films, papers, and plates used in photography. It consists principally of a silver salt or salts suspended in gelatin. (F)   A.S.

Emulsion Batch Number

A number placed on the label of film and paper packages which identifies the batch from which that particular film or paper was made. (F)   A.S.

En

One-half the width of an em. (PR)   R.A.F.

Enameled Paper

Paper coated with clay, glue, and other substances, having a glossy finish; a gloss-coated paper. (PR)   R.R.K.

Enamel Print

A print on metal with glue or cold enamel. (PR) J.S.M.

Enamel Top

An acid-resisting image of either glue or cold enamel. (PR)   J.S.M.

Encaustic Paste

A wax paste used to impart a slight gloss to matte or semi-matte prints. (F)   A.S.

115

Encode
   To transform a message from one representation into another, by operation of code rules. (C)   C.C.

English Finish Paper
   A smooth-finished, machine-made and calendered book paper with an even surface. Is soft, dull and pliable; used largely in book work. (PR)   R.A.F.

Engrave
   To cut or incise lines or designs in metal, wood and other surfaces by manual use of tools; often but improperly applied to "etching." (PR)   J.S.M.

Engraver
   One who engraves; a finisher; the term is loosely applied to photoengravers, regardless of branch or activity. (PR)
                J.S.M.

Engraver's Proof
   In photoengraving carefully executed impression of a line or halftone etching on good quality paper. (PR) J.S.M.

Engraving
   Manual engraving of any surface with tools; any plate produced by engraving and intended for use on a printing press; a printing plate produced by photoengraving. (PR)
                J.S.M.

Engravings, Sectional
   Line or halftone etchings made in sections from a large original, dividing the reproduction into sectional negatives and plates because the camera or platemaking equipment will not accommodate the reproduction as a whole unit. (PR)   J.S.M.

Enlargement
   A reproduction larger than the original itself. (F) J.S.M.

Ensemble

A collection (e.g., of possible signs, signals, messages, from a specified source, with a set of estimated probabilities of occurrence). (C)   C.C.

Entertainment Films

Films made primarily for amusement. (F)   G.W.

Entropy (in statistical thermodynamics)

The expected log probability of the states of a thermodynamic system. The term is used, by analogy, in communication theory, to refer to the information rate of a source of messages, though we deprecate its unqualified usage, in this book. (C)   C.C.

Envelope Corner Card

An address printed at the left of an envelope. (PR)
R.R.K.

Envelope Stuffer

Printed advertising material which is included with mailings of bills, statements or correspondence. (PR) H.V.G.

E.O.D.

Abbreviated instructions for inserting a newspaper advertisement every other day. (A)

E.O.W.

Abbreviated instructions for inserting a newspaper advertisement every other week. (A)

Equal Time

Impressed with the tremendous potential radio gave them for reaching and influencing people, lawmakers, under the Radio Act of 1927, required the broadcasting industry to afford "equal opportunities" to candidates for public office. Any attempt to apply precise definitions to the act (Section 18) had to wait until 1932, when a Nebraska political candi-

117

date brought action against his opposition for false and libelous statements made on the air. The Supreme Court of Nebraska held the station jointly liable with the defamer.

Thus by statutory regulation the industry was required to refrain from censorship of the news of candidates for political office who used its facilities. Also, a station found itself exposed to libel, but could not prevent the broadcast of libelous statements over its facilities.

The Radio Act of 1927 was incorporated into the Communications Act of 1934 and remains essentially the same legislation under which the broadcasting industry operates today. Section 18 of the Act of 1927 was retained as Section 315 of the new act.

Section 315 has been one of the most troublesome provisions of the act, not only because of the inherently controversial nature of politics but also because of a conflict in laws. In prohibiting the station from censoring speeches of political candidates, Congress thought that the licensees who might favor one candidate could get around the intention of the statute by censoring the speeches of his opponent. However, the individual states have jurisdiction in cases of defamation.

Although the industry continued to demand that its relations and duties to the government be defined clearly and its rights explained, Congress took no specific legislative action regarding Section 315 between 1937 and 1959. The Federal Communications Commission continued to conduct hearings and to enforce the "equal time" provision whenever a violation of this right was claimed.

Efforts were made at several House and Senate hearings in 1955 and 1956 to amend the rule governing equal time on the air, but also to clarify the liability of stations to suits for libel and slander arising from speeches of candidates that the stations had no power under the law to censor. But no new amendments came out of the hearings.

In June, 1959, however, the U.S. Supreme Court in a 5-4

decision, upheld the North Dakota Supreme Court which ruled in favor of a Fargo station, whose plea had been that it was not responsible for a certain candidate's libelous remarks because federal law required that it carry the political broadcast without censorship.

The Supreme Court ruled that radio and television stations are immune from libel action in connection with speeches made by political candidates. The decision held that Congress had granted immunity under Section 315 of the Communications Act by requiring stations to give equal time to opposing candidates, but barring broadcasters from censoring candidates' speeches. The court emphasized that all persons are still protected against defamation in that libel action may be brought against any individual making a libelous or defamatory statement.

For over three decades the consensus of opinion had been that Section 315 did not apply to news coverage of political campaigns. In spite of the many legislative proposals dealing with political broadcasting, no serious challenge had been made to the established practice by the stations of inserting recorded portions of appearances by candidates into their radio and television news broadcasts.

However, on Feb. 24, 1959, the FCC issued an interpretation relating to the applicability of Section 315 to certain newscasts carried by several television stations in Chicago. The broadcasting industry rebelled at the decision to have to give equal time in the coverage of news. The Commission could not be swayed by the overwhelming adverse opinion from the mass media, which finally resulted in a presidential pronouncement against the ruling. The Congress reacted, and on Sept. 14, 1959, it passed an amendment to 315 which provided that equal time shall not apply to news and other similar programs.

A little more than a month later, the FCC had to make a ruling on the new amendment in a suit filed by a Philadelphia politician against a television station for what the candidate considered his right to "equal time" on a local community affairs type show. The Commission dismissed the charge in the absence of proof that the show was not a bona fide news interview.

Again, as in 1927 and 1934, Congress and the FCC did not define their terms for what they considered a bona fide newscast, news interview, news documentary and news event. It would appear that the interpretation problem of the latest Section 315 (a) will have to be solved by the courts as it has been in the past. (B)   E.F.

Equivocation (of a noisy communication channel)

As used in communication theory; the rate of loss of selective information at the receiver's end of a channel, due to the noise (measured in bits per second or per signs as stated). Broadly, the receiver's average doubt about the transmitted signals. (C)   C.C.

E.T.

Abbreviation for electrical transcription (B)

Etaoinshrdlu

A pi line made by the compositor running a finger down a row of keys on his typesetting machine. (P)   B.C.B.

Etch

Acid action on a treated metal surface. (PR)   H.V.G.

Etch Proof

When type matter is to be used as "copy" for the plate-maker, in either the letterpress or offset process, it is necessary to provide him with very sharp, clear proofs of even color density, as the camera will pick up any imperfections and reproduce them in the plate. Such proofs must be made by the typesetter with special care. Etch proofs, or reproduction proofs, as they are sometimes called, must be ordered specifically from the printer or typesetter. (PR)   B.B.

Etching Bath
The solution or mordant used for etching. (PR) J.S.M.

Etching Ink
A greasy ink of resinous constituency, used as an acid resist in conjunction with etching powders applied to the inked print or plate. (PR) J.S.M.

Etching Machine
Mechanically operated apparatus for accelerating the process of etching by agitation of the mordant and discharge of the solution against the surface of a metal plate; a device in which etching is conducted by electrolysis. (PR) J.S.M.

Etching Needle
A sharp-pointed steel instrument for drawing lines into an acid-resisting surface. (PR) J.S.M.

Etching Powder
Finely ground mixtures of resins used for dusting relief plates during etching to protect the top and sides of lines and dots. (PR) J.S.M.

Etchings, Photo
Photographic etchings differ from sketches in the subjugation of the photographic image, the main part of the picture being completely redrawn in pencil. (F) A.S.

Etching Tub
A stonewear or acid proofed tray or trough, mechanically oscillated to cause an acid solution to flow back and forth over a metal plate during etching. (PR) J.S.M.

ETV
Abbrevation for Educational TV. (B)

Exchange
A distribution center for films, usually theatrical. (F) G.W.

121

Exchanges
Where one newspaper exchanges copies with another, these copies are called *exchanges,* which are examined and studied regularly. Most large papers have an exchange editor to perform this duty. (P)   B.C.B.

Exclusive
A newsstory is exclusive when it is the property of only one newspaper—a *scoop.* (P)   B.C.B.

Exciter Lamp
Light bulb in a projector which projects light through the film to the photoelectric cell. (F)   G.W.

Executive Privilege
The notion that executive officials, particularly in government, have an inherent right to withhold information from the public or the legislature. (C)

Exeltype
An early and original form of Screnline and Shadowgraph procedures. (PR)   J.S.M.

Expanded
A thick type face. (PR)   R.R.K.

Experimental Film
A film which, by subject or technique, differs from most films. (F)   G.W.

Expiration
Termination of period for which subscription was paid. (P)   A.B.C.

Exposure
Audience exposure to a specific advertisement, broadcast, or publication. Depth of exposure is an indication of audience consciousness of an advertising message. (A)

Exposure

The process of controlling the amount of light which reaches the film. (F)

G.W.

Exposure Factors

The difficulty encountered by beginners in photography may be attributed to the large number of factors which must be taken into consideration in arriving at a correct exposure time. Following is a list of the more important factors: (1) relative aperture of lens; (2) kind of film used; (3) reflecting power of the subject; (4) season of the year; (5) time of day; (6) if artificial light is used, color of the light; (7) geographical location and altitude. (F)   A.S.

Exposure Indicator

A device attached to plate-holders to show that the plate has been exposed. (F)   A.S.

Exposure Meter

An electrical or optical device that measures the amount of light reflected from or directed on a subject. This is done by converting or translating light energy to exposure units, thus indicating lens aperture and shutter speed. (F)   A.S.

Extension

Extension of the camera is the distance to which the front of the camera (lens mount) can be drawn out from the back. (F)   A.S.

Extension

Continuance by publisher of a subscription beyond its original expiration date because of lowering of subscription price or reducing the frequency of issue. (P)   A.B.C.

Extra

Edition of a newspaper other than those issued regularly each day. (P)   A.B.C.

Extra-Condensed
A very thin type face. (PR)   R.R.K.

Equivalent Exposure
The change in exposure time required when camera lights are moved from their normal position. (F)   J.S.M.

Evaporating Dish
A wide shallow vessel of porcelain, silica or enameled iron used to purify (evaporate) wet collodion silver baths by boiling off a definite volume of the solution. (PR)   J.S.M.

Eveready Case
Camera case with drop front and openings to permit viewing film window and operating various parts, so that camera can be used without removal from case. (F)   A.S.

Everset Shutter
A shutter which does not require cocking or resetting between exposures. (F)   A.S.

F

F.C.C.
The Federal Communications Commission. The Federal authority which licenses broadcasting stations and assigns frequencies.

Face
Either the part of a type that makes the impression, or a type face style. (PR)   P.W.B.

Face
The sensitized side of a photographic surface; the working surface of a photographic image or printing plate. (PR)
J.S.M.

Face Down, Face Up
Etching copper halftones in a tray of ferric chloride solution, with the plate supported in notched wooden blocks in either a face down or face up position in the mordant. (PR)
J.S.M.

Facing
The surface of the standard outdoor advertising structure upon or against which the advertising message is exhibited. (A)   R.D.L.

Facing Text Matter

Describes position given to an advertisement opposite reading matter. If requested, often costs extra. (A)   P.W.B.

Facsimile

A rather misused term to indicate a reproduction the same size of the original, and in which all detail and tone values are reproduced in a manner closely resembling those of the original. To apply the term to a reproduction of an oil painting is meaningless—a facsimile reproduction would entail furnishing an exactly duplicated painting. A highlight halftone plate in which the highlight dots have been eliminated by local etching. (PR)   J.S.M.

Fade

Taking sound out slowly by backing away from microphone or turning down the level on the audio console. A cross fade in audio occurs when one voice goes out while another moves in. (B)   N.A.B.

Fade-In (or-out)

The gradual emergence of an image on the screen from darkness or disappearance into darkness. (F)   G.W.

Fade-In (or -out)

A television control technique by which a scene is gradually brought into view or is gradually dimmed from view. (B)   H.V.G.

Fading

Variations in the intensity of radio signals received over a great distance from the transmitter. (B)   H.V.G.

Fading Area

The area where fading is most noticeable for a given station. (B)   H.V.G.

Fake

A falsified story. (P)   B.C.B.

126

Fake Color Process

A method of producing halftone color plates from a photograph or other monochrome original, the color effects in the various plates being obtained by judicious re-etching and finishing. (PR)   J.S.M.

Faked Photograph

A photograph print in which detail or tone values have been deliberately changed or altered by retouching. (F)
          J.S.M.

Family

A group of related type fonts in a series, as the "Caslon Family." (PR)   R.R.K.

Fanfare

Music which introduces the start of a show, an entrance, or a special announcement. (B)   H.V.G.

Farm Out

To sublet a process in printing, as the binding, composition, or presswork. (PR)   R.R.K.

Farm Publication

A publication directed to various types of farmers, such as poultry, dairy or general. It may be a national circulation magazine or directed to certain areas or states. (A)   H.V.G.

Fast-Slow Travel

Traffic Audit Bureau formula for checking outdoor billboard traffic exposure. Fast: over 30 miles per hour. Slow: less than 30 miles per hour. (A)   R.D.L.

Fat Head

A headline too large for space allowed for it. (P) B.C.B.

Feature

To give special prominence to a story. Any story that may not be news, strictly regarded, yet is timely and interesting may be called a feature. The word is also used to denominate the most important or interesting element in a story. (P)   B.C.B.

Feature
A full-length film of five or more reels. (F)   G.W.

Feature Issue Subscriptions
Subscriptions to periodic special feature issues only, such subscriptions being accepted at a price different from that made to those who subscribe for all the issues of the year. Also known as "intermittent" subscriptions. (PR)   A.B.C.

Fee
A specified amount charged by an agency for service rendered an advertiser which is not covered by the usual agency commission. (A)   H.V.G.

Feed
Supply a program to other stations. (B)   N.A.B.

Feed Back
The squeal occurring when the input and output of an electrical circuit are accidentally connected. (B)   H.V.G.

Feedback
A concept in human communication which evolved from machine control systems or self-governing mechanisms. Common to the idea, whether mechanical, electrical or biological, is communication of information and self-stabilizing control action, e.g., the thermostat, which controls the temperature of a room. In human communication it has come to mean keeping the message channel open and allowing for give-and-take between the sender and receiver of information. It demonstrates a behavior pattern or control action by which the sender and receiver of information remain selective toward conditions of stability or instability created by their interaction. (C)

128

Felt Finish

Antique (rough textured) paper with a surface of unusual character or design generally manufactured for some specific purpose. (PR)   B.B.

Felt Side

The correct side of the paper for printing. The top side of the sheet when manufacturing. (PR)   R.A.F.

Ferrotype

Photographic image on a sheet of black japanned iron; a tintype. (PR)   J.S.M.

Field

The photographed area that will appear in the film. (F)
                                                              G.W.

Field Strength

The intensity of the signal transmitted by a station within its coverage area. (B)   H.V.G.

15 and 2

The usual terms on which advertising media is ordered by advertising agencies for their clients, i.e. 15 per cent commission is allowed by the media on the gross cost, plus 2 per cent discount on the net amount for prompt payment. (See Cash Discount.)   (A)   H.V.G.

File

A correspondent *files* a story when he dispatches it by wire or by radio. All newspapers keep *files* of their back copies. (P)   B.C.B.

Fill

Music or ad lib inserted to bring a program up to time. (B)   N.A.B.

Filler

Short items that may be placed almost anywhere on the

129

page, as distinguished from stories bearing top heads. (P)
B.C.B.

Fill-In
The name, address and salutation added to direct mail letters to make them appear individually typewritten. (A)
H.V.G.

Fill-In Light
In portraiture or other photography by artificial light, fill-in lights are used (in addition to main lights) to fill in the dark shadow portions of the subject so that some detail will be recorded. (F) A.S.

Film
A thin layer of light-sensitive silver emulsion applied to plates, films and papers; a photographic material comprising a sensitive layer on a transparent flexible support; an image on photographic film; the thin skin-like collodion image after removal from its temporary glass support. (PR) J.S.M.

Film Chamber
The removable section of the camera that holds the film. (F) G.W.

Film Cleaner
Any liquid which may be used safely to remove dust and grease from film. One such is:

Ethyl alcohol	85%
Methyl alcohol	10%
Strong ammonium hydroxide	5%

(F) A.S.

Film Clips
Short sequences from film libraries inserted in live telecasts. Also called "film strips." (B) N.A.B.

Film Forum
A combination film showing and discussion. (F) G.W.

130

Film Library

Any institution (business, government, or educational) that circulates or distributes prints of films. (F)　　G.W.

Film Sequence

Part of a telecast composed of motion picture scenes. (B)　　P.W.B.

Filmstrips

Motion-picture film that is projected one frame at a time; also called slidefilms. (F)　　G.W.

Filter

Color filter. A porous wad of absorbent cotton or sheet of special paper through which photographic solutions are passed (filtered) to remove precipitates and foreign matter held in suspension in the liquid. (PR)　　J.S.M.

Filter

Colored glass or gelatin placed in front of the lens to absorb certain light rays so as to highlight or eliminate certain colors or shades. (F)　　G.W.

Filter

A special type of microphone that muffles sounds. (B)　　N.A.B.

Filter Neutral

A filter which has no color absorption or selectivity. (F)　　A.S.

Filter Factor

The additional exposure necessary when using a particular color filter on the camera lens. (F)　　J.S.M.

Filter Ratio Scale

A device in the form of a glass transparency designed to accurately determine the exposure factors for any color filters used in conjunction with color-sensitive photographic negative materials. (PR)　　J.S.M.

131

Finder

Eyepiece for observing what is being photographed through the camera lens. (F)   G.W.

Finder, Angle

A finder so arranged that the photographer may take a picture in a direction at right angles to the direction he is facing—used in candid camera work. (F)   A.S.

Fine Grain

Any photographic emulsion of particularly small grain; in particular, a print made from the original negative from which a duplicate is struck. (F)   G.W.

Fine Line

A thin black finishing line enclosing the image on a printing plate; also called a hairline. (PR)   J.S.M.

Fine Line Process

An indirect procedure for reproducing very delicate line originals. It involves the use of an unsharp line positive for masking the line negative made from the original, and results in a sharply defined line positive, from which a final line negative must be made by contact printing. (PR)
                    J.S.M.

Fine Papers

Bonds, Ledgers, Writing, Papeteries and Weddings. (PR)
                    R.A.F.

Fine White Line

A thin white line cut or etched into a plate. (PR) J.S.M.

Fingernails

Printer's slang for parentheses. Also called "parens."
(P)   B.C.B.

Finish

The particular treatment given outer edges of printing

plates, such as ovaling, hairline finish, square finish, vignetted finish, etc. (PR)   J.S.M.

Finish
The surface of a sheet of paper, such as "laid," "wove," "antique," "coated," etc. (PR)   H.V.G.

Finished Art
Art work which is completed and ready for reproduction. (A)   H.V.G.

Finisher
The engraver or craftsman who performs final re-etching, engraving, tooling and other operations on printing plates prior to proving. (PR)   J.S.M.

Finishing
The final work performed on a printing plate for removal of defects and to promote the best possible reproduction. (PR)   J.S.M.

Finishing Line
Border line on the outer edges of halftone plates. (PR)   J.S.M.

Firm Order
Magazine space order that is non-cancellable after a certain date. (P)   P.W.B.

First-Day Story
A story published for the first time; a story dealing with something that has just happened. (P)   B.C.B.

Fish Bowl
The reserved studio location from where the client or sponsor can view a program. (B)

Five W's
"Who, what, when, where, why." With the interrogative

"how," they represent the questions to be answered in the conventional lead. (P)   T.E.B.

Fix
  Correct; a fix is a correction (P)   B.C.B.

Fixation
  Chemical removal of undeveloped silver salts from photographic images by treatment in a fixing bath, or one comprising a solution of sodium thiosulfate (hypo). (PR) J.S.M.

Fixative
  A liquid solution sprayed on a pencil, pastel, or charcoal drawing which dries quickly, leaving a protective, transparent coating. (A)   H.V.G.

Fixed Location
  A specific space position from issue to issue. (A)

Fixing
  The removal of all undeveloped emulsion from the film. (F)   G.W.

Fixing-Hardening
  A bath in which film, plates, or prints are freed from the unaltered silver bromide and at the same time the gelatin film is toughened. (F)   A.S.

Flag
  The first-page nameplate of the newspaper; the editorial heading; a lead sticking up in the midst of a column of type to warn the printer that a correction or an addition is on the way. (P)   B.C.B.

Flag Waver
  Newspaper that emphasizes patriotism excessively. (P)
                                                       T.E.B.

Flap
  A piece of heavy paper attached to the back of artwork or layout and folded over it for protection. (A)   H.V.G.

134

Flare

Appearance of a circular disc of light in the center of photographic images when viewed on a focusing screen, the defect due either to optical errors in the camera lens or to mechanical causes. The condition known as "camera flare" is due to scattered light within the apparatus and causes fogged images, particularly in the shadow areas of halftone negatives. (PR)   J.S.M.

Flare Spot

A fogged spot, generally near the center of the film or plate. It is usually circular or arc-shaped, and may be due either to reflection from the lens surfaces or from the interior of the lens mount. (F)   A.S.

Flash

A bulletin by telephone, telegraph, or radio that conveys the first brief word of an event that has just taken place. (P)   B.C.B.

Flash

Extremely short scene. (F)   G.W.

Flash (approach to billboard)

Less than 75 ft. for slow traffic. Less than 100 ft. for fast traffic. Less than 40 ft. for pedestrian traffic. (A)   R.D.L.

Flashback

A scene that cuts in on the story to show something that has happened in the past. (F)   G.W.

Flash Exposure

A means of hypersensitizing film by exposing it very briefly, using an evenly illuminated subject such as open sky. This exposure overcomes the inertia of the film. An exposure of 1/300 second at f 16 is about right for most film. (F)   A.S.

Flash Exposure

A supplementary exposure in halftone photography with

a small lens stop to a sheet of white paper placed over the original or to the rays of a flashlamp, this for the purpose of strengthening the dots in the shadows of the negative. (PR)   J.S.M.

Flashing
Giving the flash exposure in halftone photography; sometimes called "papering." (PR)   J.S.M.

Flashlamp
Specially devised electric lamp attached to the front of a process camera and designed to transmit light through the lens during the flash exposure. (PR)   J.S.M.

Flat
The glass plate on which a number of wet collodion or strip film negatives have been transferred and arranged to promote photoprinting and etching as a single unit; a zinc or copper plate bearing a number of line or halftone images and photoprinted from a flat. (PR)   J.S.M.

Flat
The stripper's completed work in offset-lithography; negatives or positives properly assembled on a lithographic layout and ready for plate making. (PR)   R.R.K.

Flat
A wooden frame, covered with canvas and then painted —the basic unit of television scenery. (B)   N.A.B.

Flat Bed
Any typographic printing press in which the type form lies flat, and the ink and paper are conveyed to it by rollers, in making the impression. (PR)   B.B.

Flat Cast
When a "mat" is furnished for use in a publication, it is necessary to have a stereotype made from it and mounted just as an engraving would be. Inasmuch as most stereotypes

are curved for use on rotary presses, it is customary to specify a "flat cast" when it is intended to mount it for ordinary publication printing. (PR) B.B.

Flat Color
This term has no reference to the color itself, or to its appearance when printed; it means that the color is to be printed by itself, not overlaid or blended with others. (PR) B.B.

Flat Etch
The first or initial etch given a halftone plate to promote required printing depth. (PR) J.S.M.

Flatness
Lack of contrast in print or negative, generally due to flat, even lighting, overexposure, or incorrect concentration of developer. (F) A.S.

Flat Plate
An etched halftone on which no re-etching or finishing has been performed; an inferior halftone plate, i.e., one lacking in contrast. (PR) J.S.M.

Flat Proof
An impression made without makeready from an unfinished or finished printing plate; a proof lacking in quality. (PR) J.S.M.

Flat Rate
A fixed charge for space in a publication regardless of amount of space used or frequency of insertions. (A) H.V.G.

Flat Tint Plate
A sheet of copper or zinc cut to required shape for printing a solid color; tint block (PR) J.S.M.

Flat Tones
Lithographed areas of dot formation containing a single tone value, without gradations. (PR) R.A.F.

Flexichrome

A method for hand coloring a black and white photograph, similar to color toning. (A)   H.V.G.

Flimsy

A thin, carbon copy of a newsstory. (P)   B.C.B.

Flip Cards

Illustrations or titles or individual cards to be "flipped over" for TV commercials. (A)   H.V.G.

Floating

Manipulation and placement of wet collodion and strip-film negatives during stripping and arrangement on a flat. (PR)   J.S.M.

Flong

A paper matrix used in stereotyping. (PR)   R.R.K.

Floor Manager

Production—staff member who remains in the studio to relay cues from the director in the control room to performers and technical staff. (B)   N.A.B.

Flop

If you wish to have the subject of a photograph—a building, a person, or what have you—face in the opposite direction, the engraver or lithographer can "flop the negative" and get this result in the finished plate. You have to watch this, though. If a man were holding a pencil in his right hand, for instance, the flopped picture would make it appear that he was writing with his left hand. (PR) B.B.

Flowing

Coating a glass plate, negative or sheet of metal with various photoengraving solutions by flowing them over the surface; collodionizing. (PR)   J.S.M.

Fluff
An obvious error made by an actor during broadcast. (B)

Fluorescence Color Process
Method of halftone color reproduction involving the use of originals (paintings) executed with special pigments, and necessitating a special procedure of color photography. (PR)   J.S.M.

Fluorescent Lighting
Commonly used luminescent light for outdoor posters and bulletins. (A)   R.D.L.

Fluorographic Process
Procedure of highlight halftone photography, entailing the use of originals in the form of washdrawings prepared with special fluorescing (ultraviolet-absorbent) pigments. (PR)   J.S.M.

Flush
Type matter lined up and set even with the edge of a page or block of printed matter; i.e., "set flush right." (PR)   H.V.G.

Flush and Indent
A direction to printers, meaning set the first line of the copy flush, without paragraph indention, and indent the remainder one em or more at the left. (P)   B.C.B.

Flush Blocking
Trimming plate and block so that printing surface is flush with the edge of the block. (PR)   R.A.F.

Flush Cover
A cover that has been trimmed to the same size as the inside text pages. (PR)   R.A.F.

139

Flush Edge
A plate with no excess metal on one or more edges of the printing surface. (PR) J.S.M.

Flush Head
A headline set flush to the left with a ragged ending of lines to the right. (P) B.C.B.

Flush Mounted
Cuts mounted on wood without shoulders or "tack room." Up until recently, when it was necessary to mount engravings in this way for some particular reason, it involved "anchoring," which was expensive and not too satisfactory. Nowadays some engravers are actually gluing the metal to the block with a plastic adhesive, applied hot and under great pressure. When this method has been further perfected it promises to displace the use of tacking altogether, except in the case of large plates. (PR) B.B.

Flush Paragraphs
Paragraphs having no indentions. (PR) R.A.F.

FM
Frequency Modulation—a broadcasting method that eliminates electrical interference and provides greater fidelity than the more common AM (Amplitude Modulation) broadcasting. (B) H.V.G.

Focal Length
The distance of the principal focus of a lens from its optical center. Really equivalent to the size of a lens, or the factor which determines the size of the image at a given distance from the subject or original. (F) J.S.M.

Focal Plane
The plane surface on which the image transmitted by a lens is brought to sharpest focus. The focal plane on process cameras is the position interchangeably occupied by the

focusing screen and the photographic plate or film. (PR)
J.S.M.

Focus
To adjust the lens so as to sharpen the image. (F)   G.W.

Focusing
The act of bringing a camera image to correct size and proper sharpness. (F)   J.S.M.

Focusing, Automatic
Determination of the correct position of the focal plane on process cameras by mathematical calculation, or by use of scales based on the laws of conjugate foci. (PR)   J.S.M.

Focusing Glass
A small achromatic magnifying glass used for ocular examination of cameras images on focusing screens to promote sharpest possible focus. (F)   J.S.M.

Focusing Mount
The lens mount which permits the lens to be moved toward or away from the film in order to focus it accurately on given distances. All fast lenses are in focusing mounts, and the slower ones may or may not be. Focusing is accomplished by moving a rotating collar which is calibrated in feet. (F)   A.S.

Focusing Negative or Target
A developed negative consisting of a geometrical design which may be placed in the negative holder of the enlarger for focusing. The extreme contrast and detail in the negative permit exact focusing, and the negative to be enlarged is substituted after the focusing is complete. (F)   A.S.

Focusing Scale
Graduated scale on process camera for bringing images to correct size without image measurement and ocular focusing. (PR) (F)   J.S.M.

Focusing Screen
Surface on which camera images are viewed and brought to correct size and sharpness. Usually consists of a sheet of groundglass, preferably with a square or circular patch of transparency in the center to facilitate closer examination of line images and delicate detail. (PR)   J.S.M.

Fog
Photographic defect in which the image is completely or locally veiled by a deposit of silver of varying density, due either to the action of extraneous actinic light or through improper chemical action. (F)   J.S.M.

Fog Filter
Actually not a filter, but a diffusion screen, used to give the effect of fog in a picture. (F)   A.S.

Fold
The point at which the newspaper page is folded in half. All important news is *played* above this fold. (P) B.C.B.

Folio
In ordinary editorial usage, folio just means page number. Folios are almost invariably set outside the type margin on each page. (PR)   B.B.

Folio
A size of paper measuring 17"x22". (PR)   H.V.G.

Follow, Follow Up
A follow story is one based on a story previously published; it gives later developments. Same as a second-day story. Also, a subsidiary story following a big lead, and relating to the same or a similar subject. (P)   B.C.B.

Follow Copy
Directions to printers, meaning set the copy exactly as it is written. May also be used in referring proof back to proofroom for correction. (P)   B.C.B.

142

Folo

Abbreviation of *follow*. (P) B.C.B.

Font

An assortment of letters and characters of any one size and style of type. (PR) R.R.K.

Footage

The way in which film is measured and the standard of length. (F) G.W.

Footstick

The heavy metal bar at the bottom of a chase, used in locking it. The footstick provides purchase for the *quoins* or *screws* used to clamp the *form* shut. (PR) B.C.B.

Forcing

Continuing development for a long time in order to get detail or density, or treating underexposed films or prints by adding alkali. (F) A.S.

Form

Metal square (chase) into which the type to be used on a particular page is placed. (PR) T.E.B.

Format

The size, style, shape, printing requirements, etc., of any magazine, catalogue, book or printed piece. (PR) R.A.F.

Format

The form or proportion of the space to which the layout must be adapted, such as picture format. (A) H.V.G.

Format

The form or general makeup of a radio or television program. (B) H.V.G.

Forwarding

The process of binding a book after the sheets are fastened together. (PR) R.R.K.

Foto
Newspaper photograph. (P)   T.E.B.

Fotog
Abbreviation for news photographer. (P)   B.C.B.

Fourth Estate
A name given to the newspaper press, or the body of newspaper publishers and writers. (P)   R.A.F.

Foundry Proof
The final proof before sending a form to the electrotyper. (PR)   R.A.F.

Foundry Type
Individual type characters for setting by hand. Unlike machine types which are remelted after use, foundry types are made of especially hard metal and are used repeatedly. (PR)   H.V.G.

Four-Color Process
An extension of three-color reproduction, in which a fourth or "black" plate is used in conjunction with those for the primary colors. (PR)   J.S.M.

Four-Way Powdering
In the dragon's blood process of relief etching, brushing of etching powder in four different directions on the plate, thereby protecting all sides of lines and dots. (PR)
                                                              J.S.M.

Frame
Single complete television scene. (B)   P.W.B.

Frame
Each individual picture on the motion-picture film. (F)
                                                              G.W.

Frequency
The wave length assigned to a particular station by the F.C.C. (B)   H.V.G.

Frequency
The value scale of sound tones, in kilocycles. (F)   G.W.

Free-Form Cut Out
Outdoor bulletin-type display but without solid background. (A)   R.D.L.

Free Lance
An artist or writer who takes individual assignments from different advertisers or advertising agencies but is not in their fulltime employ. (A)   H.V.G.

Free Publication
One not meeting the standards of the Audit Bureau of Circulations which require that at least 70 per cent of the total distribution during a regular six month Publisher's Statement period be on a paid basis. (P)   A.B.C.

Free Sheet
Term applied to papers free from groundwood. (PR)
                                                    R.A.F.

Free Silver
Nascent silver nitrate solution on the surface of wet collodion plates during exposure and development. (PR)
                                                    J.S.M.

French Fold
Manner of folding a sheet, once horizontally and once vertically, which has been printed on one side so that only the printed surfaces are visible. (PR)   H.V.G.

Frilling
A photographic defect in which the emulsion separates from the plate or film in folds and wrinkles. Frilling usually starts at the edges of the plate, during fixing, but may occur at other stages in the photographic process. It is caused by differences of temperature between solutions, etc. See reticulation. (F)   A.S.

Frisket
Paper mask or stencil placed over dead metal and bearers of printing plates during proving. (PR) J.S.M.

Frisket
A very thin paper applied over a photograph or art work in which areas are cut away, the remaining areas acting as a mask, for retouching, etc. (A) H.V.G.

Front-of-Book
Refers to position for advertisements placed in front pages of a magazine, ahead of editorial matter. (P) P.W.B.

Front Office
The section of a small newspaper plant where the public is met, as distinguished from the *backroom*. (P) B.C.B.

Frothing Powder
A mixture of powdered gum arabic, alum or other ingredients sometimes added to nitric acid baths to accelerate zinc etching by frothing of the bath. (PR) J.S.M.

Fudge Box or Jigger
A mechanical contrivance consisting of a clamp in which linotype slugs can be locked and the whole then sent to press as a part of the first page. The fudge box is used for late news bulletins and sports scores. It obviates the necessity of frequent replates and makes for increased speed in presswork. (P) B.C.B.

Fugitive Colors
Colors or inks which are not permanent, fading or changing color when exposed to light. (PR) R.A.F.

Full-Bound
A binding completely covered with leather. (PR) R.A.F.

Full Net Program
A particular program broadcast to every station on a network. (B) H.V.G.

Full Position

Preferred position for a newspaper advertisement, generally following and next to reading matter, or top of column next to reading matter. When specifically ordered, it costs more than run-of-paper advertising. (A) H.V.G.

Full Showing

In car card advertising, usually denotes one card in each car of a line in which space is bought. In the New York subways a full showing consists of two cards in each car; a half showing, two cards in every other car. In outdoor poster advertising, a full or "100-intensity," showing indicates use of a specified number of panels in a particular market. (A)
H.V.G.

Full Time Station

A station licensed by the F.C.C. to stay on the air 24 hours a day. (B) H.V.G.

Fulltone

A highlight halftone plate with the deepest shadows represented by solids. (PR) J.S.M.

Furniture

Pieces of wood or metal of less height than type which are packed around the type, if needed, to make it possible to lock up and *justify* a form. (PR) B.C.B.

Fusing

Evaporation of a wet collodion silver bath to the crystallized form. (PR) J.S.M.

Future

A note about a story that will develop later; kept by the editor in a *futures book*. (P) B.C.B.

Fuzz

Loose fibers or lint appearing on paper surface. (PR)
R.A.F.

Fuzzy

Popular descriptive term in photoengraving for a number of defects: an original (or reproduction) showing blurred or ill-defined detail; halftone negatives with dots lacking proper opacity and sharpness; halftone plate with irregularly etched or broken dot formation; a poor impression caused by slurring during proving. (PR)   J.S.M.

FYI

"For your information." (P)

G

Gallery
The photographic department of a photoengraving plant.
(PR)   J.S.M.

Galley
A shallow tray in which type is placed for assembling or storage. (PR)   H.V.G.

Galley Press
A proofing machine for type and plates. (PR)   R.R.K.

Galley Proof
Any proof taken of type matter while it is still on a galley, before it has been made up into pages. (PR) R.A.F.

Gallup Poll
Takes its name from the inventor, Dr. George H. Gallup. A fact-finding service sold mainly to U.S. newspapers whose sole function is to measure public opinion on political, social and economic issues of the day. There are Gallup Poll affiliates in many European countries. (C)

Gamboging
Application of an aqueous emulsion of gamboge to certain areas of prints on metal prior to laying tints with benday films. (PR)   J.S.M.

Gamma
The degree of contrast or gradation in a photographic negative. (F)   J.S.M.

Gang Negative
A negative bearing a number of properly positioned duplicate images, produced either from a pasted-up original, by assembling and stripping duplicate negatives, or by direct printing from a single negative on a plate or film with a photocomposing machine. (PR)   J.S.M.

Gang Plate
A printing plate bearing a number of duplicate images as an integral unit; a plate made from a gang negative. (PR)   J.S.M.

Gate
The retainer that holds the film against the aperture in the projector. (F)   G.W.

Gatekeeper
The individual or group who "opens" or "closes" the *gate* to any message that comes along in the interlocking networks of social communication in society. Persons or groups that have a large number of message networks centering upon them tend to exercise greater influence and power in society (after Schramm). (C)

Gathering
Assembling the signatures or sheets of a book or booklet, often confused with collating. (PR)   R.R.K.

Gauge
An electrotype of the same thickness as an engraving. Known as a 16 gauge, it measures .063 inches thick. (PR)   H.V.G.

Gelatin Relief Plate
A printing plate or surface consisting of a relief image

150

of light-hardened gelatin; a cheap substitute for photoengravings. (PR)   J.S.M.

General Semantics
The study and improvement of human evaluative processes with special emphasis on their relation to signs and symbols including language. (C)

Giveaway Show
A program centering around the free distribution of merchandise to participants or to the audience. (B)

Glass Washing
Rendering glass plates chemically clean for wet collodion photographic supports. (PR)   J.S.M.

Glassine
A semi-transparent paper often used for proofing type to ascertain whether it fits properly in the space for which it is intended. (A)   H.V.G.

Glossy
The kind of photographic papers that can be ferrotyped to a high gloss. (F)   A.S.

Glossy
Photograph with a shiny finish. The glossy is preferred because it provides better detail when used for a cut. (P)   T.E.B.

Glossy Print
A photograph or photostat which has been finished with a high surface gloss, making detail within the art more definite. (A)   H.V.G.

Glue Enamel Process
Use of a solution of bichromated fish glue as a sensitizer for metal plates, development of the image with water, and burning-in of the print to convert the image into an acid resist. (PR)   J.S.M.

151

Gift Subscription
Subscription paid for by one other than the recipient. (P)   A.B.C.

Goldenrod Paper
A support for negatives used by a stripper in making flats for the albumin process of platemaking in offset-lithography. The masking of goldenrod paper prevents the exposure of the plate in the blank areas. (PR)   R.R.K.

Goodnight
A reporter takes a goodnight from his boss when he goes off duty; the word also used to indicate when the news section of a paper is closed. (P)   B.C.B.

Gouache
A method of painting with opaque colors which have been ground in water and mixed with a preparation of gum. (A)   H.V.G.

Gradation
The tonal range in prints and negatives. If there are only a few tones between the deepest shadow and the brightest highlight, the gradation is "steep"; if there are many tones the gradation is "long." (F)   A.S.

Graf
Paragraph. (P)   B.C.B.

Grafa-Tone Screen
A special type of halftone screen producing effects ranging from dot to wavy line formations. (PR)   J.S.M.

Grain
The distribution of silver particles in photographic emulsions and images. (F)   J.S.M.

Grain
As paper is manufactured the fibres of cellulose have a tendency to settle in one direction, parallel to one another,

152

as if they had been combed. The direction in which these fibres run is the grain of the paper, and wherever possible it is desirable to fold paper with the grain, not against it. In any lot of paper, the direction of the grain is marked by the manufacturer, generally by underlining one of the dimensions, as 25 x 38. To test for grain, moisten one side of a piece of the paper. It will begin to roll itself up into a cylinder; the grain runs parallel with the axis of the cylinder. (PR) B.B.

Grained Plate
An etched printing plate possessing a grained or stippled surface. (PR) J.S.M.

Grain Halftone
A halftone reproduction made with either a dust grain or by means of a grain screen. (PR) J.S.M.

Graining
Roughening the surface of a metal offset-lithographic press plate by means of marbles and an abrasive to increase its water-carrying capacity during the press run. (PR) R.R.K.

Graining Bath
A dilute nitric acid-alum solution used for imparting a matt surface to zinc plates before sensitization of the metal. (PR) J.S.M.

Grain Screen
A halftone screen embodying a grain rather than a ruled line formation; a mezzograph screen. (PR) J.S.M.

Grapevine
Miscellaneous time copy, as good six months hence as today, which is edited, headed up, set in type, and stowed away against a time when emergency filler is needed. Also called "plug" copy. (P) B.C.B.
An informal communication network with no chain of

command or formal procedure for transmitting information. (C)

Graphite Coating

The graphite coating applied to the mold in electrotyping to produce conductivity and to insure the rapid and uniform deposit of metal. (PR)   R.A.F.

Graver

Any of various cutting or shaping tools used by finishers or engravers. (PR)   J.S.M.

Graveyard Shift

Same as *dog-watch* or *lobster-trick*. (P)   B.C.B.

Gravure

One of the three major printing processes, the other two being letterpress and lithography. Gravure differs from the others in that the portions of the plate to be printed are etched out or depressed, rather than raised as in letterpress printing. The plate is covered by ink which is then scraped off, except for that remaining in the etched or depressed areas, which provides the printed impression. At the present time the high cost of making gravure (or "intaglio") plates makes the process impractical for small publications or other work where the press run is short. It is entirely possible that new developments in this field within the next few years will overcome this difficulty. (PR)   B.B.

Gray Scale

A graduated strip showing neutral tones ranging from black to white, placed at the side of colored originals during photography as a means of determining accurate exposure in separation negatives and the uniformity of such images. (PR)   J.S.M.

Greek In

Commercial artists' term for rows of dots or meaning-

154

less symbols used in a sketch or rough dummy and intended to indicate the position and weight of printed lines in the finished work. (PR)   B.B.

Green Film
Newly developed film which, although apparently dry, still contains a considerable amount of moisture. Even in a warm room film does not become completely dry in less than six to twelve hours, and it is best not to attempt printing or enlargement of film sooner than this. (F)   A.S.

Green Proof
First proof pulled after type has been set. Consequently, this proof must be read carefully for typographical errors. (PR)   T.E.B.

Gripper Edge
Grippers are devices on printing presses that pick up the sheet of paper from the paper table and hold it in position while it receives the impression. All work printed on sheet-fed presses must have a margin of about ¾″ on one edge of the form to accommodate these grippers; where this edge will come on various pages depends upon the imposition of the form. (PR)   B.B.

Gross
The published rate for space or time quoted by an advertising medium, including agency commission, cash discount and any other discounts. (A)   H.V.G.

Groundglass
A sheet of glass ground to a matte surface; a focusing screen. (F)   J.S.M.

Groundwood
A mechanically-prepared coarse wood-pulp used chiefly in the manufacture of newsprint and lowest-priced grades of book paper. (PR)   R.A.F.

Group (Mail Subscriptions Special)

Subscriptions in quantities to corporations, institutions or individuals for employes, subsidiary companies or branch offices under special conditions specified in the rules of the Audit Bureau of Circulations. (P)   A.B.C.

Group Organizer

A person who takes two or more subscriptions to the same publication from a group of individuals, collectively, and sends the order for all of the group at the same time, each member of the group thereby receiving a reduction from the regular subscription price. (P)   A.B.C.

Guideline

The indispensable *slug* or title given each newsstory as a guide to both copyeditor and printer. Thus, a political story might be called "Pol," and each section would be so marked, while the headline would bear the same designation; for example, "Add 1 Pol," "Add 2 Pol," "Pol 8 head," "Pol 2 head," "Insert Pol," "Precede Pol." Each guideline is calculated to give a hint as to the nature of the story. (P)   B.C.B.

Guider

On proof presses, means of fixing the exact position of paper to obtain register. Paper is placed in contact with guides. A preliminary sketch, colored proof or drawing to serve as guidance in making colorplates. (PR)   J.S.M.

Guillotine

A machine comprising a heavy treadle-operated steel blade, used for cutting sheets of copper and zinc, also for trimming finished etchings. (PR)   J.S.M.

Gutter

The inside margins of facing pages, the edge along which the publication is bound. (A)   H.V.G.

H

Hairline

The fine and delicate lines in a type face design or in an illustration; hairline rule is the thinnest made in letterpress. (PR)   R.R.K.

Hairline

The narrowest or finest black or white line capable of being etched or engraved on a relief printing plate; a black finishing line bordering the edges of a square finished half-tone plate. (PR)   J.S.M.

Hairline Boxes

Shallow little one-column boxes made of border rule that prints in extremely fine lines. (P)   B.C.B.

Hair Spaces

Half-point and one-point spaces made in various point sizes used to letterspace words and to justify lines of type. (PR)   R.R.K.

Halation

Spreading of light action beyond proper boundaries in photographic negatives, particularly around the highlights of the image. (F)   U.S.M.

157

Halation

Blurred image or circle of light due to reflection or dispersal of light. (B)   H.V.G.

Half Prints

Usually an 8-page newspaper supplement, 4 pages of which are blank, supplied by a feature syndicate to weekly newspapers. (P)

Half-Bound

A binding of which only the back and corners are covered with leather. (PR)   R.A.F.

Half-Diamond Indention

When successive lines are indented each slightly more than the ones above in type composition. (PR)   R.R.K.

Half-Lap

A television control technique where two pictures are held simultaneously on the screen, one on each half. (B)
                                                             H.V.G.

Half Stick

Matter set in one half-column measure. (P)   B.C.B.

Half Title

A page of a book on which appears only the title of the volume and precedes the first page of text or a division of the book. (PR)   H.V.G.

Halftone

A printing plate, made by the photoengraver or the lithographer for the reproduction of photographs or artwork. The halftone reproduction of pictures is actually an optical illusion; what the eye really sees is an area of minute dots —about 14,400 of them to the square inch. What appears to be blacks and grays and tone gradations that make a picture, are in reality only the varying sizes of the dots, as can be seen under a strong magnifying glass.

In the engraving process these dots are produced by the use of a glass screen, ruled in very fine cross lines, positioned in the engraver's camera a short distance in front of the sensitized plate or a plastic screen placed in direct contact with the light-sensitive material. The number of these lines to the inch—the same number of lines to each dimension—that can be properly used for any given illustration depends very largely upon the kind of paper upon which the picture is to be printed. For soft-surfaced, "blottery" paper, such as newsprint, a comparatively coarse screen, 60-line to 80-line, is required. For the hard-surfaced coated papers used in most smaller publications, a much finer screen, at least 100 lines to the inch, is suitable, and generally 120-line or 133-line engravings on copper are specified; in exceptional cases, even finer.

In this connection it is interesting to note that letterpress halftones on zinc are rarely made in finer screens than 100-line; the advantage in cost diminishes rapidly if a finer screen than this is specified for zinc halftones. (PR)   B.B.

Half-Tones
Middle tones between dark shadows and highlights.
(F)   G.W.

Halftone Blowup
An enlargement made from a halftone negative, print or impression, with the dot formation much coarser than that of the halftone original. (PR)   J.S.M.

Halftone Copy
Continuous tone originals, or those best reproduced by means of a halftone screen. (PR)   J.S.M.

Halftone Dot
The individual formation or element in a halftone negative, printing plate and final impression. (PR)   J.S.M.

Halftone Etching
Act of etching halftone images into relief on metal

plates, with retention of proper printing depth and accurate reproduction of detail and tone values. (PR)   J.S.M.

Halftone Negative
The image produced by photography of an original through a halftone screen. (PR)   J.S.M.

Halftone, Outlined
A silhouetted or blockout halftone plate on which the background of the subject has been eliminated. (PR) J.S.M.

Halftone, Outlined and Vignetted
A halftone plate on which part of the background is cut away and part vignetted. (PR)   J.S.M.

Halftone Photography
Reproduction of originals by photography with a half-tone screen. (PR)   J.S.M.

Halftone Plate
Relief printing plate made from a halftone negative. (PR)   J.S.M.

Halftone Positive
One made in a camera from a continuous tone negative with a screen interposed between the photographic plate and the lens. (PR)   R.R.K.

Halftone Screen
A grating of ruled, etched and pigmented (opaque) lines on two glass plates, each plate bearing a series of parallel lines of a definite number per inch, the two plates cemented together so that the lines cross each other at right angles and produce transparent apertures between the intersecting lines. Rulings range from 50 to 300 per inch. (PR)   J.S.M.

Halftone Stop
The circular or variously shaped lens apertures employed in halftone photography. (PR)   J.S.M.

Halftone Tint
Negatives and printing plates therefrom displaying only a formation of dots or single parallel lines of uniform size, shape and width. (PR)　　　　　　　　J.S.M.

Halftone, Vignetted
A halftone plate on which the tones at one or more edges of the subject gradually fade away to pure white. (PR)　　　　　　　　J.S.M.

Halftonometer
Gauge for measuring the depth of halftone printing plates; a depthometer. (R)　　　　　　　　J.S.M.

Halo Effect
A lighting effect secured by backlighting. (F)　　A.S.

Hand Painted Posters
Outdoor posters used for local or emergency advertising where only a small number of posters is needed or when speed of announcement is essential. (A)　　　　R.D.L.

Hand Press
A hand-operated proof press. (PR)　　　　　　J.S.M.

Hand Proof
Carefully executed impression taken from a printing plate on a hand press. (PR)　　　　　　.　　J.S.M.

Hand Rest
A thin board slightly elevated above a printing plate, used by etchers when spotting, staging and re-etching; bridge; (PR)　　　　　　　　J.S.M.

Hand Type
See Foundry Type. (PR)

Handbill
Small printed advertisement delivered by hand. (PR)
H.V.G.

Handout
Copy supplied by press agent. (PR)   B.C.B.

Hanging Indent
Headline having the top line flush to the left and the lower line or lines indented. (P)   T.E.B.

Hard Edge
A defect in halftone images caused by injudicious staging or a burr on the printing surface; wire edge. (PR) J.S.M.

Hard Goods
Manufactured goods such as hardware, household appliances, etc. (A)   H.V.G.

Hard Vignette
A vignette effect exhibiting a delicate but definite printing edge instead of graduating to pure white. (PR) J.S.M.

Hard-Working
Describes developing solutions which tend to produce contrasty negatives or prints. (F)   A.S.

Hardening Bath
Solution used to toughen photographic images, specifically alum baths for negatives and chromic acid or bichromate mixtures for glue prints on zinc. (PR)   J.S.M.

Hardness
Excessive contrast in the film print or negative. (F) G.W.

Headline (or "Head")
Line, usually set in large type, above body matter. (P)
        R.A.F.

Headline
A group of words which used as a title or caption is given importance in an advertisement by reason of size, position and content. (A)   H.V.G.

Head-of-Desk
Person in charge of copydesk, whether city editor, one of his assistants, or copyeditor. (P) B.C.B.

Head-on Location
An outdoor advertising bulletin facing traffic on a highway. (A) H.V.G.

Heavy Metal
Photoengraving metal rolled to 11-point thickness. (PR) J.S.M.

Hellbox
Box in the composing room wherein discarded type and other lead to be remelted may be thrown. (PR) T.E.B.

H.I.
Abbreviation for human interest. (P)

Hiatus
A period of time during the summer (usually of eight to thirteen weeks) when a sponsored program is discontinued due to the seasonal change in audience habits. (A) H.V.G.

Hickey
Slang term for slight tears or rips in wet collodion or stripfilm negatives, or for small "runs" or blemishes in sensitized coatings. (PR) J.S.M.

Hickey
A speck on the printing area of an engraving that remains after the etch. Must be routed off. (PR) H.V.G.

High Key (Photograph)
A photograph which is predominantly light in tone. (F) H.V.G.

High Key
Tones in a picture which all lie toward the lighter end

of the scale. Also applies to degree and contrast of lighting
on an image, set, etc. (B)   H.V.G.

High Leads
Leads (leds) sticking up in the columns in such fashion
that they will print. It is the printer's business to push them
down so they will not show. (PR)   B.C.B.

Highlight Dots
The formation of small dots representing the highlights
in a halftone negative and printing plate. (PR)   J.S.M.

Highlight Halftone
A halftone plate in which the highlight areas are devoid
of dots to accentuate the contrast of the reproduction. Made
either from a highlight negative, or by special etching of
the halftone print on metal. (PR)   J.S.M.

Highlight Negative
A halftone negative in which the dot formation in the
highlights has been "plugged up" or eliminated during
exposure of the original by any of various methods, including the use of special stops and employment of originals
specially prepared for highlight effects. (PR)   J.S.M.

Highlights
Where much light is used. (F)   G.W.

Highlights
The most nearly white portions of a photograph or halftone. (PR)   B.C.B.

Highlight Stop
The particular lens aperture used in halftone photography to join the highlight dots in the negative and to
record highlight detail. (PR)   J.S.M.

High Lines
Lines of uneven depth cast by faulty linotype; when they
appear in print they are particularly black. (PR)   B.C.B.

164

Hilite Lens
A process lens with special integral apertures to produce highlight effects in halftone negatives. (PR)   J.S.M.

Hitchhike
A spot announcement following a commercial program but within the sponsor's allotted time, used to promote another of the same sponsor's products. (B)   H.V.G.

Hogarth's Line
A double curve in the form of a letter S, frequently employed in photographic composition; it is sometimes called the line of beauty or "S" curve. (F)   A.S.

Hold for Release
Term endorsed on copy that is not to be published until a specified time. (P)   B.C.B.

Hold Presses
When news of superlative importance breaks, the presses may be held until it can be put in type. (P)   B.C.B.

Holdover (or Overset)
Type matter which has been set but not used and may be made use of at some future time. Mark such copy HOLD on the galley proofs. (PR)   B.B.

Hole
Any vacant space on a page. (P)   B.C.B.

Hook
In any medium, a device used to create an immediate response for a product or just to gain information for the advertiser or medium. The hook is also used in inquiry tests to check ad effectiveness. (A)

Hook, Spike
Discarded copy is placed on the hook, or spiked, by the city editor or head of the desk. Also, linotype operators

work "from the hook" on which the copycutter places the various *takes* of a story. (P)   B.C.B.

Hooper

Popularity rating of a program, as measured by C.E. Hooper, Inc. Also called Hooper rating and Hooperating. (A)   H.V.G.

Horizontal Publication

A business publication with editorial content which caters to no one business interest or function. (A)

Hot

Too much light. (F)   G.W.

Hotel Copies

Copies purchased by a hotel and distributed free to guests. Copies similarly distributed by restaurants, clubs, Pullman and dining cars are included in the same designation. They are included in bulk sales regardless of number. (P)   A.B.C.

House Agency

An agency owned solely or partly by an advertiser. (A)
                                                        H.V.G.

House Organ

A publication prepared periodically by a business organization and issued to its employees or to clients and prospects. (P)   H.V.G.

House Show

A station's or network's own packaged show. (B)

H.T.C.

Abbreviation for the expression "hed to cum." This expression is used by the copyreader or the editor to state that the story is to be set before the head is decided on. (P)   T.E.B.

Human Interest

Any pleasant little news oddity about people; stories with

166

conversation and action, but not necessarily with *straight news*. (P)   B.C.B.

Hyperfocal Distance
The distance between a camera lens and the nearest object in focus when the lens is focused on infinity. (F)   A.S.

Hypo
The most common fixing agent used in photography. (F)   R.R.K.

Hypotenuse
A book page proportion in which the depth is 50% greater than its width. (PR)   R.R.K.

I

I.F.J.
International Federation of Journalists.

INS
International News Service, now defunct. Merged with United Press. (P)

I.T.U.
International Typographical Union.

Icon (—Sign)
A sign which is considered to bear some analogy or resemblance to the form of its designatum (e.g., a picture). (C)   C.C.

ID
The station identification on television. Also, the identification of a program televised from film. (B)   H.V.G.

Illustration Board
A heavy board available in a variety of weights and surfaces, generally with only one side a working surface—used for wash and tempera illustrations. (A)   H.V.G.

Image
The object or likeness reproduced on the film. (F) G.W.

Image-Orthicon
Super-sensitive RCA tube used in television cameras.
(B)   H.V.G.

Imagic
A cheap and indirect photoengraving process involving the use of continuous tone negatives, from which halftone negatives are made by means of a contact screen, the images then photoprinted and etched into relief on zinc plates sensitized with cold enamel. (PR)   J.S.M.

Impact Reports
A measurement method developed by Gallup & Robinson which asks a reader to playback an advertiser's message once he can prove he has seen it. The objectives of this kind of readership research are to determine idea registration and potential buying urge. (A)

Imposition
The arrangement of pages in a form, for printing. (PR)
                                                       B.B.

Impression
The pressure of type forms or plates on the paper in a printing press. (PR)   R.R.K.

Impressionism
That style of photography in which the essential features are brought out forcefully, while the rest of the picture appears indefinite, in a minor tonal key. (F)   A.S.

Imprinting
Reprinting a finished printed piece to insert additional copy. (PR)   H.V.G.

Inclining
Painting on the negatives or positives to create color areas and the portions that are to overlap slightly. This hand work is essential for color register. (PR)   R.A.F.

Indent

Type matter is indented when the usual paragraph form is disregarded and lines are begun at some specified distance inward from the margins. Thus matter may be indented one em at the end of each line, creating a little white space area and emphasizing the text so treated. Matter also is indented for initials of varying size. (PR)   B.C.B.

Independent

A station which is not affiliated with a network but originates its own programs. (B)   H.V.G.

Index

An index of the day's news, usually on the front page. (P)   B.C.B.

India

A color of paper a very light buff. (PR)   R.A.F.

India Ink

An intense black waterproof ink. Used extensively for black and white drawings and lettering for reproduction. (A)   H.V.G.

Indicia

As used in the printing of publications, indicia has come to mean the mailing data required by the Post Office to be printed on envelopes or on the publication itself, such as "Sec. 562, P. L. & R. Permit No. 1000." (PR)   B.B.

Indirect Process

Halftone reproduction of a colored original by making continuous tone separation negatives therefrom, producing a set of continuous tone positives from the negatives, and final halftone negatives from the positives; the threeway process. (PR)   J.S.M.

170

Individual Location
Location for single outdoor bulletins or posters. (A)
H.V.G.

Individual Mail Subscription
Subscription served by mail and qualifying as paid in accordance with the rules of the Audit Bureau of Circulations.
(P)
A.B.C.

Industrial Advertising
Advertising of capital goods, supplies and services directed mainly to industrial or professional firms which require them in the course of manufacture. (A)
H.V.G.

Industrial Film
A film made by business or industry. (F)
G.W.

Industrial Journalism
The presentation of information about a company, an industry, employees, and the free enterprise system, with the prime purpose of building a personal identification with an organization or idea, or of winning support for certain objectives or beliefs.

Industrial Product
One that is sold and advertised in manufacturing operations. (A)
H.V.G.

Information
Nowadays, the concept of information would seem to be of value to many research workers, and as universal and fundamental as the concepts of energy or entropy. Speaking most generally, every time we perform any experiment, or make any observation, we are seeking for information; the question thus arises: How much can we know from a particular set of observations or experiments? The experimenter is really not forming a "communication-link" with Mother Nature. He is not receiving signs or signals, which are phys-

171

ical embodiments of messages, not words, pictures, or symbols. The stimuli received from Nature—the sights and sounds—are not pictures of reality, but are the evidence from which we build our personal models, or impressions, of reality. Another distinction between observation and communication is implied by the fact that Nature, as a source of information, is uncooperative—in the sense that she does not select the signs to suit our particular difficulties of observation at any time.

Information is a many sided concept. One side, at least, has been polished with mathematics, whilst other sides (semantic and pragmatic aspects) are beginning to show up, though these other aspects are not, as yet, truly distinct and clear. The formal statistical theory of communication has certainly shown, both as regards its theorems and its measure of "selective information rate," some promise of use and interpretation in those various different sciences which concern, in some way, the idea of "information"; nevertheless caution is needed in extending this existing theory outside its legitimate, and clearly defined, sphere. Information, *of some kind or order,* certainly appears to be a concept of value in many fields, but this is not to say that the one mathematical theory and one measure have indiscriminate application.

The word "information" is used, in everyday speech, in different ways. We speak of *useful* information, of *valuable* information, of *factual* information, of *reliable* information, of *precise* information, of *true* information. But none of these expressions occurs in statistical communication theory, which describes information solely as the statistical rarity of signals from an observed source . . . It may be helpful to refer to three levels of information, corresponding to the three levels of semiotic—the syntactic, semantic, and pragmatic levels. We may confine the Wiener-Shannon statistical theory to the syntactic level, since it essentially concerns signs and statistical relations between signs. But "information," in its popular use, is regarded as information *about* something other than

172

the signs themselves; it is considered to refer to designata (objects, people, times, places, events, relationships, etc., in the outside world); and it also involves users (informants, advisers, reference book compilers, etc., as well as those who act on the information). These popular interpretations are essentially semantic and pragmatic. Again at semantic level, it may be possible to infer one piece of "information" from another. ("This shop is closed only on Sundays" implies "This shop is open on weekdays," in common English.)

We have stressed that statistical communication theory abstracts from the semantic and pragmatic aspects of the set of signs used. Similarly it is possible to discuss *semantic information,* regarded as abstracted from pragmatics—information conveyed by sentences "in the language," not information for, or to, any particular person. Clearly, the adjectives *useful, useless, valuable,* and the like, applied to "information," suggest some definite user (useful or valuable to whom?) whereas *factual* or *precise* do not. As a simple illustration of such distinction between the pragmatic and semantic levels of information, the sentence, "A train will leave from somewhere, for elsewhere, soon," contains less information—is less precise—than "A train will leave from London, for Edinburgh, today." And this is even less precise than "A non-stop train will leave from King's Cross Station, for Edinburgh, at 10:00 a.m. today." These three sentences convey increasingly precise information to anybody (at least to anybody who understands English). But whether the information is useful, or valuable, depends upon a person's needs or circumstances. Whether it is *reliable* depends upon personal experience of that particular source of information (the informant, timetable, information booth, etc.).

The first statement here contains less semantic information (about trains, etc.) than the last, because it can logically be deduced from the last, but not vice-versa. The statements are rank-ordered here in increasing precision; such semantic precision, or "information," is correlated with precision of potential action on the part of any (English-speaking) recipient.

Such examples illustrate one of the principal ways in which we daily seek, or offer, information, by successive subdivision of some whole field of inquiry into smaller and smaller regions of uncertainty. Countless illustrations might be cited. A postal address seeks out one specific person by locating first *country,* then *town, street, number;* again the whole animal kingdom is classified successively into *classes, orders, families, genera, species,* et cetera; bibliographical references are given by *journal, volume, number, month, page,* or the like; times are quoted (in reverse), such as *8:00 p.m., 18 September 1955 A.D.* And so on. Such taxonomical interpretation of "information" as "successive selection" is natural and widespread.

The reader will appreciate that such successive selections are similar to those employed in defining "selective-information content" of signals in the statistical theory of communication, but there is here an essential difference. . . . But the difference is now that designata are involved; the "field of inquiry" concerns outside (extra-linguistic) things or events, and the successive subdivisions specify these more and more precisely. Usually empirical names or signs are used to correspond to each successive region of uncertainty (e.g., classes, orders, families, in the examples above); however, we can denote these regions by signs, according to some rule.

"Information" in most, if not all, of its connotations seems to rest upon the notion of *selection power.* The Shannon theory regards the information source, in emitting the signals (signs), as exerting a selective power upon an ensemble of messages. In the Carnap-Bar-Hillel semantic theory, the information content of statements relates to the selective power they exert upon ensembles of states. Again at its pragmatic level, in true communicative situations (and speaking only descriptively now) a source of information has a certain value to a recipient, where "value" may be regarded as a "selection power." Gabor, for example, observes that what people value in a source of information (i.e., what they are prepared to pay for) depends upon its *exclusiveness* and *prediction* power; he cites instances of a newspaper editor hoping for a "scoop" and a race-goer receiving information from a tipster. "Exclusiveness" here implies the selecting of that one particular recipient out of the population, while the "prediction" value of information rests upon the power it gives to the recipient to select his future action, out of a whole range of prior uncertainty as to what action to take. Again, signs have the power to select responses in people, such responses depending upon a totality of conditions. Human communication channels consist of individuals in conversation, or in various forms of social intercourse. Each individual and each conversation is unique; different people react to signs in different ways, depending each upon their own past experiences and upon the environment at the time. It is such variations, such differences, which give rise to the principal problems in the study of human communication. (C)   C.C.

Information Film
A film to inform adults on some subject. (F)   G.W.

Inherited Audience
The carry over from one program to another on the same station of a portion of the preceding program's audience. (B)   H.V.G.

Initial
The first character in a block of copy, often set in a larger size and different type face. (PR)   H.V.G.

Inker Unit or Mechanism
Assembly of rollers on proof and printing presses to achieve even distribution of ink on printing surfaces. (PR)
                                    J.S.M.

175

Inking In
Operation of drawing on a photograph or silverprint with waterproof ink. (PR)   J.S.M.

Inking Up
Rolling up an exposed albumen plate with ink before development of the image. (PR)   J.S.M.

Ink Top
The acid resist produced by dusting an inked albumen image with topping powder; the albumen process of plate-making. (PR)   J.S.M.

Inlooker
A reader who has seen at least one major story in a publication. (A)

Insert
A special page printed on superior paper stock by the advertiser and forwarded to the publisher for binding in the publication or to be inserted loose. Usually used for fine color work. (A)   H.V.G.

Insert
A scene in a picture that is different from all the rest of the picture. (F)   G.W.

Insert
Matter intended to be incorporated within the body of a story after the latter has been sent to the composing room. (P)   B.C.B.

Insert
An extra sheet placed in a book or magazine. (PR)   H.V.G.

Inserting
Act of accurately fitting one or more collodion or stripfilm negatives into another; the assembly of a number of negatives into prearranged definite relationship with each other. (PR)   J.S.M.

Insertion Order
Authorization from advertiser or agency to publisher to print an advertisement of specified size on a given date or dates at a definite rate. Copy instructions, cuts or complete plates may accompany the order or be sent later. (A)
H.V.G.

Inset
The pages cut off in folding and placed in the middle of the sheet. (PR)
R.A.F.

Inside Mortise
Opening cut entirely inside a mounted printing plate for insertion of type or other matter. (PR)   J.S.M.

Installment Subscriptions
Subscriptions, collection of subscription price being made in installments within the subscription period. (P) A.B.C.

Institutional Advertising
Advertising devoted to creating good will for the advertiser rather than the immediate sale of specific products. (A)
H.V.G.

Institutions Advertising
Trade advertising directed to industries classified as "institutional," e.g. hotels, restaurants, hospitals, schools, etc. (A)
H.V.G.

Instructional Film
A teaching film for classrooms. (F)   G.W.

Intaglio
Any kind of printing in which reproduction is effected from depressions etched into the printing surface, rather than from raised surfaces, as in typographic or letterpress printing, or from a plane surface, as in lithographic printing. Gravure, rotogravure, color-gravure, etc., are intaglio processes. (PR)
B.B.

Intaglio Etching
An image etched into a plate instead of appearing in relief, and usually made from a photographic positive. (PR)　　　　　　　　　　　　　　　　　　J.S.M.

Intaglio Halftone
A halftone plate etched in intaglio manner and made from a halftone positive. (PR)　　　　　　J.S.M.

Intaglio Proof
Impression from an intaglio plate, produced by depositing ink in the etched incisions or lines and wiping the surface of the plate clean before taking the impression on paper. (PR)　　　　　　　　　　　　J.S.M.

Intensification
Increasing the opacity of developed and fixed photographic negatives by chemical treatment of the image. (F)
　　　　　　　　　　　　　　　　　　J.S.M.

Intensifier
A chemical agent capable of intensifying photographic negatives. (PR)　　　　　　　　　　J.S.M.

Interaction
See Empathy; Feedback.

Interior
Any indoor scene. (F)　　　　　　　　　　G.W.

Interior Dialogue
The soliloquy and the aside technique used in TV. The narrator bridges sequences with a "stream of consciousness" technique. (B)　　　　　　　　　　H.V.G.

Interleaving
The placing of flat sheets together before binding. (PR)　　　　　　　　　　　　　　R.A.F.

178

Interpretative Reporting

The attempt to clarify the facts of an event without usurping the legitimate function of the editorial page. Interpretation of the news is essentially an exercise in news judgment. It includes objectivity as method, but also a new-found sense of responsibility on the part of the writer to background events, to attempt to understand events, and to try to appraise them for the reader without conscious distortion. (P)

Intertype

A keyboard typesetting machine which casts a line in one piece. (PR)   R.R.K.

Interview

A story based on an interview. (P)   B.C.B.

Iris

The adjustable diaphragm in front of the camera lens used to control the admission of light. (F)   G.W.

Iris-In (or -Out)

Gradual emergence or disappearance of a scene through a growing or diminishing circle. (F)   G.W.

Irradiation

The spreading of light in an emulsion due to reflection from the surfaces of the silver halide crystals. The slight blurring due to irradiation should not be confused with the more noticeable and extensive blurring known as halation, which is due to reflection from the back surface of the plate or film on which the emulsion is supported. (F) A.S.

Island Position

Newspaper and magazine advertisement entirely surrounded by reading matter or margin. This position is not generally sold. (A)   H.V.G.

179

Italic

A variation of a type face used to emphasize words or phrases in text matter. Italic letters slant to the right but retain all other characteristics of their Roman counterpart, e.g. Garamond, *Garamond Italic*—(PR)   H.V.G.

Itals

Abbreviation for italics. (P)   B.C.B.

J

Jacket

An extra, protective cover of a book. (PR)   R.A.F.

Jem Metal

A zinc-copper alloy (brass) or type of photoengraving metal specially intended for electrical etching. (PR) J.S.M.

Jim Dash

Hairline (usually 3 picas) between the deck and the story. (P)   B.C.B.

Jobber

A press used for small work. (PR)   R.R.K.

Job Compositor

A typesetter who sets commercial printing. (PR) R.R.K.

Job Font

A small assortment of type in any one size and style. (PR)   R.R.K.

Job Printer

A printer who does small commercial printing, such as letterheads and envelopes. (PR)   R.R.K.

Job Ticket

Usually an envelope containing copy on which directions concerning the job are given. (PR)   H.V.G.

Job Type

Type faces used in printing commercial work. (PR)
R.R.K.

Joint

Line or point of contact between joined negatives and plates. (PR) J.S.M.

Journalistic Style

Stresses short sentences, short words, simple writing, in a descending order of relative importance and interest. (P)

Journeyman

A printer who has completed his apprenticeship. (PR)
R.R.K.

Jump

The continuation of a newsstory from one page to another under another head. The part that is continued is called the *jump* and the whole story is a *jump story*. (P)
B.C.B.

Jump Heads

Headlines for a story that is continued from one page to another. Also called "runover." (P) B.C.B.

Jumplines

The continuation lines of a story jumped from one page to another: "Continued on Page 12," "Continued from Page 1." (P) B.C.B.

Junior Page Advertisement

A full page advertisement for a smaller publication which appears in a larger publication as a junior unit because it shares the page with editorial material. (A)

Junior Panel

A reduced facsimile of the standard 24-sheet poster. (A)

Justify

To arrange the spacing between letters and words in such a way that all lines of type are of equal length, so that the right hand edge of the column is flush, just as the left edge is. This is done automatically on the linotype machine, and on the monotype caster. (PR)   B.B.

Justowriter

Office composing machine for preparing justified copy. Made up of two typewriters. One has a keyboard that cuts a ribbon. The other is a printing machine set in action by the ribbon. (PR)   P.W.B.

K

Keep Standing
Instructions to printer to hold type after job is completed for further instructions. (See Kill.) (PR)   H.V.G.

Kelly Press
A two-revolution letterpress. (PR)   R.R.K.

Kemart
Process of halftone photography employing fluorescing originals, which are given a supplementary exposure with purple light for improved reproductions and highlight effects. (PR)   J.S.M.

Kern
The part of the type face that extends over and from the side of the type body. (PR)   R.R.K.

Key
To identify positions of art or copy in a dummy by means of symbols, usually letters. (PR)   R.A.F.

Key Drawing
Outline drawing containing only guide lines or those necessary for separation of colors on printing plates. (PR)
J.S.M.

Keying an Advertisement
Inserting in the address or coupon a different code for each medium used, so that inquiries can be traced and media effectiveness compared. (A)   H.V.G.

Key Plate
In a color set, the particular printing plate used as a guide for registration of other colors; the plate containing maximum detail. (PR)   J.S.M.

Key Station
The station in a network which originates the network's principal programs. (B)   H.V.G.

Kicker
An overline over the headline. (P)   B.C.B.

Kill
To break up and redistribute the type and cuts in a form. (PR)   H.V.G.

Kill
Stop. (B)   N.A.B.

Kinescope
Picture tube used in television receiver and at monitor positions in control rooms. (B)   P.W.B.

Kinescope Recording
A motion picture made from the face of a television tube for rebroadcast or reference use. Also called a "Kine." (B)   H.V.G.

Kit
An adapter. A nest or interfitting series of wooden or metal frames used as a transparency holder on process cameras. (PR)   J.S.M.

Kitsch
A German term for popular, commercial art and litera-

ture, epitomized by slick and pulp fiction, comics, popular music, calendar or cover girls, etc.; a synthetic rendering of genuine folk culture, or ersatz mass culture.

Kleig Lights
A patented type of wide angle lights famous because of their long use on the stage. Now used in TV. (B) H.V.G.

Kneaded Eraser
An eraser composed of a pliable substance for cleaning drawings. (A) H.V.G.

Kodachrome
Color transparency manufactured by the Eastman Kodak Company. Gives full color transparencies by a single exposure. (F) H.V.G.

Kodachrome Reproducer
Any of several process camera attachments or devices originally designed for producing enlarged halftone reproductions from Kodachrome and other colorfilm transparencies made on small (35 mm.) films. (PR) J.S.M.

Kodacolor
A type of colorfilm used mainly by amateur photographers and providing a negative with colors complementary to those of the subject, the print from the negative showing the proper colors of the original. (F) J.S.M.

Kodak Screens
Magenta and orange-colored halftone screens of photographic (film) type, used in actual contact with sensitized surfaces during halftone exposures; Kodagraph screens. (PR) J.S.M.

Koloroid
A photographic process of making four-color proofs from continuous tone and halftone separation negatives. Special materials in the form of colored pigment papers (carbon

tissue) are used, whereon contact exposures are made and the images successively developed on a suitable support to produce a full-color picture. (PR)　　　　　J.S.M.

Kotavachrome
Method of making color-prints from Kodachrome transparencies, the prints furnished in standard photographic sizes and processed by the manufacturer (Kodak). (PR)
　　　　　J.S.M.

Kraft Paper
A tough paper made of sulphite pulp. Usually tan in color, it is used for envelopes, paper bags and wrapping paper. (PR)　　　　　H.V.G.

Kromekote
Trade name for one of the several enamel finish papers with an extremely high gloss. These papers require special inks and special care in printing. (PR)　　　　　B.B.

Kromolite
Method of highlight halftone reproduction involving the use of specially prepared drawings. (PR)　　　J.S.M.

Krylon
A clear spray used to form a protective coating on artwork. (A)　　　　　H.V.G.

L

Label Head
Head that lacks life or originality. So called because it presents the appearance of having been seen, like a label, many times before. T.E.B.

Laboratory
The place where films are developed and prints made. (F) G.W.

Lacquering
The coating applied to a surface of a finished printed job for protectiveness as well as improving the appearance. (PR) R.A.F.

Laid
A watermark made by means of a dandy-roll with close parallel lines running at right angles to chain marks. (PR) R.A.F.

Laid Paper
Paper having parallel lines watermarked at equal distances apart. (PR) H.V.G.

Lamcote
Trade name for a process by which paper may be coated with thin sheets of cellophane after having been printed. (PR) B.B.

Laminate

The process of coating printed sheets of paper with cellophane or acetate, to impart a high gloss or soil-resistant quality. (PR) B.B.

Laminated Press Plates

A thin electrotype (shaves to one-half its original thickness) which is bonded by an adhesive plastic to a perforated aluminum base. In addition to lightness, it has the advantage of having a hard backing so important with tension lockups, whereby the hooks which hold the plate to the platen cylinder reach underneath the plate and, by tension outward, pull the plate down firm on the cylinder. (PR)

Laminated Wood

Wood for blocking which has been built up of thin layers with the grain crossing alternately. (PR) R.A.F.

Language System

A set of signs and rules representing, in the meta-language, a description of an object-language (we again distinguish *pure* and *descriptive* systems, as for syntax). (C)
C.C.

Lap

The slight extension of areas of printing surfaces to assure register of colorplates. (PR) J.S.M.

Lap Dissolve

Wiping off of the television picture and leaving another in its place. (B) P.W.B.

Lasswell "Formula"

Proposed by Harold D. Lasswell, of the School of Law, Yale University, this analysis introduces five principal variables in any act of communication as a means of classifying communication studies. Lasswell asks: Who-Says What-In Which Channel-To-Whom-With-What-Effects? This five-part question focuses upon both the discrete aspects of communi-

189

cation as well as the mutual influence and interplay among the five factors or its processlike character. Its principal use has been in mass communication situations with studies of the communicator or controller of information (Who), of content (Says What), of media (In Which Channel), of audience (To Whom), and of effects (With What Effect). (C)

Latensification
The process of increasing the sensitivity of a photographic emulsion *after* exposure. (F)   A.S.

Latent Image
What is on the exposed film before it is developed. (F)   G.W.

Lateral Recording
Where the sound vibrations in a record groove occur from side to side, or laterally. (B)   H.V.G.

Lateral Reversal
Turning of a photographic image as to right and left position, achieved either with optical reversing devices, by stripping, or placement of the image in a transparency holder during photography. (PR)   J.S.M.

Latitude
The possible degree of variations in exposure. (F) G.W.

Lay of the Case
The arrangement of letters and characters in a type case. (PR)   R.R.K.

Layout
The form in which the elements of an advertisement are combined:

1. Rough (Visual)—Preliminary sketch to show idea only.

2. Finished layout—A more well-defined sketch of the idea giving a close resemblance of art and type style.

3. Comprehensive Layout ("Comp")—a rough layout

worked to a more finished state showing as nearly as possible how the completed advertisement will look. (A)   H.V.G.

Layout
A full scale drawing of a proposed press sheet, divided into individual units of the job, containing measurements needed to position correctly the work areas in the unit, in offset-lithography; a drawing containing specifications of a proposed job in letterpress or lithographic printing. (PR)
R.R.K.

Layout
Same as "spread." (P)   T.E.B.

L.C.
Abbreviation for lower case, meaning small letters, not capitals. (P)

Lead (Leads) (Lēd)
Thin metal strips one, two, and three points thick, used to space out lines of type; also the process of spacing out. The rule of the expert printer is always to lead out from the tops of the columns and a bit around subheads, or short dashes; never between paragraphs to any great extent. (P)
B.C.B.

Lead (Leed)
Introductory sentences or paragraphs of newsstory; the big newsstory of the day; there may be substitute leads (sub leads) or new leads, adds to lead, and inserts in lead. (P)
B.C.B.

Lead (Leed)
A tip which may lead to a story. (P)   B.C.B.

Leader
Blank film at the beginning and the end of a reel of film. (F)   G.W.

191

Leader

A line of periods or bullets used to lead from headline to text or into a block of copy. (PR) H.V.G.

Lead In

The announcer's resume of the preceding episodes of a continued story or the preface leading into the drama to follow. (B) N.A.B.

Lead Mold

The process of making molds of engravings and type for electrotyping. (PR) R.A.F.

Lead Out

As an instruction to the compositor, it means to set lines further apart so they will fill more space vertically. (PR) B.B.

Ledger Paper

A strong, smooth writing paper used for records and ledgers. (PR) R.A.F.

Legend

Explanatory type matter under an illustration. (PR) R.R.K.

Legman, Legger

A reporter who gets the information and telephones it to a *rewrite* man at the home office. (P) B.C.B.

Lens

The curved-glass eye through which the scene is photographed by the camera. (F) G.W.

Lens Cap

A velvet lined covering for the protection of a camera lens. Also used for making exposures in the studio by momentarily removing the cap from the lens. (F) A.S.

Lens Coating

Deposition of a very thin film of evaporated metallic

fluorides on the uncemented glass elements of a lens, the coating tending to increase the speed of the objective and reduce reflections from glass to air surfaces. With process lenses, coating results in a slight increase of contrast and promotes somewhat sharper line negatives. (PR)   J.S.M.

Lens Flare
A light-flash on the film caused by using a very fast lens at a very small diaphragm stop. Usually happens only rarely with the better fast lenses. (F)   A.S.

Lens Scale
The chart or scale mounted above process lenses on the camera as an aid in quick and accurate setting of iris diaphragm apertures, particularly in halftone photography. (PR)   J.S.M.

Letterhead
Stationery which has a heading printed or engraved on the paper. (PR)   H.V.G.

Lettering
The hand drawing of letters for reproduction as differentiated from mechanical means such as type or photo-lettering. (A)   H.V.G.

Letterpress
Direct printing from raised surfaces consisting of type, line plates and halftone engraving. (PR)   H.V.G.

Letter Space
To add space between letters, generally in headings, to fill a given space or for the sake of appearance. The amount of space to be added is designated in points: there are 12 points to the pica, approximately 72 points to the inch. (PR)   B.B.

Level
The volume of sound. (F)   G.W.

193

Libel

A method of defamation expressed by print, writing, pictures, or signs. In its most general sense any publication that is injurious to the reputation of another. (P)

Library

Newspaper repository for cuts, clippings, editions, reference material, etc., commonly needed. Also known as the "morgue." (P)   T.E.B.

Lift

The amount of paper brought to the press at one time for printing. (PR)   B.B.

Ligature

Two or more letters tied together and cast in one piece of type, as fi, ff, fl, ffi, ffl. (PR)   H.V.G.

Light Face

Type with overall characteristics rather light in weight. (PR)   H.V.G.

Light Filter

Color filter. (PR)   J.S.M.

Light Integrator

Device for photoelectrically controlling the length of exposures, the apparatus combining an instrument for indication of light intensity and measurement of light sources; Luxometer; Totalux; Totalurne. (PR)   J.S.M.

Light-Lock

A baffle type of entrance to photographic darkrooms, preventing entry of stray light during traffic from the chamber. (F)   J.S.M.

Light-Struck

Term applied to photographic material accidentally fogged by action of actinic light, or by extraneous light

194

creeping into faulty camera equipment; light fog. (F)
J.S.M.

Light Table

A glass-topped table illuminated from underneath and used for layout work, stripping, opaquing and other operations requiring viewing images by transmitted light. (PR)
J.S.M.

Light Trap

(1) An arrangement of doors or a curved passage by which one can enter a darkroom from a lighted room without permitting actinic light to shine into the darkroom. (2) Any arrangement for preventing light passage through an opening which must admit a moving part such as the felts on plate holders. (F)
A.S.

Limbo

Dark background for TV program. Creates appearance of action taking place in a void. (B)
P.W.B.

Limited Time Station

Applied to a station that uses its facilities only certain times during a day, usually because it shares its channel with another station. (A)
P.W.B.

Limiting Capacity (of a Communication Channel)

The upper limiting rate at which (selective) information may be communicated by a specific channel, with any arbitrarily small frequency of errors. It may depend upon signal power, noise power, and other physical properties of the channel. (C)
C.C.

Linage

The amount of newspaper advertising space in terms of agate lines (14 lines to the inch). (A)
H.V.G.

195

Line
Telephone wire used for transmission of a program.
(B)   P.W.B.

Line
A measure of depth of space. Refers to agate lines. There
are 14 lines to the inch. (PR)   H.V.G.

Line and Wash Drawing
An artist's rendering employing a combination of line
and wash techniques. (A)   H.V.G.

Line Colorwork
Color effects produced by means of line images, bendaying
and the use of modern shading sheets. (PR)   J.S.M.

Line Copy
Photomechanical originals in which the design or image
is composed of lines or dots, and which can be reproduced
in the form of line etchings. (PR)   J.S.M.

Line Cut
An engraving which prints only solid lines or areas
without shades or tones. See Ben Day. (PR)   H.V.G.

Line Drawing
Drawing done in line only, usually refers to black and
white drawing without tones of gray. (A)   H.V.G.

Line Engraving
Specifically, engraving on metal or other surfaces with
tools, but in photoengraving pertaining to a printing surface
of relief lines; a line etching. (PR)   J.S.M.

Line-Halftone Combination
A printing plate comprising both line and halftone
images, sometimes in close juxtaposition to each other.
(PR)   J.S.M.

Lineholder

Oblong iron clamp in which small blocks or mounted plates are tightly held during trimming. (PR) J.S.M.

Line Negative

Photographic image made directly from a line original without interposition of a halftone screen, the image represented more or less in the form of a stencil, with opaque background and completely transparent lines. (PR) J.S.M.

Line Photography

Direct photography of line originals on negative material of high contrast and without use of halftone screen. (PR) J.S.M.

Line Positive

A transparency or diapositive of a line original. (PR) J.S.M.

Line Screen

Halftone screen. (PR) J.S.M.

Line-Up

The careful alignment of pages, in the form of type, engravings and "furniture" prior to locking them together in the chase for printing. "Line-up and lock-up" are generally regarded as one operation. (PR) B.B.

Linear Enlargement

When the degree of enlargement is figured on the basis of increase in one dimension, such as length, it is referred to as a linear enlargement of so many times. This alternate basis is the increase in total area. Enlarging a 4x5 in. negative to 8x10 in. is a two-time linear or a two-diameter enlargement, but a four-time area enlarging. (F) A.S.

Linen Finish

A paper finished with a surface similar to linen. (PR) R.A.F.

197

Linen Tester

Small magnifying glass mounted at a distance above its base equal to the focal length of the lens. Originally designed for counting threads in linen, modern achromatic glasses of this type are widely used for examination of negatives, plates and proofs. (PR)   J.S.M.

Lineplate

A relief etching or engraving on metal direct from a line original. (PR)   J.S.M.

Linguistics

The comparative study of the elements, forms, structure, nature, interrelations, historical development and principles of growth and change of language.

Elements: Ex., seme, sememe, episememe, glosseme, macrosememe, phone, phoneme, phonetic sounds, etc.; *Forms:* Ex., word, vocabulary, gender, etc.; *Structure:* Ex., grammar, syntax, etc.; *Nature or types:* Ex., agglutinating, isolating, inflective, polysynthetic, etc.; *Interrelations:* Ex., ethnolinguistics, exolinguistics, sociolinguistics, psycholinguistics, comparative linguistics, etc.; *Historical development:* Ex., language origins, glottochronology, language drift, diffusion, etc.; *Growth and change:* Ex., assimilation, dissimilation, loss, lag, merger, borrowing, creation, blending, distillation, meaning change, etc. (C)

Lining

The aligning of type faces at the bottom of the letters in different sizes. (PR)   R.R.K.

Lining Beveler

A beveler with an attached auxiliary tool for cutting straight lines in the borders of printing plates. (PR) J.S.M.

Lining Tool

A graver having a number of cutting points matching the rulings of standard halftone screens, and used by finishers

198

for "shooting through" or cutting between the dots of a half-tone plate. Also known as "multiple graver" or "shooter." (PR) J.S.M.

Linograph
A keyboard linecasting machine, not now manufactured. (PR) R.R.K.

Linos
Abbreviation for linotype, a typesetting machine. (PR) B.C.B.

Linotype
A typesetting machine that produces a complete line of type at one automatic operation. Using a keyboard much like that of a typewriter, the operator strikes the desired letters, whereupon the machine selects and sets up a matrix for each, arranges them so that the length of each line is equal ("justified"), casts the type from molten metal, planes it, and returns the matrices to their proper places. The longest line that can be set on a standard linotype machine is 30 picas, or five inches. (PR) B.B.

Lip Synchronization
Simultaneous shooting of sound and photography. (F) G.W.

Listening Area
The geographical area covered by a station's signal, usually divided into primary and secondary areas. (B) H.V.G.

Lithography
Any form of printing from a plane surface; this includes the reproduction method generally referred to as "offset" and planographing. In typographic printing (or "letterpress") the impression on the paper is made from raised surfaces; in gravure, or intaglio, printing the impression comes from depressions in the surface of the printing plate. Lithographic plates have neither raised nor recessed areas; the antagonism

of grease and water is the principle involved in separating the printing areas from the non-printing areas. The printing image is laid down in a greasy substance, dampness is applied to the whole plate and then the ink. The ink adheres only to the greasy (printing) area. In lithography the printed image is generally first applied to a rubber "blanket" and transferred or "offset" from this to the paper. Hence the term "offset printing," which is not properly descriptive of the process; the correct expression is, of course, offset lithography. (PR)   B.B.

Little Merchant
Synonymous with independent carrier. (P)   A.B.C.

Live
An instantaneous broadcast as opposed to a broadcast by delayed recording or on a film. (B)   H.V.G.

Live
A printing form still in use. (PR)   R.R.K.

Lobster Trick
Same as "dog watch." (P)   T.E.B.

Local
A local newsstory; often a brief item, a *personal*. (P)
B.C.B.

Local Advertising
Newspaper advertising by local retailers, usually at a lower rate than that charged national advertisers. (A) H.V.G.

Local Control
Term which applies to dodging and burning in as practiced in enlarging. (F)   A.S.

Local Intensification and Reduction
The application of an intensifier or reducer with a brush or swab to one portion of a negative or print. (F)   A.S.

Localize
To stress the local angle of a story (P) B.C.B.

Local News Room
The *city room,* the workshop of the city staff. (P) B.C.B.

Location
Any place outside the studio where films are made. (F) G.W.

Location (Outdoor)
A lot, premise, building, wall or any place whatsoever upon which a standard outdoor advertising structure is erected, constructed and maintained on leased or owned property. (A) R.D.L.

Lock-Up
Type matter and cuts locked into a rigid form preparatory to printing or electrotyping. (PR) H.V.G.

Log
The official, chronological listing of a station's programs. (B) H.V.G.

Logical Connectives (In Symbolic Logic)
For example, the signs of *negation* ~ (not, of *conjunction* & (and), of *equivalence* ≡ (if and only if), of *disjunction* V (or) , etc. (C) C.C.

Logical Syntax
The purely *formal* parts of syntax (after Carnap). (C) C.C.

Logon
The shortest distinguishable signal element which may be received through a specified channel. A dimension or degree of freedom of signal space. (C) C.C.

Logotype
The special design of the name of an advertiser or pro-

201

duct made into a cut and used repeatedly in advertising and promotion. (A)   H.V.G.

Logotype
A single type containing two or more letters, a syllable, an entire word, thus: *ff, fi, ing, the*. Some cuts, such as a miniature reproduction of a newspaper's nameplate, or a signature, are also called logotypes. (P)   B.C.B.

Long Shot
The photographing of a whole scene so that a distant view of some objects is included. (F)   G.W.

Loose
Artwork sketchy in appearance. (See Tight.) (A) H.V.G.

Lower Case
Small letters as opposed to CAPITAL LETTERS (PR)   H.V.G.

Low Key (Photograph)
Photograph which is predominantly dark in value. (F)   H.V.G.

Ludlow
A machine (typograph) casting slugs from hand set matrices, from 6 to 72 points in size. Generally used for display advertising or headlines. (P)   B.C.B.

Luminous
Paint or other substance used on signs and bulletins to intensify light and color especially by reflection at night. (PR)   H.V.G.

Luxometer
Photoelectric device for controlling the duration of camera exposures according to actinicity and fluctuation of camera lamps. (F)   J.S.M.

M

M.A.B.
Magazine Advertisers Bureau. A division of M.P.A. The promotion organization of the magazine publishing industry.

M.P.A.
Magazine Publishers Association.

Machine Composition
Any type composition done mechanically. (PR)   H.V.G.

Machine Etching
Operation of etching printing plates in a machine by mechanical application of the mordant to the metal surface, or by electrical action. (PR)   J.S.M.

Machine Finish
A smooth paper used in printing books. (PR) R.R.K.

Magazine
That part of a typesetting machine which contains the brass matrices of the different letters and characters. Every time the operator presses a key on the keyboard, he releases a matrix from the magazine. (PR)   B.C.B.

Magazines
The film containers of the camera. (F)   G.W.

Magazine Standards

Individual specifications for making printing plates to adapt them to the special requirements of the particular publication. (PR)   J.S.M.

Magnesium Plate

A halftone or line plate made of magnesium which is light in weight, strong, and adaptable to high-speed etching made 11 points thick. (PR)   R.A.F.

Magnifier

Small lens or combination of lenses possessing the property of magnification, and used to examine dot and line structures in negatives and printing plates: linen tester. (PR)   J.S.M.

Mail Distribution

Copies served on subscriptions which have failed to qualify as paid circulation according to the requirements of the Audit Bureau of Circulations. (P)   A.B.C.

Mail Order Advertising

Type of advertising in which the complete sales transaction is handled through advertising and by mail. (A)
                                                              H.V.G.

Make-Good

Free run or re-run of a print advertisement that publication mishandled. (A)   P.W.B.

Makeready

One of the most important words in the letterpress printing business. It refers to the process of adjusting the pressure on the various parts of a form so that the entire form will print evenly. It is necessary because there are almost always very minute variations in the height of type, engravings, and rules, so that they present an uneven surface, and also because the construction of most presses is such that even though a perfectly level form were to be printed, more pressure would be exerted on the edges than in the center. A job is made ready by taking an impression of the form on a sheet of paper, upon which the weak areas are "marked out." Pressure is built up on these areas by pasting on patches of tissue—called "spotting up" —then registering this spot-up sheet in the packing on the press.

The time spent on good makeready is always a wise investment; generally speaking, the quality of the printed job is dependent upon the quality of the makeready. Moreover, the better the makeready the less wear there will be on type and engravings, so that they will give sharp, clean, impressions over a longer press run. Excessive pressure on highlight dots in halftones causes them to wear down and print larger, giving a muddy appearance to areas intended to be light. Undue wear in middle tones makes the plate shallower in these spots, so it tends to fill up with ink and loses detail. Engravers sometimes blame unsatisfactory half-tone reproduction on poor makeready by the printer; printers, in turn, sometimes accuse the engravers when hasty makeready is at fault. Very often you can put the blame where it belongs by comparing the finished work with the engravers' proofs. (PR)   B.B.

Make-Up
Assembling of type and plates into complete pages. (PR)
                                                          R.A.F.

Makeup
The art of arranging pictures and news matter in the most effective and artistic manner throughout the paper. (P)   B.C.B.

Makeup Man
The printer who makes up or assembles one or more pages. He is not to be confused with the editorial worker

205

known as the *makeup editor,* often called the news editor, who plans the makeup. (P)   B.C.B.

Margin
The space between the print and the edge of the paper. (PR)   H.V.G.

Market
People, grouped by geographical, social or other category who may be considered potential purchasers of an advertiser's specific product or service. (A)   H.V.G.

Marketing
Putting a product on the market. A broad term which usually covers market research, advertising, distribution, merchandising, sales planning and other phases which follow manufacture. (A)   H.V.G.

Markets
The general name given to the pages of columns devoted to news of the financial, grain, livestock and product markets. Market boxes are characteristic to these pages and market tables are set in agate type. (P)   B.C.B.

Mask
A cut-out placed behind the lens to limit the size or shape or contents of the scene to be photographed. (F)
                                                                        G.W.

Masking
The addition or subtraction of light through designated areas of a given film by the use of a photographic mask. Its purpose is to correct for printing ink, reduce density range of the copy, remove undercolor for high speed wet printing, produce a corrected black printer, preserve highlight detail, etc. Camera masking uses corrective film in contact with the film separation; that is, more than one piece of film per color is superimposed on another to correct for printing deficiencies. In electronic color separation the color correction

206

(masking) is done in the electronic circuits. The addition and subtraction of density for any given area is done with electrons rather than film. Thus, each color is separated and masked on only one piece of film. (PR)

Masking Out
Blocking out certain areas of a drawing that are not desired for reproduction. (A)   H.V.G.

Masking Tape
Tape which has good sticking quality but which can also be pulled up or removed easily and which does no damage to the art work or paper. (A)   H.V.G.

Masking Tape
Special opaque black or red cellulose tape for masking photographic negatives. (PR)   J.S.M.

Master Control
The central control room of a broadcasting station which feeds programs originating in all studios to the station's transmitter. (B)   H.V.G.

Master Layout
A ruled sheet, usually on white paper, which serves as a guide for stripping identical flats in offset-lithography. (PR)   R.R.K.

Master Scene
The first take of any scene shot as directed in the script. (F)   G.W.

Masthead
The matter printed in every issue of a newspaper, usually at the top of the editorial column, stating the title, publisher, place of publication, etc., from the nautical term indicating the top of the mast from which a flag is flown, hence also called *flag*. (P)   B.C.B.

Mat

A composing room term to describe the matrices used in type-casting machines; linotype, Ludlow, monotype or Thompson caster. The design of the character is engraved or punched in a properly shaped piece of copper or brass in "positive" or reading position and becomes the die for casting the hot metal into type. (PR)   B.B.

Mat Amplifier

See Video-Scene Process.

Mat Board

Board available in various types of surfaces and colors used for art work and layout mats. (A)   H.V.G.

Mat Knife

Knife with a razor-sharp blade used for cutting mats for art work and layouts. (A)   H.V.G.

Mat Print

Print of a photograph or photostat with a dull surface. (A)   H.V.G.

Mats

Frames made of mat board for finished art and layouts. (A)   H.V.G.

Mats

Lightweight molds of an advertisement or engraving made of papier-mâché. They are used as an economical substitute for news electros and mailed to newspapers to be cast into stereotypes. (PR)   H.V.G.

Mat Surface

A dull-surfaced paper or photograph. (P)   H.V.G.

Matt Surface

Designating those photographic plates and films bearing an emulsion with a matt surface, the slight grain of which aids in pencil retouching of images thereon. (PR)   J.S.M.

Maximil

Highest newspaper rate on which no discounts are to be applied in contrast to minimil rate which constitutes the lowest rate—a rate made possible through the application of all possible discounts. (A) P.W.B.

M.C.

Also, master of ceremonies, or emcee. Individual who introduces act in television or radio show and who keeps show moving. (B) P.W.B.

McKittrick's Directory

A quarterly publication showing listings of advertising agencies, their accounts and key personnel. (A) H.V.G.

M.E.

The managing editor. (P)

Measure

Width of type matter in picas. (PR) R.A.F.

Mechanical

An accurate assembly of the various elements of an advertisement or printed piece indicating the size, position and placement preparatory to reproduction. (A) H.V.G.

Mechanical Focusing

Focusing of process cameras by means of scales. (PR) J.S.M.

Mechanical Halftone

Printing plate of halftone character made by various "automatic engraving machines," none of which have proven entirely successful. (PR) J.S.M.

Media Buying Function

To present an advertising message in a vehicle for communicating at the right time to the largest number of possible prospects at the lowest possible cost and with the greatest possible effect or response. (A)

Media Director

The person in an agency responsible for the selection and purchasing of all media. (A)   H.V.G.

Media Survey

A survey to measure the penetration of a particular medium into one or several markets. (A)   H.V.G.

Medium

Means used to convey an advertising message such as newspaper, magazine, direct mail, radio, television, billboards, etc. (Plural: media.) (A)   H.V.G.

Medium Shot

Between a close-up and a long shot. (F)   G.W.

Merchandising

Arrangement of window, floor, counter and shelf displays at the retail level—often tied in with the advertising— to help move the product. Also, explaining the advertising program to salesmen, dealers, stockholders and other groups to acquaint them with the product and gain their cooperation. (A)   H.V.G.

Mercurography

Treatment of partially etched copper or zinc plates with a mercuric chloride solution to form an amalgam on the metal, the amalgam repelling greasy ink and permitting the plate to be rolled up with ink without depositing it on the sides and bottom of the etching. (PR)   J.S.M.

Mercury Vapor

A form of illuminant comprising a long narrow glass tube in which the vapor of mercury is raised to incandescence by passage of an electric current. The light produced lacks red rays but exerts strong actinic action on photographic surfaces. (PR)   J.S.M.

Merg.

A linotype. abbreviated from Mergenthaler, the inventor of the linotype. (PR)   B.C.B.

Message

An ordered selection from an agreed set of signs (alphabet) intended to communicate information. (C) C.C.

Meta-Language (Observer's Language)

The language used by an observer for describing an observed object-language. Language used for expressing rules, laws, relationships. (C)   C.C.

Metal

As ordinarily used around print shops "metal" refers to the alloy used as type metal. (PR)   B.B.

Metal Base

A block of solid type metal on which relief plates are mounted type high in substitution of a wooden base. (PR)

J.S.M.

Metal Print

Line or halftone image on a copper or zinc plate intended for relief etching. (PR)   J.S.M.

Metallic Posting

Used of metallic foil for decoration and emphasis on poster panels in standardized outdoor advertising. (A) R.D.L.

Metropolitan Plan

Plan used by some newspapers, mostly in large cities, of showing their city circulation in totals instead of analyzing it under various headings, such as "carriers," "dealers," "street vendors," etc. Also called "Total City" plan. (P)

A.B.C.

Metzograph (Mezzograph)

A halftone screen embodying a grain formation instead

211

of a system of ruled lines; a printing plate made with such a screen, or one in which details and tones are translated by means of a grain formation. (PR)　　　　J.S.M.

Microphone or Mike
The instrument through which sound is converted into electrical waves. (F)　　　　G.W.

Micro-Wave
Method of interconnecting TV stations by a directional beam. Also used in remote broadcasts for relaying program to station transmitter. (See Coaxial Cable.) (B)　　　H.V.G.

Middle Break
Station announcement of identification in the middle of a program. (B)　　　　P.W.B.

Middle Distance
That portion of a scene, especially of a landscape, which lies between the foreground and the background. (F)　A.S.

Middle Tones
The range between highlights and shadows of a photograph. (F)　　　　R.A.F.

Middletone Stop
The lens aperture used in halftone photography to register the middletones, the diameter of which is midway between that of the highlight and detail stops. (PR) J.S.M.

Miehle
A flat-bed letterpress of the two-revolution type; also trade name. (PR)　　　　R.R.K.

Miehle Vertical
A printing press, letterpress, in which the type form stands vertically. (PR)　　　　R.R.K.

Mike Stew
Sounds not supposed to be picked up by the microphone. (F)　　　　G.W.

Milky

A term used to describe the appearance of developed and unfixed film, or film which has been incorrectly or insufficiently fixed. (F)   A.S.

Mill

A reporter's typewriter. (P)   B.C.B.

Milline Rate

Cost of advertising space per agate line per million circulation. Calculated by multiplying quoted line rate by one million and dividing by the circulation of the publication.
(A)   H.V.G.

Milling

Beveling a plate, also routing away dead metal from the printing area of the plate. (PR)   J.S.M.

Mill Run

Paper requirements with a minimum of 5,000 pounds at a time are regarded as a mill run and can be ordered in special sizes without penalty. (PR)   B.B.

Minion

Seven-point type, used by some newspapers as a body type. (P)   B.C.B.

Miscellany

The name applied by country newspapers to plate matter consisting of miscellaneous filler items, short and long, in handy shape to fill space on dull days. (P)   B.C.B.

Misprint

A typographical error. (PR)   R.R.K.

Mix

Recording or re-recording of sounds, so as to blend them together. (F)   G.W.

Mix

Blending music, sound, and/or voice together on the console. (B)   N.A.B.

Mixer

Sound-recording engineer; also called a monitor. (F)
G.W.

Mixer

Panel for control and blending of sound picked up by multiple microphones. (B)   P.W.B.

MM (Millimeter)

Measurement of width of motion picture film. 35 mm is standard (theatre) size. 16 mm is the size generally used for TV film commercials and kinescopes. (B)   H.V.G.

MM Factor

A method proposed to standardize the basic weight given to all print papers independent of the cut size of the stock or the ream count. By this method all paper weights would be figured on the basis of 1,000 sheets of 1,000 square inches. This would yield an "MM Factor" which would be the actual weight for MM square inches. Ex.: Bond (basis 17 x 22 = 20 lb., 500 sheets) equivalent would be 32 x 44 sheet equals 1,408 sq. in., and 1,408 times 107 (MM Factor) = 150.656 or 151 lbs. for 1,000 sheets of 32 x 44. Decimal is 3 positions to the leftin example since weight is for each 1,000 sq. in. (PR)

Mobile Unit

A miniature transmitter, usually housed in a truck, and employed to relay on-the-spot programs to the station's transmitter. (B)   H.V.G.

Model Release

A form signed by a model releasing the photograph in which he or she appears for advertising or editorial purposes. (A)   H.V.G.

214

Modeled Plate

Halftone plate made direct from a bas-relief. (PR)
J.S.M.

Modern

A class of type faces which had its beginnings in the 18th Century, the most widely used example of which is no doubt *Bodoni,* with all its variations (*Bodoni Book, Ultra Bodoni, Bodoni Campanile,* etc.). Modern faces may be distinguished from "Old Style" or "Transition" faces by their thin lines, thicker stems, and flat serifs. (PR)   B.B.

Moire

A very apt descriptive word, moire in printing refers to an undesirable effect exactly like the pattern in moire silk. It occurs when halftone screens are superimposed on one another with the incorrect degree of tilt. It is most likely to plague an editor if he has occasion to order a half-tone made from a halftone reproduction. If the engraver is not careful to tilt the screen at exactly the right angle, the dots in the new halftone may coincide with those in the old, resulting in a displeasing, wavy, "moire" effect. (PR)
B.B.

Mold

That part of a linecasting machine or monotype in which the line or type is cast against the matrix. (PR) R.R.K.

Mold

A wax, lead or plastic impression used in making electrotypes. (PR)   H.V.G.

Monarch

Stationery, the letter measuring 7¼" x 10½" and the envelope 3⅞" x 7½". (PR)   H.V.G.

Monitor

A screen on which control-room personnel judge quality or content of the picture. Control of volume level and

picture shading in transmission of a television program.
(B)   N.A.B.

Monochrome
A photograph, picture or reproduction in a single color; monochromatic; monotint. (PR)   J.S.M.

Monotype
A machine which casts individual type characters and assembles them into even lines of any desired length. (PR)   H.V.G.

Montage
A rapid succession or superimposition of pictures using dissolves or wipes to create an over-all effect; also sometimes used synonymously for the process of editing. (F)   G.W.

Montage
Group of photographs or drawings blended together to produce the effect of a single illustration. (A)   H.V.G.

Montage
Usually three or more television images transmitted simultaneously by means of dissolve techniques. (B) H.V.G.

Montage
A series of sounds in rapid succession, usually used to cover a long period of time in a short sequence. (B) N.A.B.

Monthly Payment Subscriptions
Subscriptions for which the subscriber is not required to pay in advance for the whole term but in monthly installments within the subscription period. (P)   A.B.C.

Mordant
In etching, an acid or other corrosive liquid capable of eating into and dissolving a metal surface (PR)   J.S.M.

216

More

Written at the bottom of a page of copy indicates *more to come*. (P)   B.C.B.

Morgue

The newspaper's repository for clippings, photos and all types of reference material. (P)   B.C.B.

Morse Code

The code used by telegraphers. (P)   B.C.B.

Mortise

An open space in a plate into which smaller cuts or type matter may be inserted. (PR)   H.V.G.

Mortising

Operation of cutting out sections of mounted printing plates, usually by means of a drill and jig saw. (PR)

J.S.M.

Mottling

Marks which often appear on negatives when they are not sufficiently agitated to keep the developer in motion. (F)   A.S.

Mount

The wood or metal base on which a printing plate is permanently fastened for use on a press (PR)   J.S.M.

Mounting

Operation of attaching printing plates to mounts or supports of wood or metal. (PR)   J.S.M.

Mounting Machine

An apparatus for applying adhesives to wooden blocks and mounting printing plates thereon by means of heat and pressure. (PR)   J.S.M.

Moviola

A small machine for viewing film and listening to the sound without projection. (F)   G.W.

217

M.R. (Motivational Research)
Psychologically oriented research attempting to establish the subconscious motives that prompt people to buy. (A)
H.V.G.

Mr. and Mrs. Show
The name given a type of program involving a married couple using an over-the-breakfast-table format. (B) H.V.G.

Muckrakers
A derogatory tag placed by Theodore Roosevelt on the magazine writers in the early 1900's who crusaded against big business, corruption, and for social justice. He had intended to compare their pre-occupation with exposés to the Man with the Muckrake in *Pilgrim's Progress,* who continued to rake the filth rather than look upward at heavenly virtue. (P)

Mug Shots
Closeup of faces. (P)   B.C.B.

Multicolor Board
A shading sheet bearing two latent but developable patterns of benday nature, the material intended for the preparation of line originals for color reproduction. (PR)
J.S.M.

Multiple Color Presses
Printing presses capable of printing two or more colors at one time. (PR)   H.V.G.

Multiple Exposure Camera
Process camera fitted with an attachment of shutters or flaps to permit up to four exposures being made on a plate or film. (PR)   J.S.M.

Multiple Negative
Gang negative. (PR)   J.S.M.

Musical Clock

An early morning program containing music separated by time signals and commercial announcements. (B)   H.V.G.

Must

When "must" is written on copy by the proper executive, it must be published. BOM means business office must. (P)

B.C.B.

N

N.A.B.
National Association of Broadcasters. The national association of radio and TV stations and networks.

N.I.A.A.
National Industrial Advertisers Association. An organization of advertisers, agencies and media, formed to promote the effective use of industrial advertising and marketing.

N.O.A.B.
National Outdoor Advertising Bureau, Inc., acts as a central outdoor department for more than 200 advertising agencies, and it helps them to buy, place and service outdoor advertising.

Nameplate
The large heading giving the paper's name, on the front page. (P)   B.C.B.

Narrator
A voice that is in the background or off-camera. (B)
H.V.G.

Narrator
A voice which delivers the commentary or tells the story. (F)   G.W.

National Advertising
Advertising directed to markets that are not merely local or regional but national in scope. (A)   H.V.G.

Near Point
The nearest object point lying between the camera and the object in critical focus which is reproduced without perceptible unsharpness. (F)   A.S.

Neck
The part of a type between the shoulder and the face. (PR)   R.R.K.

Negative
A photographic image of originals on paper, film or glass in reverse from those of the original copy. (F)   R.A.F.

Negative Glass
Chemically clean sheets of glass coated with a substratum and intended as supports for wet collodion images. (PR)   J.S.M.

Negative Inserting
Combining different negatives into one design by stripping one into another. (PR)   J.S.M.

Negative Paper
Photographic paper coated with a contrasty or process emulsion and intended for the production of paper negatives. (PR)   J.S.M.

Negative Plate
A printing plate made from a positive, or one showing tones in reverse to those of the original; "reverse plate." (PR)   J.S.M.

Negative Tint
Halftone tint. (PR)   J.S.M.

Negative Varnish

Any of various solutions applied to the face of photographic negatives as a protecting film. (PR) J.S.M.

Nemo

A program originating outside of the station's studios. (B) H.V.G.

Neon

A gas filled glass tube bent in shape of letters or designs. Used as a means of electrical illumination on displays and outdoor signs. (PR) H.V.G.

Net

The amount paid to the advertising medium by the advertising agency after deducting the agency commission. (A) H.V.G.

Net

Abbreviation for radio network, which is merely a group of stations joined by wires to release a given program simultaneously. (B) N.A.B.

Net Advertising Circulation

A weighted measure of circulation designed to estimate the actual number of people who see a specific standardized outdoor advertisement. It is computed by multiplying the Daily Effective Circulation by the Average Space Position Value, i.e., 100,000 DEC × 9.8 SPV equals 980,000 NAC. (A) R.D.L.

Net Press Run

Total of perfect copies printed suitable for distribution. (P) A.B.C.

Network

A chain of stations over which a program is broadcast simultaneously. (B) H.V.G.

222

Network Affiliate
A station belonging to a radio or television network and broadcasting network programs locally. (B)   H.V.G.

Network Option Time
Time on network affiliates for which network has selling priority. (A)   P.W.B.

News
In the generic sense, news is timely, significant and new. In newspaper practice, news is history, timely report, sensation and human interest. A psychological view believes it satisfies the human need for reward, immediate or delayed. In the communist sense, it has social significance only if it maintains and extends the dominant social order. In the scientific, objective sense, news is a report of an event. (P)

News Agent
A distributor of papers or periodicals at wholesale. (P)
A.B.C.

Newscolor
Colorplates for newspaper printing; color printing in newspapers. (P)   J.S.M.

Newsdealer
A merchant with fixed place of doing business who buys papers or periodicals to sell again at retail. (P)   A.B.C.

Newshole
The number of columns of space in a newspaper available for editorial matter after the advertisements have been scheduled. (P)

News Leak
Information or an opinion released by a public official who wants it publicized but does not want it attributed to him. A variation of this is the "plant" or question which

a public official asks a reporter to ask him at a news conference so the official can give the impression that he did not disclose the information on his own. (P)

News Peg

That part of the dramatic feature style lead which contains the actual news about an event and which gives credence to the story. (P)

Newsplate

Line, halftone or combination etching specially intended for newspaper printing; plates for newspaper advertisements. (P)   J.S.M.

Newsprint

A soft paper made from woodpulp used for printing newspapers. (PR)   H.V.G.

Newsreel

A timely report of current events on films. (F)

News Release

A written account or notice of a newsworthy subject sent to newspapers and other publications for editorial use. (A)   H.V.G.

News Stick

A composing stick with a fixed measure. (PR)   R.R.K.

News Summary

An index or a summary of the day's news, usually on the front page. (P)   B.C.B.

Newstone

Halftones up to 100-line, etched on zinc, and intended as newspaper illustrations or for printing on cheap paper. (P)   J.S.M.

Newtonian Rings

Rainbow-like rings or formations of color occurring when

224

negatives are locked into contact with sensitized metal plates in printing frames, and caused by interference of light waves. Popularly assumed to indicate perfect contact, but really indicative of a film of air between the two surfaces. (PR) J.S.M.

Next-to-Reading Matter
Position of an advertisement directly next to editorial matter in a publication. When specifically ordered, it takes preferred rate. (A)   H.V.G.

Nick
A notch in type which acts as a guide to the compositor. (PR)   R.R.K.

Nickeltype
An electrotype on which the first deposit is of nickel and the remainder of the shell is copper. Commonly called "steelfaced." (PR)   R.A.F.

Nielsen Rating
Popularity rating of a program, similar to Hooperating. (A)   H.V.G.

Night Side
Newspaper employes on night shifts are on the night side. (P)   B.C.B.

Nine Column Newspaper
Eight column wide newspapers which have changed from the traditional 12 pica column width to an 11 pica column width, the cumulative space gain of which equals an extra 11 pica column. The change has lessened the newsprint requirement of most U.S. dailies. (P)

Noise
Disturbances that alter the message after it has left the sender, or that interfere with the efficient decoding of communication. Noise factors in the process of communication include actual noise (physical); physiological noise (pain,

headache, deafness, etc.); psychological noise (prejudice, hate, etc.); semantic noise (sender-receiver differences in language meaning, presentation, abstraction, etc.). (After Shannon-Weaver). (C)

Noise (in Telecommunication)
Disturbances which do not represent any part of the messages from a specific source. (C)　　　　　C.C.

Nonactinic
Said of light rays which do not affect photographic surfaces during a given or reasonable length of time. (F) J.S.M.

Nondeductible From Dues
Association subscriptions of members of an association which allow no deduction of the subscription price of the publication from the dues in case the member does not desire the publication. (P)　　　　　A.B.C.

Nonpareil
Six-point type. Also, the unit of measurement for type widths in newspaper composing rooms—thus a cut may be 50 agate lines deep and 20 nonpareils wide. The pica (12 point) unit is used generally for display advertising widths. Also nonpareil slugs for spacing between columns. (P)　　　　　B.C.B.

Nonreturnable
Not subject to credit on being returned. Said of sales plan in which dealers or other distributors purchase their copies with the understanding that they must pay for all copies purchased whether they sell them or not. (P) A.B.C.

Nontheatrical Film
A film for audiences outside theaters. (F)　　　　　G.W.

Nonwrinkle Posting
Dampening an outdoor poster before or during a posting operation, and stretching it while posting so that when

dried it presents a smooth surface. (A)   R.D.L.

Normal Stop
Detail stop in halftone photography. (PR)   J.S.M.

Notch
An area cut out of an engraving for insertion of type. Differs from a mortise in that it is open on one or two sides. (PR)   H.V.G.

No. 10
Common size of business stationery—the letter measuring 8½″ x 11″ and the envelope 4⅛″ x 9½″. (PR)   H.V.G.

Numbering Machine
A type-high printing machine which is locked with type in regular printing forms, and prints numbers in consecutive order, forward or backward as wanted. (PR)   R.R.K.

O

O.A.A.A.

The Outdoor Advertising Association of America, Inc.
Organization composed of standard poster advertising and
painted display advertising plant operations.

O.A.I.

Outdoor Advertising Incorporated is a non-profit organization, the national sales organization representing plant
owners in the United States. It represents the medium to
advertisers, agencies and selling companies; it collects market
information, conducts surveys, plans campaigns, arranges
schedules and does many other things helpful in selling outdoor advertising.

Obit, Obituary

A biography of a dead person. (P)   B.C.B.

Object-Language

A language under observation and study (not to be confused with Meta-Language). The language of communication
events. (C)   C.C.

Objective

A term sometimes applied to the image-forming lens of
an optical instrument; for example, the lens used on a camera
or enlarging apparatus. (F)   A.S.

228

Objectivity

A characteristic of conventional newswriting style with the definite purpose of limiting the writer to a simple report of an event; a newsstory supposedly without meaning, evaluation, editorializing or slant. (P)

Observer

(We distinguish between external observer and participant observer.) The former is quite detached from the communication event he is observing; his reportings are entirely objective. The latter reports upon communication events, in which he is one partner; he may use cognitive terms. Both observers report in a meta-language. (C)   C.C.

Occupational Classification

Segregation of subscribers into groups according to their business or professional callings or according to the position they occupy in a business organization. (P)   A.B.C.

Off Camera

A voice heard during a scene while the actor is out of view. (B)

Off Mike

Talking just outside the live area of the microphone. (B)   N.A.B.

Off the Record Information

Facts disclosed by a news source for the newsman's own information, but not for publication. This device has been used to muzzle the newsman about facts that ought to become public and with informants who don't want to be quoted. Information accepted on these terms does help produce added insight into complex news situations. (P)

Office Collect System

System of newspaper operation by which accounts with subscribers are kept in office of the paper and collections are made by the paper's own employes. (P)   A.B.C.

Official Organ

A periodical which is owned by an association organized for other purposes than to publish the periodical or which is appointed as the mouthpiece of an association in return for special privileges granted the association. (P)   A.B.C.

Offset Lithography

A printing process in which the impression is transferred from the printing plate to a rubber blanket and then onto the paper. (See Lithography.) (PR)   H.V.G.

Offset Paper

As the designation of a certain kind of paper, "offset" is a smooth, but not coated, sheet, bulkier than most book papers, with a surface quite similar to that of bond paper in appearance, but not as hard. Almost any paper properly "sized," that will resist the effect of water and which is entirely free from fluff or fuzz is suitable for offset printing. (PR)   B.B.

Offset Printing

This term is inaccurate (and incorrect) when used to designate lithographic printing. "Offset" refers to the process of transferring the printed image from a rubber "blanket" onto the paper; although this procedure is used more widely in lithography, it might also be used in typographic printing. The proper term is Offset Lithographic Printing. (PR)   B.B.

Oil

Pigment with an oil base, which can be used either opaquely or transparently, depending on the amount of thinner or oil used. The medium used for oil paintings. (A)   H.V.G.

Oil Transfer Process

A photographic process similar to the bromoil transfer or collotype process, in which the pigmented image produced in the oil process is transferred to another support by means of pressure. (F)   A.S.

Old Style

A classification of type faces the design of which is based on types used in the 16th and 17th centuries. A distinguishing characteristic of Old Style faces is their slanting serifs. *Garamond* and *Granjon* are among the many Old Style letters. (PR)   B.B.

On the Air

A term describing a program or a person who is actually broadcasting. (B)   N.A.B.

On the Head

The starting of a program on scheduled time, made possible by the proper timing of the preceding broadcast. (B)
                                                         J.C.W.

One Shot

Programs that go on the air only once; not part of a series. (B)   N.A.B.

One-Shot Camera

Small portable color camera capable of making continuous tone three-color separation negatives with a single exposure through a single lens. (PR)   J.S.M.

One-Time Rate

Rate paid by an advertiser who uses too little space or too few insertions to earn a contract rate discount. Sometimes called "open rate." (A)   H.V.G.

One-Way Screen

A halftone screen bearing a single series of parallel lines instead of intersecting lines. (PR)   J.S.M.

One-Way Tint

A halftone tint consisting of parallel lines of uniform width, usually produced by photography through a standard

231

halftone screen with a slit stop in the camera lens; a one-way halftone is a plate in which the tones are translated by means of a single series of parallel lines. (PR) J.S.M.

Onionskin
A thin bond paper primarily used for carbon copies of letters and business forms. (PR) H.V.G.

Op. ed.
Page opposite the editorial page. (P) B.C.B.

Opacity
In photographic negatives, the suppression or absorption of light by the silver deposit of the image; really the percentage of light transmitted by the image. (F) J.S.M.

Opal Glass
A translucent milk glass used in enlargers to diffuse light before it reaches the negative. (F) A.S.

Opaque
Photographically, the state or condition of not permitting the passage of light. The red or black pigment applied to areas and blemishes in photographic negatives to render them opaque for impeding the passage of light during printing. (F) J.S.M.

Opaque
A still picture or photograph viewed by reflected light, and generally transmitted via television projection equipment. (B) N.A.B.

Open End
An envelope with flap that opens on the short dimension. (PR) H.V.G.

Open End Transcription
A recorded program usually sold on a syndicated basis in various cities and produced so that local commercial an-

nouncements may be inserted at various points throughout the show. (B)   H.V.G.

Open Matter
Type lines very widely spaced. (PR)   R.R.K.

Open Rate
See Flat Rate. (A)

Open Side
An envelope with flap that opens on the long dimension. (PR)   H.V.G.

Optical
A photographic process for duplicating films, in which tricky effects are obtained by combining frames, using wipes, dissolves, etc. (F)   G.W.

Optical Axis
The imaginary line joining the centers of the two spherical surfaces of a lens; also called the principal axis. A ray of light entering the lens along this path will continue through the lens and emerge without being bent or refracted. (F)   A.S.

Optical Center
The center of a rectangle as it appears to the eye; two-fifths from the top of the rectangle. (PR)   R.R.K.

Optical Flat
A color filter consisting of a sheet of dyed gelatin cemented between two sheets of optically surfaced glass. (PR) J.S.M.

Optical Glass
Fine glass used to make lenses. (F)   G.W.

Optical Reversal
Lateral inversion of camera images by means of optical reversing devices. (F)   J.S.M.

Optical Sensitizing
Rendering photographic emulsions color sensitive by addition of sensitizing dyes. (PR) J.S.M.

Optics
That branch of physical science relating to the nature and properties of light, its modification by opaque and transparent substances, and the laws of vision. (PR) J.S.M.

Original
The photograph, drawing, painting, design, print or other matter submitted for photomechanical reproduction; usually referred to as "copy." (PR) J.S.M.

Orthicon
Main picture tube used in television camera. (B) P.W.B.

Orthochromatic
A negative or reproduction of a vari-colored original showing correct monochrome rendition of the color values and natural tones of the subject. (PR) J.S.M.

Orthochromatic Film
Sensitive to blue and green, but not to red and orange. (F) G.W.

Out of Register
The state in colorwork when the constituent negatives or plates of a color set are not of identical size or when they do not superpose in proper relation to each other. (PR) J.S.M.

Outdoor Advertising
Display-type advertising (billboards, posters, signs, etc.) placed out-of-doors, along highways and railroads, or on walls and roofs of buildings. (A) H.V.G.

Outdoor Advertising Plant
An organization which builds and maintains outdoor dis-

plays consisting of painted bulletins and/or poster panels.
(A) H.V.G.

Outdoor Circulation

The number of people passing by an outdoor structure or group of structures to whom an advertising display presents a message. The Traffic Audit Bureau computes the "Effective Circulation" of outdoor advertising as one-half the number of pedestrians plus one-half of the automobile traffic, plus one-fourth bus and rapid transit passengers that pass a given display in an 18-hour day. (A) R.D.L.

Outline Engraving

An engraving or printing plate devoid of tints or shading, and whereon only the outer boundaries of the figure or subject are shown. (PR) J.S.M.

Outlined Cut

A halftone of which the background has been cut away. See *vignette*. (PR) B.C.B.

Outlining

Cutting a thin line of separation with a tint tool on blockout halftones for guidance of the router in removing the background. (PR) J.S.M.

Outside Mortise

A notch (mortise) cut into one or more sides of a mounted printing plate from the outer edges, but in such manner that the aperture is not completely enclosed. (PR) J.S.M.

Ovaling

Cutting a printing plate to the shape of an ellipse. (See Ellipsograph.) (PR) J.S.M.

Over-Etched

A relief etching in which lines or dots have been damaged or partially etched away by excessive etching or action beyond normal period of time. (PR) J.S.M.

235

Overexposure
Film exposed too long, resulting in a print that is too light. (F)   G.W.

Overhang Cover
A cover larger in size than the enclosed pages. (PR)   R.A.F.

Overhead
News sent by telegraph or telephone. (P)   B.C.B.

Overlapping Circulation
Duplication of circulation when advertising is placed in two or more media reaching the same prospects. Sometimes desirable to give additional impact to advertising. (A) H.V.G.

Overlay
A dealer identification strip pasted upon an outdoor poster. See "Dealer Imprint." (A)   R.D.L.

Overlay
In letterpress makeready, a piece of paper placed in the packing to make part of the form print more heavily in that place; in offset-lithography, the transparent or translucent covering on the copy on which directions or work to be over-printed are placed, in the preparation of artwork. (PR)   R.R.K.

Overlay Negative
A photographic negative superposed on another to effect results impossible to get with a single image. (F) J.S.M.

Overline
The caption above the cut. (P)   B.C.B.

Overmatter
Synonymous with "overset."

Overprinting
Double-printing or surprinting work on an area that has already been printed upon, in platemaking. (PR)   R.R.K.

Overruns

Buyers of any sort of printing are expected to accept up to 10% more copies than they ordered when necessary, and to pay for them on a pro rata basis. The reason for this is that a certain amount of paper stock, over the quantity specified, must be allowed for spoilage, and press runs are always set somewhat higher than the quantity required, for the same reason. If the spoilage is not as great as was anticipated, the quantity ordered is exceeded. (PR)   B.B.

Overrunning

Setting type backward or forward in making corrections, as when copy is left out, or added in the paragraph. (PR)
R.R.K.

Overs, Overset

Type set in excess of the amount allotted and therefore crowded out of the paper for lack of room. Each editor —city, telegraph cable, and sports—is given a stipulated amount of space for his news; any type in excess of this is *overmatter, overset, overs.* Where there is an insufficient quantity of matter in type, the paper is *underset.* (P) B.C.B.

Overset

Type matter that has been set and not used. Such type will be charged for over and above the price set for printing any publication. Prices are based upon setting enough type to properly fill the specified number of pages; if more type has been set than there is room for it increases the cost and must be paid for as an extra charge. (PR)   B.B.

Oxidation

The action of oxygen and air on metals, causing discoloration and marring of surfaces, together with the formation of rust or other coatings. Treatment of a zinc plate with a graining bath or dilute acid solution. The chemical effect taking place during etching. (PR)   J.S.M.

237

Oxidation

The deterioration of a developer caused by its contact with air. (F)   A.S.

Oyster Shells

Certain peculiar blemishes occurring in the form of extraneous deposits of reduced silver on wet collodion plates, the curious shapes of the markings resembling somewhat the color and appearance of oyster shells. (PR)   J.S.M.

Ozachrome

Process of making photographic color proofs from separation negatives with diazotype (Ozalid) materials. (PR) J.S.M.

Ozalid

Photographic process employing materials sensitized with diazo compounds, the exposed images usually developed with gaseous ammonia. (PR)   J.S.M.

238

P

P.A.A.A.
Premium Advertising Association of America, Inc.

P.I.B.
Publishers Information Bureau, Inc. An organization of magazine publishers.

P.I.O.
Public Information Officer; also P.R.O. or Public Relations Officer. (P)

P.M.
An afternoon paper. (P)

P.P.A.
Periodical Publishers Association. An organization of large national magazine publishers, which handles industry relations and credit information for its members.

P.P.A.I.
Point of Purchase Advertising Institute, Inc. An association of producers and users of display material.

P.U.A.A.
Public Utilities Advertising Association. An association of utility companies throughout the world interested in advertising and public relations.

P.R.
Public relations. (P)

P.S.A.
Abbreviation for Photographic Society of America. (F)

Package
A program property in which all elements from script to finished production are owned and controlled by an individual or organization, commonly known as a "packager." Most of the popular radio and TV shows are package programs. (A)   H.V.G.

Package Goods
Mostly food, soap, and household products that are marketed in the manufacturer's package, wrapper or container. (A)   H.V.G.

Package Inserts
Separate advertising material included in packaged goods. (PR)   H.V.G.

Package Show
Complete radio or television show that is bought as a unit. (A)   P.W.B.

Pad
Put more material into a show that needs it for timing purposes. (B)   N.A.B.

Pad
Round, flat, sand-filled leather cushion on which engravers and finishers support printing plates while working on their surface. (PR)   J.S.M.

Pad
To make a story long by padding it out with words. (P)   B.C.B.

240

Padding
Colloquial term for the flash exposure in halftone.
(PR)   J.S.M.

Page Proof
Proof of the entire page. Such a proof is rarely taken of
news pages but is frequently pulled on feature material pages
of the Sunday edition. (P)   T.E.B.

Paid
A classification of subscriptions or purchases, based upon
payment in accordance with the standards set by the Audit
Bureau of Circulations. (P)   A.B.C.

Paid-On-Delivery Subscription
Subscription, for which the price of each issue is collected
when it is delivered or, in case an advance payment is made
with order, the pro-rated balance is collected at time of delivery of each issue. (P)   A.B.C.

Paid Subscriber
Purchaser of publication on a term contract, whose subscription qualifies as paid circulation in accordance with the
rules of the Audit Bureau of Circulations. (P)   A.B.C.

Paid Subscription
A subscription made in accordance with Audit Bureau
of Circulations rules defining a paid subscriber. (P) A.B.C.

Painted Bulletin
A standardized outdoor advertising structure upon which
the advertisement is reproduced in paint. (A)   R.D.L.

Painted Wall
An advertisement painted on the wall of a building so that
it shows to passing traffic. (A)   R.D.L.

Painting In
Applying acid-resisting varnish with a brush to certain
areas of line and halftone plates before etching. (PR) J.S.M.

241

Pam (Pan) Head
The mechanism at the top of a tripod which permits the camera to be moved in horizontal or vertical planes. May be fixed to the tripod, or detachable. (F)   A.S.

Pamphlet
Several sheets of paper stitched together. (PR)   R.R.K.

Pan
A gradual swinging of the camera in any direction, up or down or from left to right. (F)   G.W.

Pan
Abbreviation of "panorama"—to move the TV camera from side to side or up and down. (B)   H.V.G.

Panchromatic
A black and white print of color art that interprets the various colors in shades of gray. (PR)   H.V.G.

Panchromatic Film
Sensitive to all colors. (F)   G.W.

Panel
A square or rectangular design made up of rule or border. (PR)   R.R.K.

Panel
To depress the center area of a sheet of paper that contains a block of copy or an illustration. (PR)   H.V.G.

Paperback
A book with a paperlike covering or binding as contrasted with the standard hardcover book. It is seldom the binding which contributes to the lowered cost of paperbacks. Rather the reduction in price is achieved by printing large editions, reducing promotion and distribution costs, and paying less royalties.

Paper Negatives
Negatives on a paper base rather than a film or glass

242

base, generally used in enlarging. They can be made by two methods, one in which a small positive transparency on film is first made from the small negative. This is projected to the desired size just as a bromide enlargement is resulting in a negative on paper. Another method is to make a large positive (in reverse) on a smooth paper from which a paper negative is made by contact printing, the light passing through the paper base to the sensitized paper which has been placed in contact with it. The use of paper negatives permits a great deal of modification and retouching which is done with pencil. The mechanical grain due to printing through the paper base lends a pictorial quality to the finished contact print. (F)   A.S.

Paper Type
Several houses manufacture pads of alphabets which are intended to be used in pasting up headlines, either for reproduction in offset printing or for zinc etchings; their use is intended to save the cost of hand lettering or setting type. They are prepared with blue guide lines which will not reproduce in the finished plate. The only difficulty lies in the fact that it takes considerable practice to achieve the desired effects. (PR)   B.B.

Parallax
Displacement of one object with respect to another when viewed from different positions. (F)   J.S.M.

Parallel Action
Alternate shots of action supposedly occurring at the same time. (F)   G.W.

Parallel Panel
Outdoor advertising panel parallel to the line of travel; naturally viewed by traffic moving in both directions. (A)
                                                                            R.D.L.

Parallelism
The condition in process cameras when the copyboard,

lensboard, halftone screenholder and focal plane are all exactly parallel and square with each other. (PR)   J.S.M.

Parens
Abbreviation for parentheses. (P)   B.C.B.

Participation Program
(1) A commercial program sponsored by a number of "participating" advertisers. (2) A program in which the audience participates, e.g., quiz show. (B)   H.V.G.

Part-Time Station
Station authorized by the F.C.C. to broadcast only during certain hours. (B)   H.V.G.

Paste Lines
Shadows and marking created by illustrations and type proofs pasted into an original as additions. (PR)   J.S.M.

Paste-Up
Artwork on which proofs of type and photostats have been pasted so that all may be reproduced together. (See Mechanical.) (PR)   H.V.G.

Pastels
Colored and black and white chalks used for layout purposes. (A)   H.V.G.

Patch
Connections made in the control room to tie one circuit to another. (B)   N.A.B.

Patching
Cutting, fitting and soldering several plates together to form a single printing plate; repair work performed on plates by finishers. (PR)   J.S.M.

Patent Base
Sectional metal blocks used as supports for printing plates and provided with means for holding the plates in position on the press. (PR)   J.S.M.

Patent Insides
Name given to *ready-print* inside pages. See *Boilerplate.* (P) B.C.B.

Pattern
The specific moiré occurring when a halftone reproduction is made from a halftone proof. (PR) J.S.M.

Pattern Plate
An electrotype with an extra heavy shell backed with hard metal used for producing mats and additional electrotypes. (PR) H.V.G.

Payola
A traditional method of song plugging; the payment of money to secure the performance of a song or record. It has become standard trade jargon for bribes. (B)

Pebbling
A process of graining or crimping gloss-coated paper after printing halftones to give an antique paper effect, now generally out of date. (PR) R.R.K.

Pencil Reproduction
Line or highlight halftone reproduction of a drawing made with a lead pencil. (PR) J.S.M.

Pen Drawing
A line sketch or drawing made with a pen and India Ink. (PR) J.S.M.

Penumbral Shadow
A theory of halftone photography in which the halftone dot formation is presumed to be formed by shadows cast on the plate or film by the opaque lines of the standard halftone screen. (PR) J.S.M.

Perforations
Holes in the edge of the film that engage the sprockets in the camera and the projector. (F) G.W.

Periodical

Publication of regular periodic issue, except newspapers. (P) A.B.C.

Permastat

A photostat print on special antique finish paper. The effect is soft in tone. (A) H.V.G.

Perry-Higgins Process

Method of assembling negatives for newspaper reproduction into page form, then etching plates therefrom as integral units on sheets of magnesium metal, followed by direct newsprinting from the etched plates. Modified form of Alltone process. (P) J.S.M.

Perspective

Perspective, in radio, is the relationship of sounds to one another. In TV, perspective is the depth acquired in the image. (B) H.V.G.

Phantom

An original or reproduction therefrom in which certain details are depicted in ghost-like manner to direct attention to the other parts of the subject or illustration. (PR) J.S.M.

Phat, Fat

To phat type is to hold it for possible repetition; it is then called phatted type. A fat take or a fat page is a take or page with many cuts or other matter that does not require setting, making the printer's work easy. Fat type is extended type and thin type is extra-condensed. A fat line is a line that cannot be set in the allotted space; a thin line is a line that is too scant. (P) B.C.B.

Phillips' Code

A system of abbreviated Morse Code symbols by old-time telegraphers. To them, "prans" meant "the President today sent the following nominations to the senate." (P) B.C.B.

Phonemes

There are several *schools of thought*. We distinguish here: (1) a minimal set of shortest segments of a language which, if substituted one for another, convert one word (or "meaningful segment") to another; (2) sets of distinctive features (after Jakobson); (3) the quantal cells of a language attribute space, the axes of which represent distinctive features. Phonemes are essentially abstracted, linguistic elements, not physical utterances. (C)   C.C.

Photo Essay

A photojournalistic interpretation done leisurely which attempts to build an atmosphere as well as present facts, to register a predetermined impression or a deeper understanding of some person, idea or subject of significance. (P)

Photochemistry

That branch of chemistry which treats of photographic effects and the production of images on sensitized surfaces by the agency of light. (PR)   J.S.M.

Photocomposing Machine

Apparatus wherewith duplicate exposures can be made on sensitized surfaces by accurately controlled placement of the negative or positive, or for photoprinting an image in any specific position on the plate. Also known as step-and-repeat machine. (PR)   J.S.M.

Photocomposition

Type composed on film rather than on metal. (PR)   B.C.B.

Photoelectric Cell

A device through which light is converted into electric current proportionate to the amount of light that falls on it (P.E. cell). (F)   G.W.

Photoelectric Effect

The action or effect of light in decreasing the electrical resistance of metals and other substances when exposed to illumination of certain wave-lengths. (PR) J.S.M.

Photoelectric Engraver

An automatic engraving machine; Scan-a-Graver. (PR) J.S.M.

Photoelectrotype

Early photoengraving process in which electrotype printing plates were made from gelatin relief images. (PR) J.S.M.

Photoengraving

A picture photographed on metal, which is then given relief for printing reproduction by being etched either chemically or electrolytically. A *halftone* is a photoengraving photographed through a screen, with the dots in the light sections etched away to offer little printing surface. A *line engraving* or *zinc etching* is a *photoengraving* made without *photographing* it through a screen. (PR) B.C.B.

Photoetching

A photoengraving. The process of relief or intaglio etching of a photographic image on a metal plate. (PR) J.S.M.

Photoflood

Incandescent lamp of high actinicity, sometimes used as an illuminant for lighting originals on process cameras. (PR) J.S.M.

Photography

The science and art of obtaining images of objects by the action of light on sensitized surfaces. (F) J.S.M.

Photogelatin

Continuous tone printing process utilizing a gelatin-coated plate. Also known as colotype. (PR) H.V.G.

248

Photogravure

Any of several processes by which an intaglio engraving is made in a metal plate by photographic means. The meaning of intaglio is that what is to be printed is recessed or etched into the plate. When this type of plate is covered by ink and then scraped off, the ink remaining in the depressed lines and areas makes the printed image on the paper. (PR)

B.B.

Photointaglio

An incised printing surface produced by photographic means, and distinguished from a relief etching. (PR) J.S.M.

Photojournalism

Emphasis on pictures as a means of relating news. (P)

T.E.B.

Photo Lettering

Photographic method by which letters can be combined and extended or contracted to fit the needs of a layout. A print is provided for reproduction. (A)   H.V.G.

Photomechanical

Pertaining to all processes in which printing surfaces are produced by photography. (PR)   J.S.M.

Photomontage

The combination or blending of several photographic images into a single print to present a variety of views or subjects. (F)   J.S.M.

Photopaper

Paper sensitized with a photographic emulsion and intended for either contact or projection printing. (F) J.S.M.

Photopolymer Printing Plates

In this platemaking method, matter to be printed—text, line, halftone—is incorporated into a high-contrast, right-reading (from the emulsion side) photographic negative. The negative is placed and held in intimate contact with an unexposed plate, which has been stored for 24 hours in a carbon dioxide atmosphere. The plate is exposed through the negative to a light source which is rich in ultra-violet, such as a carbon arc lamp. When the light strikes the intended printing areas of the plate, it makes these areas relatively insoluble. Unexposed plastic is removed from the plate by a pressurized water spray containing sodium hydroxide, leaving the printing areas in relief. No acid and no etching are needed. Such a plate can be made from a prepared negative in less than 20 minutes. (PR)

Photoprinting
Exposure of a sensitized surface under a negative or positive in a printing frame. (PR)   J.S.M.

Photoresist
An acid-resisting image produced on metal plates by the agency of photography or the hardening action of light on sensitized surfaces; enamel print. (PR)   J.S.M.

Photostat
A cheap and quickly made photographic reproduction in the form of either a negative or positive print, both made with special camera apparatus bearing the name. (PR)
J.S.M.

Phototelegraphy
Electrical transmission of photographic images; wirephoto. (P)   J.S.M.

Phototextyping
Composing or setting type or text matter by means of photographic apparatus for the purpose. (PR)   J.S.M.

Phototypecomposing Machine
A keyboard device for assembling images of type faces

photographically on film, rather than in metal type forms. (PR) R.R.K.

Pi

Type that is mixed, disarranged and therefore impossible to use; a jumbled heap of type, as when a page form is dropped and broken up. (PR) B.C.B.

Pic

Picture. (P) T.E.B.

Pica

A printer's term to denote measure of width. There are 6 picas to the inch. (PR) H.V.G.

Pica Master

A band saw or plate trimmer designed to accurately trim cemented printing plates to pica or point measurements without leaving a burr on the trimmed plates. (PR) J.S.M.

Pickup

The point of origin of a broadcast; an electronic device, instrument or arm which picks up sound from a record; also the process of picking up action and sound by a TV camera and/or microphone. (B) H.V.G.

Pickup

A wad of dry rubber cement used to pick up excess cement from a paste-up. (A) H.V.G.

Pickup

Same as remote. (B) N.A.B.

Pickup

Type already set that is to be incorporated with a new lead or other fresh matter—"End new lead; pick up old story as trimmed and corrected." (P) B.C.B.

251

Pickup Point
In radio or television the place of origin of a telecast or broadcast. (B)   P.W.B.

Pickup System
Method of halftone photography employing three successively smaller lens apertures for highlight, middletone and detail exposures; 3-stop exposure. (PR)   J.S.M.

Pictorial Journalism
Relating a story through a sequence of pictures. (P)
T.E.B.

Picture Editor
The editor in charge of pictures. His duty may be simply to write the lines for all pictures used in the paper, or he may have further duties extending to being in full charge of a corps of photographers. (P)   T.E.B.

Picture Line Standard
The standard for US television is 525 lines, the standard being the number of horizontal lines scanned per second for each image or frame. (B)   H.V.G.

Picture Series
A photojournalistic approach where a group of pictures present details of which the cumulative effect is that the viewer gets the feeling that he has inspected a locale or has become acquainted with a personality. (P)

Picture Story
A photojournalistic narration which records and interprets a developing event as if the viewer were an eyewitness to a happening. (P)

Pig Iron
Heavy, serious newspaper copy. (P)   B.C.B.

Pigment
Substance used for coloring in printing ink. (PR) H.V.G.

Pilot Film
A demonstration film used to provide a sample of the content of a TV program series. (B)

Pinholes
Minute transparent spots occurring as blemishes in photographic negatives and prints, and due either to dust or chemical action. (PR)   J.S.M.

Pinhole Theory
A theory of halftone photography in which each tiny aperture of the ruled halftone screen is supposed to act in the rôle of a pinhole lens and form a vignetted image (dot) of the lens aperture. (PR)   J.S.M.

Pix
Pictures. (P)   T.E.B.

Placement Positions
Position of outdoor display related to traffic:

Angled—one end of display is six (6) or more feet farther removed from the line of travel than the other end.

Decked—positioned above another standard structure.

Head-on—positioned directly in frontal line of vision of traffic.

Parallel—positioned parallel to the line of traffic.

Roof—positioned on a roof top.

Semi-head-on—positioned slightly to the right or left of the direct line of vision of approaching traffic.

Shopping center—positioned alongside buildings or parking area of a shopping center.

Wall—positioned on or immediately adjacent and parallel to the wall of a building. (A)   R.D.L.

Plagiarism
Exact or approximate copy of the language of source without quotations, footnote designation or acknowledgment. (P)

Plane

Wooden block used by the printer to make certain that the type surface of the page is smooth. The printer slides the block over the type, tapping the block lightly with a mallet. (PR) T.E.B.

Planograph

All lithographic printing is planographic; the word means printing from a plane surface, neither raised as in letterpress or recessed as in gravure. By usage, however, planograph has come to mean the least expensive form of lithographic reproduction. (PR) B.B.

Plant

The physical structures for standardized outdoor advertising; these include poster panels, painted displays and spectaculars; also the necessary company buildings for operating these structures. (A) R.D.L.

Plant Operator

A person or company that operates an outdoor plant. (A) R.D.L.

Plastic Binding

A solid back comb rolled to make a cylinder of any thickness. Book is punched with slots along the binding side and plastic comb is inserted through the slots. (PR) R.A.F.

Plastic Plates

Relief printing plates made from plastic materials instead of metal, the plates usually produced by molding, or by direct engraving or treatment of plastic surfaces; Scan-a-Graver. (PR) J.S.M.

Plate

Metal page of type made by the stereotype department to be placed on the presses. (P) T.E.B.

254

Plate

Photographically, a sensitized sheet of glass on which negatives or positives are made; a dryplate; a wet collodion plate. A piece of metal bearing a relief or intaglio printing surface, electrotypes, photoengravings. (PR)　　　J.S.M.

Plate Base

A specially designed and machined metal plate for supporting and registering unmounted printing plates while taking proofs therefrom. Any wooden or metal support on which relief printing plates are either temporarily or permanently attached; block; mount; patent base. (PR) J.S.M.

Plate Cementing

Attachment or mounting of relief printing plates on wooden or metal supports by means of adhesives, usually with the aid of heat and applied pressure; mounting machine. (PR)　　　J.S.M.

Plate Cleaner

A solution or detergent for removing ink, etching powder and acid-resisting images from the surface of relief etchings. (PR)　　　J.S.M.

Plate Cooler

Apparatus for cooling heated plates during the process of relief etching. (PR)　　　J.S.M.

Plate Finish

A fine, smooth hard finish. (PR)　　　R.A.F.

Plateholder

The light-tight frames or case used for transporting photographic plates to and from the camera, and for holding the sensitized material in position during exposure. (PR)　　　J.S.M.

Platen Press

A style of letterpress which makes impressions from a flat surface. (PR)　　　R.R.K.

Platter

Informal term used by broadcast people to refer to records or transcriptions. (B) P.W.B.

Playback

Ability of respondent to remember content of advertisement. (A) P.W.B.

Playback

The reproduction of a recording immediately after it has been recorded. Also a term used to denote the turntable and pick-up mechanism employed in playing back the record. (B) H.V.G.

Play Up

To emphasize an angle of a story or to emphasize any material that is being placed in print. (P) T.E.B.

Plug

Filler copy. (P) B.C.B.

Plug

Short commercial, often unplanned, that is made in behalf of a product not sponsoring the radio or television program on which the plug is made. (B) P.W.B.

Point

A unit of measurement in printing material and type; .014-inch on linecasting machines, and .0138 in foundry type; there are 72 points to the inch; any mark of punctuation, as the period, comma, etc. (PR) R.R.K.

Point-Set

Letters of a type font which are cast to point multiples. (PR) R.R.K.

Point System

Refers to the point as a unit of measurement; see *Point*. (PR) R.R.K.

256

Polarized Light
Light that is vibrating in only a single plane. Light can be polarized by a filter over the light source or, if that is impractical, by a filter over the lens. (F)　　A.S.

Pola Screen
An instrument in the form of a neutral gray light filter, transmitting plane polarized light of all visible colors, but absorbing ultraviolet. Used on camera lenses and lights to eliminate or subdue undesirable reflections from originals. (PR)　　J.S.M.

Police Blotter
Record kept in police stations of arrests. The district man checks the police blotter for information. (P)　　T.E.B.

Policy Story
A story written to serve the publisher's policy. (P) B.C.B.

Polyvinyl Process
Method based on the suggested employment of polyvinyl alcohol as a substitute for albumen and glue in photo-mechanical sensitizers. (PR)　　J.S.M.

Pop Test
A test of the bursting strength of paper while under pressure. (PR)　　R.A.F.

Pork
Matter saved from one edition and reprinted in another. Also used with regard to time copy. (P)　　B.C.B.

Portrait Attachment
A supplementary lens which shortens the focal length so that near objects may be brought into sharp focus. (F)　A.S.

Portrait Panchromatic Film
A high-speed panchromatic film whose color sensitiveness

is approximately the same as that of the human eye. It is somewhat less sensitive to red than supersensitive panchromatic film. (F)   A.S.

Positive

A photographic image giving a natural representation of the light and shades of the subject or original; the reverse of a negative. A positive on an opaque support (paper, metal) is a print, whereas one on a transparent support (glass or film) is a transparency. (PR)   J.S.M.

Positive

The true picture—a print made from the negative. (F)
G.W.

Positive Film

A non-color-sensitive film, much slower than negative film but faster than positive plates. It is used as an intermediate in making a copy negative. (F)   A.S.

Positive Image

An image that corresponds, in light and dark tones, to the original. (As distinguished from a negative, in which dark tones are light, and light tones dark). (F)   A.S.

Postage Saver

An envelope with a tuck-in flap that may be opened for postal inspection. (PR)   H.V.G.

Poster

A sign affixed to a wall or board. Sizes generally used are 24" x 42" (full-size), 21" x 38" (half-size), and 14" x 21" (quarter-size). (A)   H.V.G.

Poster Panel

A standardized outdoor advertising structure upon which an advertisement reproduced on paper is pasted. Poster panel ordinarily refers to a structural unit 12'3" x 24'6" overall used for displaying 24-sheet posters. (A)   R.D.L.

258

Poster Plant

The organization which builds and services poster panels and hangs poster sheets on them displaying illustration and/or message of advertiser. (A)   H.V.G.

Poster Showing

The group of outdoor poster panels used to provide geographical coverage of any given market; this is usually expressed as a "100 showing," "75 showing," "50 showing," etc. (A)   R.D.L.

Poster Stamps

Small advertising illustrations in the form of perforated and detachable stamps. (A)   J.S.M.

Poster, Twenty-Four Sheet

An advertisement measuring 8 feet, 10 inches high by 19 feet 8 inches long which is usually lithographed or screen-process printed on several large sheets of paper to be pasted on the face of a standardized poster panel to be viewed outdoors. (While the name "24-sheet poster" is the commonly used terminology in the industry, it is no longer exactly descriptive of the number of sheets used—now usually ten or twelve.) (A)   R.D.L.

Posterizing

A method of reproducing continuous tone originals by opaquing and treatment of continuous tone negatives, from which solid colorplates are made, with the detail and gradation broadly represented by means of different colors, so that the final result lends a poster effect. (PR)   J.S.M.

Posting Mechanics

Blanking—The white border on a 24- or 30-sheet poster panel.

Custom made—A poster produced by manugraph or hand painted.

Imprinted—A poster carrying the local dealer's name.

Non-wrinkle posting—Damp application and stretching to produce smooth result.

Overlay—A dealer imprint pasted on a poster. (A) R.D.L.

Posting Period
Number of days that an advertiser's message appears on an outdoor poster panel—usually 30 days. (A)　　R.D.L.

Potter-Cushing Process
Method of photographic color proving involving chemical reversal of stripfilm separation negatives, dyeing of the positive images and super-position in register on a white support. (PR)　　J.S.M.

Powdering
Application or brushing of dragon's blood or etching powder on plates during relief etching, especially in the dragon's blood process. (PR)　　J.S.M.

Powdering Machine
Power-driven apparatus for mechanically applying etching powder to plates. (PR)　　J.S.M.

Powderless Etch
Method of controlling the action of acid on metal which eliminates the use of dragon's blood. (PR)　　H.V.G.

Pragmatics
That branch of semiotic (or of linguistics) which specifically concerns the *user* of signs. (C)　　C.C.

Precede
Matter intended to precede a newsstory. It may be a bulletin or merely some pleasant or noteworthy feature of the main story; it may be enclosed in a box or it may be plain type. (P)　　B.C.B.

Predate
(a) An edition, of an evening newspaper, carrying the date line of the following day. (This really should be called

a "post-date," but the term has become established by many years' use.) (b) An edition, of a Sunday paper, going to press before 12 o'clock noon of the Saturday preceding the Sunday the issue is dated. When the word is used in this sense it is usually called a "Sunday predate." Sunday predates are printed from several hours to several days preceding their date in order to reach distant points on or before publication date. Sometimes Sunday predate editions are sold before Sunday. (P)   A.B.C.

Preferred Position
Desirable advertising space in a newspaper or magazine for which the publisher charges a premium rate when the position is specifically ordered. (A)   H.V.G.

Premium
An offer of merchandise, either free or at a reduced price, as an incentive to buy a product. (A)   H.V.G.

Premium
Anything, except periodicals, offered to the subscriber, either free or at a price, with his own subscription, either direct, through or by agents. (P)   A.B.C.

Prescoring and Postscoring
Recording the sound before or after the picture has been taken. (F)   G.W.

Presentation
An accumulation of facts, figures, and ideas, both graphic and written, usually used in presenting and selling an advertising campaign to a client. (A)   H.V.G.

Press
A machine which holds a printing form, inks and makes an impression on paper. (PR)   H.V.G.

Press Agent
A person hired by an institution, corporation, actor, etc.,

to *contact* the press and secure publicity. He issues *releases.*
(P)   B.C.B.

Press Proofs

Press proofs are not really "proofs" at all in the ordinary sense; they are samples of the printed work taken from the press at the beginning of the run. An editor or advertiser who insists on O.K.-ing press proofs, unless he is in the printing plant to do so, is probably running up a terrific bill. The press and its crew are standing idle while they wait for his authorization to go ahead with the job, and he will be expected to pay for this time, just as if the work were being printed. (PR)   B.B.

Pressbook (kit)

A portfolio which contains mimeographed news releases, pictures, articles, speeches, and background material related to a specific event and which is distributed to the press for its free use. (P)

Preview

Advance showing of a movie before it has been released or the screening of a film prior to a formal screening of some sort. (F)   G.W.

Preview-for-Purchase

A film sent free of charge to be viewed before making a purchase decision. (F)   G.W.

Primary Colors

The fundamental colors used for explaining the process of color vision, and for reproduction of colored originals by means of printing. Applied to light or those concerned with light phenomena, the true primary colors are violet, red and green; but the primary colors of printing inks or those involved in subtractive three-color reproduction are broadly termed yellow, red and blue—green being formed by a mixture of blue and yellow. (PR)   J.S.M.

Principal
An owner, partner or officer of an advertising agency or other business organization. (A)   H.V.G.

Print
A photographic image from a negative (or positive) made on paper, metal or other opaque supports; the line or half-tone image on metal intended for relief etching. (PR)
J.S.M.

Printer
A machine that makes final positives from the negative. (F)   G.W.

Printing Depth
The minimum depression (relief) of an etching necessary to permit clean impressions. (PR)   J.S.M.

Printing Frame
The heavy glass-covered frame in which images are locked in contact with sensitized surfaces for exposure to light. (PR)   J.S.M.

Printing-In
Combination printing of two or more negatives on a single positive; especially the "printing-in" of some detail from one negative on the background from another negative. (F)   A.S.

Printing Lamp
The arc lamp or other high-powered illuminant furnishing the source of light when photoprinting line and half-tone negatives on sensitized metal or other surfaces. (PR)
J.S.M.

Printon
A multilayer material (Ansco) intended for making inexpensive full-color prints direct from colorfilm transpar-

encies by a reversal procedure which permits processing of the pictures by the photographer himself. (F)   J.S.M.

Prism
An optical instrument in the form of a triangular piece of glass, silvered on one side, and attached to the lens of a process camera for lateral inversion of the image projected by the lens. (F)   J.S.M.

Prismatic Eye
A device which may be attached to some view-finders permitting the scene to be viewed and filmed while the operator is facing 90° away from it. (F)   A.S.

Privacy Rights
Closely related to libel protection. Protects an individual against exposure of his person or affairs who has no importance or interest to the general public. Prevents the use of pictures or names in advertising without consent. The right does not apply to candidates for public office, public officials, actors, or criminals since by their actions they have invited public interest. (P)

Private Brand
A product labeled and sold under the wholesaler's or retailer's own trademark as opposed to nationally advertised brands sold by them. (A)   H.V.G.

Process Camera
A heavy type of copying camera specially designed for the particular requirements of line and halftone photography. (PR)   J.S.M.

Process Coated
A classification of printing papers which includes enamels of various grades, and which are suitable for printing fine-line halftones. In their manufacture clay, casein, or other filling and hardening components are worked into them, and they are ironed out by heated, highly polished metal cylinders

to achieve a more or less impervious surface glaze. (PR)
B.B.

Process Developer
A developer promoting high contrast and intended for line and halftone negatives on dryplates and films. (PR)
J.S.M.

Process Engraving
Common term for photoengraving. (PR)   J.S.M.

Process Film, Plate
Photographic surfaces sensitized with very contrasty emulsions to promote sharp line and dot formations. (PR)   J.S.M.

Process Film
A slow film of steep gradation, useful in making photographs of line drawings, type matter, etc., in which there are no middle tones. It may also be used in copying monochrome originals when it is desirable to increase the contrast. (F) A.S.

Process Glue
Clarified fish glue for photoengraving purposes. (PR)
J.S.M.

Processing
Developing and printing the film in the laboratory. (F)
G.W.

Process Lens
A special type of photographic lens giving sharp definition and adapted for line, halftone and color photography. (PR)
J.S.M.

Process Plates
Color plates, two or more, used in combination with each other to produce other colors and shades. Usually involves the use of the four colors: yellow, red, blue and black. (PR)   R.A.F.

Process Printing
Printing from four sets of color plates to achieve a full range of color. Colors of ink used are yellow, red, blue and black. (PR)   H.V.G.

Process Shot
Photographs of actual scenes combined with projected backgrounds or model sets or drawings. (F)   G.W.

Processwork
The operation and finished product of photoengraving. (PR)   J.S.M.

Producer
A company that makes films or the executive in charge of all the business and administrative aspects of the film-making. (F)   G.W.

Production
The process of rehearsal and broadcast of a radio or TV program. (B)   H.V.G.

Profile
Biographical sketch. (P)   B.C.B.

Program Opposite
A competing program broadcast over another station at the same time and in the same area. (A)   H.V.G.

Progressive Proofs
Proofs of color plates showing each color separately then in combination with one another. Used as a guide to the pressman. (PR)   H.V.G.

Progs
Short for Progressive Proofs. In making three or four color process engravings, the engraver furnishes to the printer proofs of the colors as each is added. The term applies only to process printing. (PR)   B.B.

Projectall

A machine used in television to project opaque slides through the system. (B)   H.V.G.

Projection

The act of projecting a photographic image onto a sensitized surface or viewing screen; the manner in which enlargements are produced. (F)   J.S.M.

Promotion

Efforts other than space and broadcast advertising further to promote sales of the advertiser's product or service, e.g. direct mail promotion, point-of-sale promotion, etc. (A)
H.V.G.

Proof

A sheet of paper imprinted from type or plates for correction, approval or for use in reproducing the type. (PR)
H.V.G.

Proof Press

A machine used to make proofs of type matter and plates. (PR)   R.R.K.

Proofreader

One who corrects mistakes in typesetting by reading proofs and sending them back to the printer for revision. (PR)   B.C.B.

Proofreader's Marks

Signs used by proofreaders to denote errors and corrections to be made. (PR)   H.V.G.

Proofreading

All proofs should be read carefully, of course, because an editor's "O.K." absolves the printer—legally, at least—from responsibility for serious or minor errors. Galley proofs require close comparison with the copy submitted. It's a good idea to carefully check anything that the printer's proofreader has marked with an interrogation, because these experts have developed a sixth sense for grammatical construction and spelling, and while a typesetter may "follow the copy out of the window" as they say, most professional proofreaders will question anything that seems to violate good usage. Frequently, too, they will catch proper names that may have been spelled differently in different parts of the copy. There are plenty of charts of proofreaders' marks available; it pays to familiarize oneself with them and to use them correctly.

Use a soft pencil (or a ball-point pen) in correcting proofs, and try to use the Golden Rule in marking them: make your notes as legible to the typesetter as you would like to have them come to you.

In checking page proofs it is often a temptation to skim through fast, on the grounds the proofs have already been read in galley form. True enough, except for the fact that if corrections have been made in the galleys, any number of lines following the correction may have been re-set and are subject to error.

Always mark correction on *all* copies of each proof— and mark "Printer's Error—See Copy" when it applies. (PR)

B.B.

Propaganda

Broadly speaking, propaganda is a symbolic activity designed to advance a cause through enlightenment, persuasion, or a dedicated sense of mission. Propaganda is not to be confused with publicity, advertising or promotion, although it is sometimes a valuable adjunct to these special public pleadings.

Propaganda rests upon the clarification of objectives in terms which dramatize and categorize the issue—without regard to its truth or accuracy. It is characterized less by sober facts than by images or impressions which are derived by association, in suggestion rather than in detail. Propaganda has appealed not so much to what people think about themselves, but what they would like to think about themselves. The propaganda activity is a function of the free society as often as that of the authoritarian state. (C)

Proportional Rule, Scale
A rule, instrument or device for determining the exact proportions or dimensions of an original at any given scale (size) of enlargement or reduction. (PR)   J.S.M.

Props
The physical properties needed for a television production, such as room furnishings, paintings or other objects required by the script. (B)   H.V.G.

Proving
Operation of taking trial impressions from printing surfaces and performed on small hand-or power-operated presses. (PR)   J.S.M.

Public Domain
Artistic material that is open to public use because protecting copyrights have expired. (P)   P.W.B.

Public Opinion
The expression of all those members of a group who are giving attention in any way to a given issue. The process starts with more than individual opinions. There has been an interaction of attitudes, mind-sets, beliefs, and other subjective states on an issue.

The personification of "public opinion" or "publics" is a common practice. It is essentially the product of a collective mental life, which in a democracy includes the expression of the majority (if there be a majority) and the minority or all minorities at any given time. In a totalitarian state, tolerance of minority views is forbidden. The masses

in such a society are conditioned to uniform expression.
(C)   W.A.

Public Record
The term record is ordinarily applied to public records only. The right of inspection, in the absence of specific statute of broader effect, is limited to public records. The mere fact that a document, writing, paper, or memorandum made by a public officer is deposited or on file in a public office or is with, or in the custody of, a public officer does not make it a public record. There commonly are many papers or documents, etc., in public offices made by public officers in connection with public business which are not public records.

Generally there is no single test which may be applied to determine what are not public records.

The primary source of determination is definition. In some states the primary source of definition is statutes; in most states the primary source is court decisions on common law; in all states the courts are the final source. As elsewhere, court decisions are of two kinds: those which declare common law, and those which interpret statutes. (P)   H.L.C.

Publication
Any piece of printed matter of regular periodic issue.
(P)   A.B.C.

Publicity
Information of public interest released as a "news release" for editorial (unpaid) publication. (A)   H.V.G.

Public Relations
The management, government or organization function which attempts to maintain favorable public attitudes, to foster greater public understanding and acceptance of procedures and policies, and to identify such institutions with the public interest through a sustained program of planned personal and mass communication. (C)

Public Service Posters

24-sheet posters supporting such organizations as Red Cross, religious groups, American Cancer Society, National Safety Council, etc., and for which advertising space is donated by the standardized outdoor advertising industry on a national basis. However, local operators also prepare and display such posters on a strictly local basis. (A)   R.D.L.

Publisher's Interim Statement

Certified statement of publisher, made to the Audit Bureau of Circulations at the publisher's option and issued unaudited (but subject to audit) by the Bureau. (P) A.B.C.

Publisher's Statement

Certified statement of circulation data made to the A.B.C. by a publisher member of the Audit Bureau of Circulations and issued unaudited (but subject to audit) to members of the Bureau. (P)   A.B.C.

Puff

A personal publicity story. (P)   B.C.B.

Pull a Proof

To make a print for reading proof. (PR)   R.R.K.

Pull In

To publish matter without waiting for the proofroom's typographical corrections is to *pull* in the type. This is rarely done except in emergency cases where the story is important, press time is near and there is need for great haste. Such type is also said to be *railroaded*. (PR)   B.C.B.

Pulp

The mass of material used to make paper. (PR) R.R.K.

Pulse

A rating service similar to Trendex, measuring TV viewing by personal interview and recall methods. (A)

Punch

Stories and headlines with punch are those with vigor, strength, snap, instantaneous appeal. Punch words are short and full of action—nab, trap, plot, etc. (P)   B.C.B.

Put to Bed

A paper has been put to bed when plates or type have been *locked up* and the press is *ready to roll*. (P)   B.C.B.

Q

Q-A
Question and answer material. This kind of material is used in stories telling of extensive questioning. Examples are court proceedings, congressional investigation hearings, and lengthy interviews. (P)   T.E.B.

Quad
Blank type used to space out at the ends of lines in type composition, and to indent paragraphs. (PR)   R.R.K.

Quadder
Short name used to denote special linecasting machine equipment which centers, sets flush left or flush right automatically, without keyboarding. (PR)   R.R.K.

Quadrichromatic, Quadricolor
Consisting of four colors. (PR)   J.S.M.

Quartertone
A highlight halftone of the blowup variety. (PR)   J.S.M.

Quarto Size
An old-time bookbinders' term, not now in ordinary

usage. It means literally, an eight-page (four sheet) form, size 9½" x 12". (PR)   B.B.

Query

A brief mail or telegraphic synopsis of a story sent to a newspaper by a correspondent, who also states the number of words available, as: "Seven killed, ten hurt in powder mill explosion here—1,000." The news executive then orders the quantity desired and the correspondent is paid on this basis. (P)   B.C.B.

Quoin

A small wedge or expanding device used for locking type forms in chases in letterpress. (PR)   R.R.K.

Quotation Furniture

Small sizes of metal furniture used by compositors. (PR)   R.R.K.

Quotes

Quotation marks; a part of a story quoted. (P) B.C.B.

R

R.A.B.

Radio Advertising Bureau. An offshoot of N.A.B. Organized to promote radio broadcasting to the advertiser.

R.D.G.

Radio Directors Guild.

R.E.C.

Radio Executives Club.

R.P.S. Royal Photographic Society

Founded in England in 1853, it was the first photographic society. (F)   A.S.

Rack

(1) A metal strip with cogs on the upper surface. These cogs engage the cogs on a pinion, permitting the two to be moved relative to each other. Many camera and enlarger adjustments, such as focusing, are made by means of a rack and pinion. (2) Wood or metal frame upon which film is wound during processing. (3) Term applied to the movement of the camera lens toward or away from the film plane as the focusing ring is turned. The lens is said to be "racked" in or out. (F)   A.S.

Rack

Cabinet in which galleys of type are kept. (PR)   B.C.B.

Rack Folder
A folder designed to fit into a rack displaying numerous folders. (A)   H.V.G.

Rack Sales
Sales of papers from racks or boxes, placed on street corners, in street cars or at other convenient points, and unattended by salesmen, the customer depositing coin in payment in a box provided for the purpose. Same as box sales. Sometimes spoken of as "the honor system." (P) A.B.C.

Railroad
To rush copy to the composing room without reading it carefully; the copyeditor pauses only to see that it contains no dangerous or inaccurate statements and to write subheads and a headline. See *Pull in.* (P)   B.C.B.

Railroad Showing
An outdoor bulletin or station poster conspicuously located to attract attention of train passengers. (A) H.V.G.

Rapid Fixer
A fixing bath which dissolves the undeveloped silver halides in prints and films in minimum time. Such a fixer is useful in hot weather when the tendency of gelatin to soften is increased by long soaking. (F)   A.S.

Rate Book
Space rates and other data on advertising in various media, compiled in book form. Standard Rate & Data Service is one of the principal organizations publishing this information. (A)   H.V.G.

Rate Card
A card issued by a publication giving the space rates, mechanical requirements, closing dates, etc. (A)   H.V.G.

Rate Class
The time charge in effect at a specified hour. The Class

A rate is highest, and usually covers the period from 6 p.m. to 10 p.m., when the listening audience is greatest. (A)

H.V.G.

Rate-Holder
A minimum-sized advertisement placed in a publication during a contract period to hold a time or quantity discount rate. (A)   H.V.G.

Rates
The charges established by a station for the sale of various segments of time on the air. (A)   H.V.G.

Rating
The popularity test for a specific show; a percentage of viewers or listeners obtained by telephone check, personal interview or through diaries kept by individual viewers or listeners. (A)   H.V.G.

Ratiometer
An instrument for determining the correct factors of tricolor filters under given conditions of work. Filter ratio scale. (PR)   J.S.M.

Raw Film (or Stock)
Unexposed and underdeveloped film. (F)   G.W.

Readability
A test of those factors of writing style that can be measured to check the complexity of writing and increase the probability of comprehension for specific audiences, e.g., sentence length, long words, familiar words, abstract words, personal references, strong verb forms, simple sentences, etc. Readability research into these factors has produced practical suggestions for clear and readable writing. (C)

Reader Confidence
The allegiance and support of a group of regular readers to a particular publication. (A)   H.V.G.

Readership

The actual number of people who read a publication as distinguished from the circulation or number of copies distributed. (A) H.V.G.

Read-In

Printed material, two or more columns wide, that reads into one column to the right. (P) T.E.B.

Reading Notice

Brief all-type newspaper advertisement set up in editorial style to simulate news matter. Must contain abbreviation "Adv." at end of text. Charged at higher rate than regular advertising. (A) H.V.G.

Read-Out

Printed material, two or more columns wide, that reads into one column to the left. (P) T.E.B.

Ready Print

Inside sections of newspapers bought already printed with feature articles, advertisements, etc. (P) R.R.K.

Ream

Five hundred sheets of paper.

Rebiting

Reetching. (PR) J.S.M.

Rebroadcast

A separate radio broadcast timed to reach a different audience or a different time zone at a favorable hour. These are often transcribed. (B) H.V.G.

Reciprocity Failure

At low levels of lighting, the reciprocity law (illumination decreases can be compensated for by proportionate increases in exposure time) fails to work. This failure has to be corrected by much greater increases of exposure at low light levels than would be expected on the basis of the reciprocity law. (F)   A.S.

Recognized Agency

An advertising agency which meets certain standards and qualifications and therefore is allowed agency commission by media on the space or time the agency purchases for its clients. (A)   H.V.G.

Recommended Agency

An advertising agency which has been investigated by a media association and is favorably reported to the association's members. (A)   H.V.G.

Recording

The process of putting sound on film. (F)   G.W.

Recording Channel

All sound equipment, from mike to film track. (F) G.W.

Red Fog

Same as dichroic fog. (F)   A.S.

Reducer Cutting

An oxidizing agent which removes equal amounts of silver from all parts of the negative, therefore removing a larger proportion of the silver image from the shadows than from the highlights. Such a reducer will increase contrast, and is suitable for negatives which have been overexposed. Also called subtractive reducer. (F)   A.S.

Reducer, Flattening

A reducer which reduces highlights without affecting the detail in the shadow; ammonium persulfate is most commonly used for this purpose. (F)   A.S.

Reducer, Proportional

A reducer which acts on each portion of the negative in proportion to the amount of silver deposited. Since this is exactly the reverse of the developing process, a negative which ts correctly exposed but overdeveloped should be treated with a proportional reducer. (F)   A.S.

Reducer, Superproportional
A reducer which removes a greater amount of silver from the denser portions of a negative than from the lighter portions. Used to reduce contrast. (F)   A.S.

Reducing Glass
A double concave lens for viewing originals in reduced sizes. (PR)   J.S.M.

Reduction of Density
Act of lessening the opacity of a photographic negative by chemical removal of some of the developed silver forming the image; cutting a wet collodion negative. (PR)   J.S.M.

Redundancy
The part of a message which by virtue of an excess of syntax makes it increasingly unlikely that mistakes in reception will occur. Repetition in the message increases the probability that the communication will be understood. (C)

Reel
The spool on which film is wound; also, a unit of film length—1,000 feet for thirty-five millimeter and 400 feet for sixteen millimeter film. (F)   G.W.

Reengraving
Embellishing an etched halftone plate by cutting decorative lines or patterns into the relief dot formation. (PR)   J.S.M.

Reetching
Supplementary or local etching of halftone plates to satisfactorily render the detail, tones and color values of the original in the printed reproduction. Lightening a tone or local area by additional etching. (PR)   J.S.M.

Reference Media

Books or publications of periodic issue giving statistical data designed to be kept for reference. (A)   H.V.G.

Referent

That which a sign "refers to," or "stands for," or denotes, more especially when this is a physical or imagined thing, event, quality, et cetera. The term designatum is used more generally. (C)   C.C.

Reflection

The change of direction experienced by a ray of light when it falls upon a surface and is thrown back into the medium from which it approached. (F)   J.S.M.

Reflector Buttons

An element (reflecting glass) used to form letters and designs in outdoor advertising for night-time visibility. (PR)   H.V.G.

Refraction

The deviation of a light ray from a straight path when passing obliquely from one medium into another of different density, or in traversing a medium whose density is not uniform. (F)   J.S.M.

Register

The alignment of successive plates in printing more than one color. (PR)   H.V.G.

Register Marks

Guides in the form of small crosses or marks placed or drawn on an original before photography to facilitate registration in platemaking and proving. (PR)   J.S.M.

Relative Aperture

The ratio between the effective aperture of a lens and its focal length. This ratio is usually given in numbers, not fractions. For example, a lens with a relative aperture of $\frac{1}{2}$ is known as an $f2$ lens. (F) A.S.

Relay Stations
A group of pick-up and re-broadcast relay stations, approximately 30 miles apart, used in lieu of a coaxial cable to pass along a television program to stations on a network. (B) H.V.G.

Release
A completed film made available for distribution. (F) G.W.

Release
A statement signed by a person authorizing the advertiser and agency to publish his photograph or testimonial statement for commercial purposes. (A) H.V.G.

Release Copy
Copy received by the newspaper to be held until a specified date. Examples of release copy are speeches of well-known people, wire service feature stories, and important statements. The purpose of release copy is to enable the newspaper to have the material in type at the time of release. (P) T.E.B.

Relief Effect
Dry effect in collodion negatives. (PR) J.S.M.

Relief Plate
A printing plate in which the non-printing areas have been etched or cut below the surface of the material, leaving the relief presentation of the design in positive form. (PR) J.S.M.

Relief Printing
Letterpress printing from type, electrotypes, stereotypes, and photoengravings. (PR) P.W.B.

282

Rembrandt Lighting

Portrait lighting, three-quarter view, in which the shadow side faces the camera, named after the painter who used this kind of lighting for many of his portraits. (F)　　A.S.

Remote

A program originating away from the studio. (B) N.A.B.

Remote Pickups

Events broadcast away from the studio by a mobile unit or by permanently installed equipment at the remote location. Also called "Nemo" broadcasts. (B)　　H.V.G.

Renewal

A subscription which has been renewed prior to or at expiration or within six months thereafter. (P)　　A.B.C.

Renewals

Extra outdoor posters usually sent to plant operators; these are sometimes needed to replace any posters that may become damaged. (A)　　R.D.L.

Repaints

The repainting of copy of outdoor painted displays, usually every 3 months; the same copy or new copy may be used. (A)　　R.D.L.

Replate

To recast a page of type to insert an important but late story. (P)　　B.C.B.

Reproduction

The process of duplicating an original by photographic or photomechanical means; the copy of final impression obtained from the original by photoengraving procedure. (PR)　　J.S.M.

Repro Proofs

Carefully-made type proofs that are photographed for re-

production in engraving, gravure printing, or offset. (PR)
P.W.B.

Rescale
To redesign and proportion an advertisement to fit a larger or smaller space. (PR) H.V.G.

Research
Market studies, consumer tests, program or media tests in behalf of the client as an aid in directing advertising and business promotion. (A) H.V.G.

Research Director
Head of the research department. (A) H.V.G.

Residual Reclamation
Recovery of hypo, silver salts and other materials from exhausted fixing baths, photographic solutions and wastes by chemical or electrical treatment of the residue-containing substances. (F) J.S.M.

Resist
Acid resists used in photoengraving. (PR) J.S.M.

Resolving Power
The ability of a lens and the sensitized surface of a photographic material to sharply transmit and record very fine detail or lines. (PR) J.S.M.

Restrainer
Any of various chemical substances used in photographic developers to retard too energetic action of the solution on the exposed image. (F) J.S.M.

Retail Trading Zone
Retail trading zone is the area beyond the city zone whose residents regularly trade to an important degree with retail merchants in the city zone, in sufficient volume to justify advertising expenditures by the merchants in maintaining this trade (A) H.V.G.

Reticulation
A network of minute depressions or corrugations in a negative, produced—either accidentally or intentionally—by any treatment resulting in rapid expansion and shrinkage of the swollen gelatin. Reticulation may be produced by solutions which are too warm or too alkaline, or by forced drying in an air current which is too hot. When a reticulated negative is printed, the corrugations show up as a network of fine lines due to the scattering of light by the uneven gelatin surface. See frilling. (F)   A.S.

Retopping
Act of replacing faulty acid or photoresists on partially etched relief plates by application of glue enamel or by rolling up the plate with etching ink, thereby permitting etching to be completed without damaging the plate. (PR)   J.S.M.

Retouching
Corrective treatment performed on photographic negatives and prints with pencils, crayons, airbrush and dyes for elimination of flaws and imperfections, and for general improvement of the final result before plating. (PR)   J.S.M.

Retouching Dye
Special black or red dyes used for retouching and spotting of negatives and prints. (PR)   J.S.M.

Returnable
Copies of publications sold to distributors under agreement to take back those unsold. *Fully returnable* means that all copies sold to any and all distributors may be returned if unsold. *Limited returnable* is used in two senses. First, when a part of the distribution is sold on a returnable basis and part on a nonreturnable basis; second, when distributors are allowed the return privilege but only of a certain percentage of the quantity purchased. (P)   A.B.C.

Returns

Copies returned to publisher by dealer or other distributor for credit. Frequently, to save transportation charges, complete copies are not returned but only paper headings or covers. (P)   A.B.C.

Reuters

The British news agency which offers world news coverage and news distribution at home, in the British provinces, the commonwealth group, and abroad through news exchange agreements. It is an internationally owned trust. (P) (B)

Reversal

Film that can be made directly into positives without the use of a negative; used largely in sixteen-millimeter production. (F)   G.W.

Reverse Plate

As most ordinary printing consists of black type on a white background, reverse means that the type matter will be in white on a black background. To secure this effect it is necessary to have the type set in the ordinary way and a reproduction proof pulled. This is turned over to the engraver, who makes a line engraving of the solid color background, in which the letters are etched out, so that in printing the background area is covered by ink, the white paper showing through for the type matter. Reverse zincs are twice the price of straight zincs. (PR)   B.B.

Reverse Print

An image on a metal plate which has been chemically reversed from its original character or manner of tone representation. (PR)   J.S.M.

Revised Proofs

Corrected proofs of advertisements or printed material to verify changes. Also called "Revise." (PR)   H.V.G.

Rewind

A device for transferring film from one reel to another; also, to wind the film onto the original reel after screening it. (F)   G.W.

Rewrite

Each large newspaper has a battery of rewrite men, picked for their ability as writers, who receive information over the telephone and write it up, rewrite poorly written stories of all kinds and boil down the matter received from news agencies. (P)   B-C-B

Ribbon Mike

Microphone of high velocity. (B)   H.V.G.

Riding the Showing

Checking the space position, locations, time of posting, and the condition of outdoor billboards. (A)   R.D.L.

Right of Privilege (Shield Laws)

A legal right of privilege which places conversations between a reporter and a news source in the same privileged class as conversations between doctor and patient, lawyer and client. The so-called "shield laws," although adopted by some states, have been opposed by many newspaper publishers on grounds that no good reporter would write a story based on a confidential source without checking facts with other sources. (P)

Right to Know Laws

Legislation enacted primarily at the state level to clarify the multiple interpretations, both permissive and restrictive, centering around the supposed constitutional right to investigate and report governmental affairs and the right of access to public meetings and public records. (P)

Rim

The outer edge of the copydesk *horseshoe,* where copyeditors sit, as opposed to the slot, or inside where the executive or *sit-in man* has his post. (P) B-C-B

Ring
To draw a ring around some word or symbol in news manuscript; a ring around an abbreviation indicates to the printer that it should be spelled out; in other cases it means the word should be abbreviated; some copyeditors "ring" each period. (P) B-C-B

Ring Bank
The composing room stands at which corrections are made in type. (P) B-C-B

Ring Machine
Linotype machine used for making corrections. (P)
T.E.B.

Ring Man
Linotype operator who makes corrections. (P) T.E.B.

Ripple Finish
A paper finish similar to ripples on water. (PR) R.A.F.

Rising and Falling Front
An adjustment provided on some cameras which makes it possible to raise or lower the lens in relation to the film, in order to increase or decrease the amount of foreground included. This adjustment is very useful in photographing tall buildings. It is essential that the principal plane of the lens and the focal plane be kept strictly parallel in order to avoid distortion. (F) A.S.

Roll Holder, Roll-Film Adapter
An accessory permitting the use of roll film in cameras designed for plates or cut film. (F) A.S.

Rolling Up
Applying ink to metal plates with a roller, either for the purpose of creating an acid resist, or for depositing ink on

the surface of a printing plate to take an impression therefrom. (PR) J.S.M.

Roll-Leaf Stamping
A process of stamping gold, silver, or other colors on covers of books, stationery, and like work. (PR) R.R.K.

Rollup Process
A special method of etching halftone plates, involving rolling up the heated plate after the flat etch with a roller charged with etching ink, the heat of the plate causing the applied ink to melt and run down the sides of the dots. (PR) J.S.M.

Roman Type
The regular style of type used in book and newspaper composition as distinguished from *italic*. (PR) H.V.G.

Roof Panel
Refers to location of poster panel or bulletin. (A) R.D.L.

R.O.P.
"Run-of-paper." Position of advertisement to be determined by the publisher, usually in the general news section. (A) H.V.G.

Rotary Bulletin
An outdoor painted bulletin of special construction permitting rapid removal and assembly of the panel segments at new location. A bulletin to be shown in several locations in a showing. (A) R.D.L.

Rotary Press
A press in which the printing surfaces are curved into cylindrical shape; this cylinder revolves in making the impression on the paper. Used only for high-speed, long run printing. (PR) B.B.

Rotation

The process of continuing a series of advertisements over and over again in a regular order. (A)   H.V.G.

Roto

Abbreviation for rotogravure.

Rotogravure

Gravure printing on a web-fed press. (PR)   H.V.G.

Rough

As used by commercial artists, a rough is a preliminary sketch intended only to visualize a finished layout or drawing. Roughs are rarely drawn to a careful scale, and should not be used to measure engraving sizes or type measures. (PR)   B.B.

Rough Cut

An assembly of scenes that have not gone through the final cutting process. (F)   G.W.

Rough Proof

A quickly made impression on poor grade paper without recourse to makeready or special care in proving. (PR)

     J.S.M.

Roulette

A finisher's tool comprising a handle bearing on one end a rotating wheel or knurl, this possessing a serrated cutting pattern corresponding to the ruling of halftone screens. (PR)

     J.S.M.

Rouletting

Operation of indenting the surface of a printing plate with a roulette to lighten or modify tone values. (PR)   J.S.M.

Round Robin

A network of stations forming an "electrical loop" and permitting switching between points of program origination. (B)   H.V.G.

Roundup

Comprehensive story from several sources. (P) B-C-B

Router

Device used to cut away surplus metal from printing plates. (PR) H.V.G.

Routing

Removing non-essential metal from non-printing parts of a plate. (PR) B-C-B

R.P.M.

Revolutions per minute. A phonograph record revolves at 78, 45 or 33⅓ r.p.m., a transcription usually at 33⅓ r.p.m. (B) H.V.G.

Rubber Cement

An adhesive made with a rubber base, used widely in the graphic arts, which does not wrinkle or stain paper and is removable. (A) H.V.G.

Rubber Plates

Printing plates consisting of an engraved or molded surface of rubber, made either by manual engraving or by molding from relief etchings. (PR) J.S.M.

Rule

A line, commonly used as a border to separate elements. Thickness may be hairline or in various point sizes. (PR)
  H.V.G.

Rule for Insert

A direction to the printer, meaning that he shall turn a rule as a sign that type already set shall be picked up and incorporated with the story. (P) B-C-B

Run

A story already printed has been run; a reporter's run is his *beat* or the route he takes on his regular coverage. (P)
  B-C-B

Run-Around

Body of type to be set around odd-measure cut, as in fiction or feature magazines. (P) B-C-B

Run Flat

To set the manuscript in type as it stands, without revision. When this direction is given to a copyeditor, it means that he shall leave the story unchanged. (P) B-C-B

Run In

To the typesetter, run in means to set copy in continuous lines, from margin to margin, regardless of natural breaks in meaning. For instance, a column of names might be set one to a line, but if the copy were marked "run in" they would appear one right after the other, clear across the column. Such an arrangement would, of course, save space, but at the sacrifice of readability and appearance. (PR) B.B.

Running Head

The title of a book printed at the head of each page.

Running Stories

These are stories sent to the composing room in short sections, each of which ends with the end of a sentence or paragraph and is marked "more," to signify that additional copy is to be sent along. (P) B-C-B

Running Through

Cutting through connected dot formations in etched halftones with a graver to lighten tone values or to bring the dots to proper size, also to introduce dots in solid spots or blemishes in the etching. (PR) J.S.M.

Run Out

Proofreader's mark indicating that the printer make a hanging indention. (PR) H.V.G.

Run Through

In TV the first rehearsal of the cast on camera with sound,

292

music, etc. In radio a complete reading of the script. (B)
H.V.G.

Rush
Copy to be handled quickly is so marked. (P) B-C-B

Rushes
Scenes just shot; same as dailies. (F) G.W.

Rush Job
The following definition has appeared in print shops and editorial offices for years:

"I AM A RUSH JOB. . . . I belong to no age, for men have always hurried . . . I prod all human endeavor . . . Men believe me necessary—but falsely. I rush today because I was not planned yesterday. I demand excessive energy and concentration . . . I override obstacles, but at great expense . . . I illustrate the old saying, 'Haste Makes Waste.' My path is strewn with the evils of overtime, mistakes and disappointments . . . Accuracy and quality give way to speed. Ruthlessly I rush on—I am a RUSH JOB." (PR) B.B.

S

S.A.G.
Screen Actors Guild, a union of performers important to the television and motion picture industries. (B)   P.W.B.

S.E.S.A.C.
Society of European Stage Authors and Composers.

S.N.P.A.
Southern Newspaper Publishers Association.

S.S.
Same size. Marked on copy to be photographed with no reduction or enlargement. (PR)   H.V.G.

Sacred Cows
Personalities or institutions given special newspaper favor. (P)   B-C-B

Saddle Wire Stitch
Bindery term for the setting of wire stitches exactly in the fold of a publication's pages. Used in practically every case where the number of pages is not too large to permit penetration. The alternative type of wire stitching is called side-wire; this calls for an entirely different arrangement of the pages in printing. (PR)   B.B.

Safelight

A darkroom light that does not affect sensitive photographic materials. (F)   A.S.

Safety Shell

The copper facing of an electro which is made and held in reserve in case of loss of or damage to an original engraving. (PR)   H.V.G.

Salted Paper

Plain photopaper impregnated with a gelatinous chloride solution, and sensitized by application of a silver nitrate solution. (PR)   J.S.M.

Sample Copies

Copies distributed free to prospective subscribers or prospective advertisers. Copies delivered as part of a contractual arrangement shall not be counted as sample copies. (P)

A.B.C.

Sampling

The distribution of free samples of a product to encourage its use or to introduce it for future sale. (A)   H.V.G.

Sans Serif

A type face which has no fine cross strokes at the top or bottom of the letter. Ex: Futura, Gothic, etc. (PR)   H.V.G.

Satellite Station

Television station which obtains all its live talent programming from a network. It may service a community outside the service area of the master station. (A)   P.W.B.

Sawtooth Edge

A peculiar effect experienced in reproducing lines by means of the halftone screen, also when the edge of the illustration crosses the screen line at such angle as to cause the symmetrical series of dots to break into an appearance similar to the teeth of a saw. (PR)   J.S.M.

Scale
The full range of tones which a photographic paper is capable of reproducing. (F) **A.S.**

Scale Focusing
Bringing an image to correct size on process cameras by use of focusing scales. (PR) **J.S.M.**

Scale Rates
Standard cost rates for photoengraving, electrotyping, composition, etc. (PR) **H.V.G.**

Scaling Copy
Calculating the percentage of enlargement or reduction of artwork; determining proportional width or depth of artwork to needed depth or width. (PR) **R.R.K.**

Scaling Photographs
Practically every photograph used in a publication has to be either reduced or enlarged in reproduction to meet space requirements, and the matter of determining the ratio of width to depth is the job known as scaling. There are a number of ways of doing this, from slide rules to algebraic equations; the simplest and most commonly used method involves a slanting line drawn from corner to corner and measured off. There are several types of computing rules designed for scaling pictures. (PR) **B.B.**

Scan-a-Graver
An automatic engraving machine for photoelectrically producing relief halftone printing plates on sheets of plastic by an electrically actuated and heated stylus, the action of the stylus controlled according to the tone values and gradation of the photographic image or original undergoing reproduction. (PR) **J.S.M.**

Scanning
The electronic process of breaking down the optical TV image into horizontal lines. (B) **H.V.G.**

Scans

Abbreviation for electronically scanned color separations. (PR)

Scenario

A complete written script containing camera action, dialogue, and story development; usually used for theatrical films. (F)   G.W.

Scene

Subdivision of the sequence; one or more shots of the same action, objects, or subjects. (F)   G.W.

Schedule

The list of available stories and pictures compiled each day by the city, telegraph, cable, sports and news editors; the draft of a page, showing each story and picture in the position in which it is to appear; a *dummy* page, with the heads, type and pictures pasted in as they will appear. (P)   B-C-B

Schedule

The chronological listing of various programs and announcements broadcast by a station. (B)   H.V.G.

Schmalz

An overemotional or oversentimental treatment of program material. (B)   J.C.W.

Scoop

A story that is the exclusive property of one newspaper, possession of which means a victory over a competitor; a *beat*. (P)   B-C-B

Scoop

The degree of cut or removal of material effected by a router bit. (PR)   J.S.M.

Score

A mechanical impression made to crease a sheet of paper so that it folds neatly. (PR)   H.V.G.

297

Scratchboard Drawing

A method of rendering a black and white drawing by scratching off parts of the blackened surface of a special chalk-coated stock to allow the white portions of the paper to show through. (A)   H.V.G.

Scratcher

A square steel point used by etchers for scraping away spots and blemishes on metal plates, also such parts of the image as are not desired in the final etching. (PR)   J.S.M.

Screamer

Large, bold headline covering all or nearly all of a page. This term is synonymous with "streamer" and "banner." (P)   T.E.B.

Screen

Plate glass with cross-ruled opaque lines used in cameras to break continuous-tone illustrations and artwork into half-tone screens; refers also to the number of lines to the inch on printed illustrations. Offset screens are generally 120, 133, or 150; letterpress screens run from 50 to 175 generally, depending upon the roughness of the paper stock used; gravure screens are generally 150. (PR)   R.R.K.

Screen Angle

In color reproduction, the particular angle at which the halftone screen (or original) is placed for each of the color-plates of the set, so as to avoid pattern or moiré in the completed impression. (PR)   J.S.M.

Screen Credits

All announcements of who did what on the screen titles which precede or follow the film. (F)   G.W.

Screen Distance

The separation or space between the surface of a halftone screen and that of the plate or film during halftone photography, the specific distance varying with screens of different ruling. (PR)   J.S.M.

Screenholder
In process cameras, the mechanism or carrier for rectangular and circular halftone screens and for adjusting the screen distance. (PR)   J.S.M.

Screen Indicator
A ruled or lined instrument or device for determining the ruling of the screen employed for any halftone reproduction. (PR)   J.S.M.

Screening
Stripping a halftone tint on the transparent portions of another negative. (PR)   J.S.M.

Screen Lineplate
A line etching made from a pen drawing and bearing a screen or tint effect in the lines and solids of the design; a skiagraph. (PR)   J.S.M.

Screen-Plate
A plate for color photography bearing a mosaic or arrangement of grains or lines colored violet, red and green, the tricolor mosaic acting in the capacity of color filters and imparting a full-color effect to the photographic positive made on the material. Screen-plates and films have been largely superseded by colorfilm transparencies as originals for color reproduction. (PR)   J.S.M.

Screen Process
A printing process frequently used where a smaller number of 24-sheet outdoor posters is required. (A)   R.D.L.

Screen Separation
Screen distance. (PR)   J.S.M.

Screen Sweating

Condensation of moisture on halftone screens when using wet collodion plates, the sweating due to difference in temperature between the plate and the surface of the screen. (PR) J.S.M.

Screeny Negative

A halftone image in which the dot formation or screen lines are unusually prominent or too much in evidence. (PR) J.S.M.

Screnline Process

A special procedure of producing outline and shadow effects in line and halftone illustrations by use of extra negatives, stripping, multiple photoprinting and other operations. Exeltype; Shadowgraph. (PR) J.S.M.

Screw Mount

Term applied to lenses or filters which screw into camera and lens, respectively. (F) A.S.

Script

The detailed shot-by-shot and sequence-by-sequence written guide to the making of the film (also, shooting script, final shooting script, and post-production shooting script). Term is used instead of "scenario" for nontheatrical films. (F) G.W.

Script

The written dialogue, music and sound effects from which a program is produced. (B) H.V.G.

Script Girl

A clerk who keeps a detailed written record of all the minutiae of the actual shooting, set, costumes, action, dialogue, and so forth. (F) G.W.

Script Type

Style of type similar to handwriting. (PR) H.V.G.

300

Script Writer

A writer who develops the dramatic, musical and other entertainment portions of a program as opposed to the commercial portions. (B)   H.V.G.

Scum

A superficial form of fog on wet collodion plates, in which the surface or image is covered with a thin removable deposit of reduced silver. A thin film or veil of semi-soluble glue adhering to the bare (unexposed) areas of prints made with glue enamel. (PR)   J.S.M.

Scumming

When the nonprinting parts of an offset-lithographic plate pick up ink or become dirty. (PR)   R.R.K.

Sears Process

An indirect method of highlight halftone photography. (PR)   J.S.M.

Second-Day Story

A follow story based on one that already has appeared. This type of story also carries a second-day head, conveying the hint that it records not a fresh event, but developments. (P)   B-C-B

Second Front Page

The front page of a second section. (P)   B-C-B

Sectional Announcements

Announcements which are appropriate to various regions of the country made simultaneously over certain portions of a national network during the broadcast of a single program. (B)   H.V.G.

Sectional Story

A story sent to the printer *in takes* or one with various angles played up under different headlines. (P)   B-C-B

See Copy

A direction to the proofroom, meaning look up the original manuscript and compare it with proof, which appears to be wrong or to have something omitted. (P)　　　B-C-B

Segment (of Text or Utterance)

Any continuous part of a text or utterance. See quantum. (C)　　　C.C.

Segue

Transition from one musical selection to another without interruption. (Pronounced seg-way) (B)　　　H.V.G.

Selective-Information Content (in Communication Theory)

The least number of binary digits (*yes, no*) required to encode some particular message (or alternatively to specify its selection from an alphabet). See entropy for definition of *average* rates. (C)　　　C.C.

Selective-Information Rate, of a Source (in Communication Theory)

The minimum average number of binary digits required to encode (represent, specify) the source messages—per second, or per sign, as stated. This refers to selective information as opposed to semantic information. (C)　　　C.C.

Selectivity

Capacity of a radio set for receiving signals of a station without interference of other stations on adjacent channels. (A)　　　P.W.B.

Self-Cover

A cover of the same weight paper as the inside text pages. (PR)　　　R.A.F.

Self-Mailer

A folder, booklet or other direct mail piece which provides space for addressing, postage and sealing, and therefore requires no envelope for mailing. (A)   H.V.G.

Semantic Differential

An operational method for indexing connotation and internal judgments that people make to a given stimulus, which may be a word, a phrase, a picture, a name of a person, etc. The standard research instrument uses polar opposites (good-bad, fair-unfair, strong-weak, etc.) placed at each end of a seven-interval rating scale along which people are asked to place a check mark. The scale helps to specify the connotative meaning which an individual has for any stimulus and to isolate statistically significant dimensions of connotation such as evaluation (good-bad), activity (active-passive), and potency (strong-weak). After Charles E. Osgood). (C)

Semantics

There are different *schools of thought*. We refer to (1) the branch of semiotic (sign theory, linguistics) concerned with "meaning" of signs; (2) study of the non-causal, imputed relations (rules) between signs and their designata. We distinguish descriptive semantics (study of semantic features of historical languages) and pure semantics (analysis of semantic rules of freely invented or set-up systems). After Carnap. (C)
                                                                        C.C.

Semiotic

The theory of signs (i.e., of linguistics, logic, mathematics, rhetoric, etc.). Subdivided into syntactics, semantics, pragmatics (after Charles Peirce and Charles Morris). (C)   C.C.

Semi-Spectacular

A painted outdoor bulletin with the addition of special lighting and/or animation. (A)   R.D.L.

Sensitizing

Making a plate sensitive to light. In offset-lithography, coating the plate with bichromated albumin solution; in the

deep-etch lithographic process, coating the plate with bichromated glue or gum. (PR) R.R.K.

Separation

In three-color photography, the separation or division of
the colors of the original into their primary hues (negatives),
each subsequently printed in a color complementary to that
of the color filter used for exposing the particular negative.
The gradations or steps in the tone values of an original or
halftone reproduction. The act of separating or introducing
colors on printing plates by manual means. (PR) J.S.M.

Separation Negative

One of the images of a color set, especially one taken
through a color filter. (PR) J.S.M.

Sequence

A series of scenes that develop one major part of the story
or content. (F) G.W.

Serif

The short cross-line at the ends of the main strokes of
some styles of type faces. (PR) H.V.G.

Service Fee

A retainer sometimes paid to the agency by the advertiser
(see FEE) or an amount paid for particular jobs beyond the
agency's usual service. (A) H.V.G.

Set

Mental expectancy corresponding to preformed hypotheses concerning a future event. (There are different *shades of
opinion.*) (C) C.C.

Set

A studio-constructed scene. (F) G.W.

Set and Hold for Release

A direction to the printer to set matter in type and hold
for orders. (PR) B-C-B

Set Flush

This order means to set without paragraph indent or margin. Lines may be set flush to the left or to the right, but generally it is the former. (PR)　　　　　　　　B-C-B

Sets-in-Use

Homes (usually expressed in percentage) where at least one set is operating at a given time. Reported by research organizations for television and radio advertisers. (A)　P.W.B.

Setting a Stick

Adjusting a composing stick to pica measure or half-pica measure. (PR)　　　　　　　　　　　　R.R.K.

Set-Up

The position of the camera as arranged for shooting. (F)
　　　　　　　　　　　　　　　　　　　　　G.W.

Setup

Term for a flat or arrangement of negatives which have been stripped together in specified position. Applied to double printing, the term indicates separate line and halftone negatives bearing register marks to facilitate photoprinting both images in correct superposed register on the same sheet of sensitized metal. (PR)　　　　　　　　J.S.M.

70-Lb. Paper

Most small publications are printed on 70-lb. or 80-lb. paper, the figures designating the thickness of the sheet, and everyone soon learns to distinguish between them fairly accurately by "feel." What the weights mean, though, is just a little complicated. (For instance 80-lb. book paper is thicker and heavier than 70-lb., but 65-lb. cover paper is thicker than either.)

The types of paper used for publications are almost invariably in the classification known as "book papers." The standard size of book papers, as delivered by the paper house to the printer, is twenty-five inches by thirty-eight inches.

The term "70-lb. paper" means that 500 sheets (one ream), size 25″ x 38″ weigh seventy pounds. (PR)   B.B.

Shading Machine
A benday machine or apparatus for holding and adjusting shading mediums while transferring tints or patterns to various surfaces. (PR)   J.S.M.

Shading Medium
A benday film or one bearing a relief pattern for inking and subsequent transfer of the pattern by pressure. (PR)
                                                                    J.S.M.

Shading Sheets
Any of various photomechanical drawing materials, bearing either a visible or latent (developable) pattern of lines or dots, and used in the preparation of line originals for introduction of tint or tone effects. (PR)   J.S.M.

Shadow
Shade within defined limits. The dark areas of an original, negative or reproduction. (PR)   J.S.M.

Shadowgraph
A process akin to Screnline, in which special effects are obtained in line and halftone illustrations by supplementary photographic and platemaking operations. Exeltype is another method of this type. (PR)   J.S.M.

Shadow Stop
The flash stop in halftone photography, or one used to strengthen or introduce small opaque dots in the shadows of halftone negatives. (PR)   J.S.M.

Shank
The main body or stem of a unit of type. (PR)   B-C-B

Shannon-Weaver Communication Theory
An analysis of the original materials of Claude E. Shannon, mathematician, on the technical problem of transmit-

ting symbols with accuracy, by Warren Weaver, scientist. Weaver suggested applications of Shannon's mathematical theory of communication to the problem of social interaction. To communicate, an encoder must manipulate symbols in a way that maximizes the chances of reception and the decoding process. Communication occurs only when codes of the sender and receiver of the message are similar.

A prime reason for dissimilarity is the idea of "noise" or, broadly speaking, physical, semantic or psychological disturbances in the communication channel. Noise supposedly can be counteracted by repetition, by strengthening the signal (message), by targeting the signal more specifically, and by reinforcing the signal with other symbol processes or structures.

This idea suggests feedback, which exemplifies a behavior pattern or control action on the part of the sender and receiver of information by which they remain selective toward different conditions of stability or instability created by their interaction (a give-and-take atmosphere). (C)

Share-Of-Audience
The proportion of total radio or TV sets tuned to a particular program on a station. (A)   H.V.G.

Sheet
A single unit in an outdoor poster advertisement. A "24-sheet" is a standard size poster. A "3-sheet" poster is 82" x 41". (A)   H.V.G.

Sheet
Slang for "newspaper." (P)   T.E.B.

Sheetwise
Every page in a publication has, of course, a "front" side and a "reverse" side. If page 3 is the front, page 4 will be the reverse, and so on. When the various pages are assembled in a form for printing, if all the "front" pages are printed from one form on one side of the paper, and it is then turned

over and the "reverse" pages printed from another form back to back with the others, they are called "sheetwise forms." "Work and Turn" is the opposite term to "Sheetwise." (PR)

B.B.

Sheet-Writer

Name applied to a class of subscription salesmen who receive high percentage of subscription price, often 100 per cent, and sometimes a bonus. While subscriptions obtained by a sheet-writer are often fully paid by subscribers the conditions under which he works sometimes result in his accepting less than the subscription price. Frequently he works on a contract which requires him to turn in a certain quota per day, which induces him at times to send in names of persons who have not subscribed. Sometimes also he carries several publications, some of which he throws in free in order to get a subscription for a publication upon which he gets a bonus. (P)

A.B.C.

Shield Laws

See Right of Privilege. (P)

Shoot Board

A metal table fitted with a squaring plane and used for squaring and trimming plates. (PR)

J.S.M.

Shooting

The actual camera work. (F)

G.W.

Short

A brief item; a *filler*. (P)

B-C-B

Short-Factor Developer

A developer in which the image comes up slowly but builds up density rapidly when it does appear. Hydroquinone is an example. (F)

A.S.

Short-Rate

The additional charge incurred when an advertiser contracts to use a certain amount of space within a definite period at a reduced rate, but fails to use enough space to earn the contract discount. (A) H.V.G.

Short Term Subscription
Subscription for less than a year. (P) A.B.C.

Shortstop
Dilute acetic acid solution used as an intermediate bath between development and fixing of photographic negatives and prints. (F) J.S.M.

Shot
The television picture as seen by one camera for a determined length of time. (B)

Shot
The indivisible first unit in the film (shots, scenes, sequences) which consists of a single continuous run of the camera. (F) G.W.

Shoulder
The portion of a piece of type on which the raised image sets. (PR) H.V.G.

Shoulder
In relief etching, the projecting ledge left at the sides of lines and dots after four-way powdering and etching. Excessive shoulder is considered a defect. (PR) J.S.M.

Shouts
Slang for exclamation marks. See *astonisher*. (P) B-C-B

Show Card
A large advertising placard. (PR) R.R.K.

Shutter
A mechanical device that revolves between lens and film. (F) G.W.

Sibilance

Strong "s" sounds on the microphone. (B) N.A.B.

Side Wire Stitch

Used in cases where a publication is too thick, has too many pages, for the more usual saddle wire method. In side wire stitching, the various "signatures" which go to make up the publication are assembled one on top of the other, instead of interleaved, and the wire stitches are driven through from top to bottom, instead of through the fold. (P) B.B.

Sign

A transmission, or construct, by which one organism affects the behavior or state of another, in a communication situation. (C) C.C.

Signal Service Zone

The primary wave area in which an AM station signal is strongest and not subject to bad interference or sudden fading. In TV the zones have been identified as concentric rings: City Grade Service, A Contour, B Contour. (B)

Sign-Event

(See sign-token). (C)

Sign-Token

A physical sign-event; a written, spoken, gestured sign. The physical embodiment of a selected sign-type on some one specific occasion. Also called *sinsign, sign-event.* (C) C.C.

Sign-Type

(A universal; not a physical event.) A sign as it is listed in an alphabet, dictionary, et cetera. Also called *legisign, sign-design.* (C) C.C.

Signal

The physical embodiment of a message (an utterance, a transmission, an exhibition of sign-events). A sign-event or a sequence of sign-events. (C) C.C.

Signature

Magazines or books which contain so many pages that they cannot all be printed on one form are divided into sections for printing and binding. These sections are called signatures. They generally consist of sixteen, thirty-two or sixty-four pages. (PR) B.B.

Signature

The advertiser's name as used on advertising material. (A) H.V.G.

Signature

The musical theme identifying a program. (B) H.V.G.

Significs

Inquiry into questions of meaning, expression, interpretation, and of the influence of language upon thought. (C) C.C.

Silhouette

The outline form of an object. Also used as a verb meaning to block out the background of a photograph. (A) H.V.G.

Silhouette

A halftone from which the screen surrounding any part of the image has been cut or etched away. (PR) R.A.F.

Silk Screen

Process of printing in which colors are printed one at a time through separate silk screens prepared so that ink passes only through that area which is to be printed. It is similar to a stencil technique. Used for the reproduction of show cards, placards, etc. (A) H.V.G.

Silk Surface

A term used to describe the texture of the surface of a photographic paper. This surface has a texture which simulates silk fabric. (F) A.S.

Silver Bath
The acidified silver nitrate solution used for sensitizing plates in wet collodion photography. (P)   J.S.M.

Silver Print
In either photoengraving or lithography the first step is to make negatives on film by photography. Prints made by the silver bromide process from these negatives can be furnished more quickly than proofs of the actual plates. (PR)
B.B.

Simulcast
To broadcast a program simultaneously by both radio and television. (B)   H.V.G.

Single-Line Effect
One-way tint or half-tone illustration showing detail represented by a single series of parallel lines. (PR)   J.S.M.

Sit-In Man
The assistant who substitutes for the city editor or other news executive as head of the copydesk. (P)   B-C-B

Sixteen Gauge
For a variety of reasons it is sometimes impractical to lock up type with engravings in the usual way; for instance, when a layout calls for lines of type to be used as picture captions and slanted at a number of different angles. In such circumstances the type is sent to an electrotype foundry— this requires a "foundry lock-up"—and cast into solid metal of the same thickness of the engravings, which are 16-gauge copper or zinc. These metal plates of the type can then be tacked into position on the blocks on which the engravings are mounted. (PR)   B.B.

Sked
Abbreviation for schedule. (P)   B-C-B

Skeletonize

In copy sent by wire unnecessary words are omitted, hence it is skeletonized. (P)   B-C-B

Skiagraph

Term applied to lineplates in which a screen effect has been introduced by stripping a halftone tint over the line negative before photoprinting and etching. (PR)   J.S.M.

Skyline

Headline across top of page over nameplate. Also called over-title and over-the-roof. (P)   B-C-B

Slander

Base and defamatory spoken words tending to prejudice another in his reputation, business or means of livelihood. "Libel" and "slander" both are methods of defamation, the former being expressed by print, writings, pictures or signs, the latter orally. (B)

Slant

Angle or perspective taken on a story. Also, the practice of preparing magazine articles or other material with the purpose of submitting it to a specific publication. Hence, the material is slanted toward the particular publication. (P)
                                                          T.E.B.

Slapstick

Fast action comedy, employing knockabout humor, chases, and profuse properties and sound effects. (F)

Sleeper Effect

An initial rejection of a communicator's point of view followed, after a period of time, by an acceptance of his position.

Slide

Art work or titles on film mounted for projection. (A)
                                                          H.V.G.

313

Slide
Photographs, films, art work or titles which are projected on a camera tube. (B)   H.V.G.

Slidefilm
Filmstrips which are projected one frame at a time. (F)
G.W.

Slogan
A sentence or phrase which through repeated usage becomes identified with the advertiser's product or service. (A)
H.V.G.

Slopover
Type crowded out of a form. (PR)   B-C-B

Slot
Copydesks generally are built roughly in the form of a horseshoe. The small enclosure is the slot and here the head-of-the-desk holds forth. (P)   B-C-B

Slotman
The head of the copydesk. (P)   B-C-B

Slow Motion
Slow motion: the film is speeded faster than normal through the camera, so that the action appears to be slowed down. (F)   G.W.

Sludge
A muddy or slushy precipitate formed in a photographic solution, generally upon standing or when it has been used too long. (F)   A.S.

Slug
A thick lead, 6 points and upward, used for spacing.
A line cast on a typesetting machine. (PR)   H.V.G.

Slug
Guideline or catchline name by which a story is known. (P)   T.E.B.

Slugline

See *Guideline*. (P)

Slurred

Said of blurred or imperfect impressions because of uneven pressure or movement of the plate or paper during proving or printing. (PR)   J.S.M.

Small Caps

Small capital letters, part of each font, as opposed to full size capitals.

THIS LINE IS IN SMALL CAPS.

THIS LINE IS IN REGULAR CAPS.

(PR)   B-C-B

Snap-On Mount

Method of mounting lens on camera by means of spring clips concealed within the camera housing. (F)   A.S.

Snap, Snappy

The condition of brilliance or representation of a wide range of contrast and middletones in a negative, print or reproduction. (PR)   J.S.M.

Sneak Preview

A film tryout in advance of the public showing to determine audience reaction. (F)

Sniping

Advertising signs of any size or type which are established or erected without consent of the property owners or operators. Such advertising is not approved by the Outdoor Advertising Association of America and is not carried on by members of the association. (A)   R.D.L.

Soap Opera

A term loosely applied to popular daytime serial programs because the early sponsors of these programs were often soap manufacturers. (B)   H.V.G.

Soc
Abbreviation for society, used to designate copy intended for society columns. (P)   B-C-B

Soft
Pertaining to an image showing detail and gradation, but lacking proper contrast. (F)   J.S.M.

Soft Focus
A photographic lens giving soft or diffused images. (F)
J.S.M.

Soft Goods
Manufactured goods, principally textiles. (A)   H.V.G.

Soft-Working
Developers or papers yielding a long tone scale from normal negatives or normal prints from contrasty negatives. (F)   A.S.

Solarization
A reversal of the image in a negative or print caused by great overexposure. Partial solarization is often intentionally obtained in a print for odd or pictorial effect. (F)   A.S.

Solid Matter
Type composition which has had no spacing inserted between lines. (PR)   H.V.G.

Solid Plate
A plate having an even printing surface and bearing no etched or engraved design. Used for printing solid tints or uniform depositions of ink in any color. (PR)   J.S.M.

Solotone
A shading sheet intended for use on monochrome line originals. (PR)   J.S.M.

Sound Effects
Any sound that is neither speech nor music. (B) H.V.G.

316

Sound Man

The engineer in charge of sound effects which are produced either from recordings or with special apparatus. (B) H.V.G.

Sound Track

The edge of the film on which the sound is recorded. (F) G.W.

Soup

The developing mixture. (F) G.W.

Source (of Message-Signals)

That part of a communication channel where messages are assumed to originate (where selective action is exerted upon an ensemble of signs). (C) C.C.

Space

Blank units of type used to space between words; the linotype operator handspaces between the letters of the words when he finds a line too short for the *spacebands* to fill it out. (PR) B.C.B.

Space

The pages or parts of pages in newspapers and magazines where advertisements may be placed. (A) H.V.G.

Space Charge

The charge for space bought in publications, signs, posters, car cards, etc. (A) H.V.G.

Space Discount

Discount allowed by publisher when the advertiser contracts for and uses a certain amount of linage. (A) H.V.G.

Space Position

The space position of an outdoor poster panel is the measure of efficiency with which it dominates the effective traffic circulation to which it is exposed. Its numerical value is established by T.A.B. formula and is expressed in descending values from 10.0 to 0. (A)   R.D.L.

Space Schedule
A schedule sent to the advertiser by his agency, showing the media to be used, the dates on which advertising is to appear, size of advertisements and cost of space. (A) H.V.G.

Special Representative
An individual or organization which represents and sells space and time for media in other cities. (A)   H.V.G.

Special Six-Month Statement
A statement issued by the Audit Bureau of Publications instead of Publisher's Statement. It is based upon data already audited. (P)   A.B.C.

Spectacular
Out of the ordinary form of outdoor display which attracts the eye through its size, illumination or motion. Examples: Display signs in the Times Square area in New York City. (A)   H.V.G.

Speedball
Flat, square or round pointed pens of various sizes used for quick lettering. (A)   H.V.G.

Spherical Aberration
Inability of a photographic lens to convey marginal (not oblique) rays to a point at the same distance as the central rays, a defect manifesting itself by impairment of contrast and definition in the projected image. (PR)   J.S.M.

Spike
To decide not to use a story. This term arises from the fact that usually the story is placed on the editor's spindle file. (P)   T.E.B.

Spill
A colloquial term applied by photographers to the mar-

318

ginal rays from a photographic light. The concentrated light from a spotlight has no "spill"; a floodlight has a great deal of "spill." (F) A.S.

Spiral Binding
A book bound with wires in spiral form inserted through holes punched along the binding side of the book. (PR) R.A.F.

Splice
Cementing two pieces of film together; also, the joint that results. (F) G.W.

Split Focus
Achieved by adjusting television camera between two objects when one is in foreground and other in the background. (B) P.W.B.

Split Page
A second front page. (P) B.C.B.

Split Period Audit
Audit covering a period other than that covered by the regular Publisher's Statement period. (P) A.B.C.

Split Run
Method of testing two different copy appeals by running a keyed version of each in the same publication, same date—each version appearing in one half of the edition. (A) H.V.G.

Split Run Circulation
The insertion of an advertisement in only a part of the total copies of a publication distributed. (P)

Split Screen
A single picture composed of two separate camera images seen side by side. (B)

Spoilage
A certain amount of paper stock is inevitably wasted in any printing job, and in every impression or color involved

in production. If you ever have occasion to estimate the amount of paper to be used in a publication, be sure to include about ten per cent for spoilage—more, if the job is complicated or if it is to be printed in more than two colors. (PR)   B.B.

Sponsor
Advertisers who use TV and/or radio to inform and sell their individual products and services to the public. (A)
H.V.G.

Sponsored Film
A business or industrial film. (F)   G.W.

Sponsored Subscriptions
Subscriptions obtained through cooperation between publisher and an organized local civic or charitable organization, members of schools, churches, fraternal or similar organizations, publisher donating a percentage of the subscription price to the organization involved. (P)   A.B.C.

Spot Announcements
Brief commercial statements usually varying from 30 to 125 words, interspersed within or between programs on the air. (B)   H.V.G.

Spot Drawing
A small illustration used in connection with a block of text. (A)   H.V.G.

Spot News
News obtained firsthand on the spot where it happened, hence fresh and live news. (P)   B.C.B.

Spot Radio
The use of stations in selected markets, without regard to network affiliation. Sometimes called "selective radio." May involve spot announcements or complete programs. (A)   H.V.G.

Spots

Pertaining to those opaque or transparent (black or white) formations of regular or irregular shape and size occurring as blemishes in photographic images. (F)   J.S.M.

Spotting

Removing spots from negatives, photographs and printing plates. (PR)   J.S.M.

Spread

An elaborate pictorial layout; a double spread is one across facing pages; a spread may also be a big story and auxiliary stories. (P)   B.C.B.

Sprockets

The teeth in the camera or projector that hold the film in the holes punched for this purpose. (F)   G.W.

Squared

Halftone plates having four straight edges which can be mechanically cut or beveled in straight lines. (PR) J.S.M.

Squared (Finish) Halftone

A halftone plate presenting an unbroken screen printing surface, and which can be finished in square or rectangular shape with or without a border line. (PR)   J.S.M.

Squib

A short news item; a *filler*. (P)   B.C.B.

Staggered Schedule

Several advertisements scheduled in two or more publications, arranged so that the dates of insertion are alternated or rotated. (A)   H.V.G.

Staging

Application of acid-resisting varnish or staging solution to local areas of line or halftone etchings so as to permit further etching of the untreated surface of the plate; painting out certain areas of etched halftone plates which have

321

arrived at proper tonal value, but with the remainder of the plate requiring additional etching. Crayoning. (PR) J.S.M.

Stain
Local or general discoloration of photographic negatives and prints. The discoloration formed on zinc and copper plates by short immersion in dilute acid or graining baths. Oxidation. (PR) J.S.M.

Stain Print
A line or halftone print on metal which has been subjected to a dilute acid bath just sufficiently long to stain or discolor bare metal areas. After removal of the print proper, the stained image on the metal serves as a guide in bendaying and for painting in or cutting solid tints for colorplates. (PR) J.S.M.

Stamping Die
Deeply etched or engraved relief plates on brass or zinc for stamping bookcovers, brass plates being used when the stamping process requires heat. (PR) J.S.M.

Stand By
Signal from the control room for silence in the studio prior to commencing a rehearsal or broadcast. (B) N.A.B.

Stand By
Television or radio program—but more often the latter —that is available when a program scheduled for a certain time has been cancelled or interrupted for some reason. (B) P.W.B.

Standard Advertising Register
The so-called "Red Book" of advertisers listed by industries. This publisher also issues an agency list as well as other information concerning advertisers and their expenditures. (A) H.V.G.

322

Standard Outdoor Showing

Any one of the recognized numerical outdoor advertising showings:

Fractional—Regarded as the smallest showing available.

Number 100—Sufficient panels to expose the advertised message to all or most of the important traffic arteries in a given market in a 30-day period.

Number 75—Seventy-five per cent of a No. 100 showing.

Number 50—Fifty per cent of a No. 100 showing.

Number 25—Twenty-five per cent of a No. 100 showing.

Number 150—A saturation showing; it approaches maximum intensity.

Number 200 to 400—A "Supersaturation showing."

Neighborhood—Coverage of one or more neighborhood shopping centers. (A)   R.D.L.

Standard Rate and Data Service (S.R.D.S.)

A monthly publication service which provides rates and other media data for newspapers, consumer magazines, business publications, radio, television, weekly newspapers, films for television and transportation advertising. (A)

Standard Type

Type of standard width. See *Condensed type.* (PR) B.C.B.

Standing

Material kept in type because it is used frequently. Boxes are kept standing for such material as baseball statistics; some heads, such as the box head over the columnist's writings, are kept standing because they are used daily; many ads are kept standing because there is frequently little or no change. (P)   T.E.B.

Standing Type

Type which has been set and printed from (or from which electros have been made) is customarily held for a short period in case it should be necessary to reprint from

323

it; then, in the absence of any instructions to the contrary, it is melted down so that the metal can be used again. The printer has no obligation to keep used type "standing" unless he has been instructed to do so. The cooperation of editors is always appreciated when they issue "hold" or "kill" orders promptly regarding the disposition of standing type. (PR)

B.B.

Starch Report
Readership survey relating to selected ads in a given issue of a publication, to establish the number of persons who have noted an advertisement to the extent of recalling having seen it, and the name of the product advertised. (A)

H.V.G.

Start
A newspaper subscription order. (P)   T.C.M.A.

Stat
See "Photostat." (PR)

Static Marks
Dark streaks found on developed negatives, due to static discharge when the film was drawn too quickly from the pack, etc. (F)

A.S.

Station Break
Period between television and radio programs which may contain commercials and a station identification. (B) P.W.B.

Station Identification
The announcement made to identify a radio or television station and its location. (B)

H.V.G.

Station Log
A record of commercials and programs presented on a specific day. (B)

N.A.B.

Station Rep
A sales organization representing individual stations to

national advertisers. Abbreviation of Station Representative.
(B)   H.V.G.

Stationary Source
A source of messages (or signals) the statistical properties
of which are invariant under a shift of the time origin.
(C)   C.C.

Stayflat
Metal or glass plate bearing a tacky or adhesive coating
on which films are squeegeed and held in position during the
camera exposure. (PR)   J.S.M.

Steel Die Engraving
Printing from a steel plate on which the image has been
engraved below the surface; commonly used for engraved
cards, formal announcements, etc. (PR)   H.V.G.

Step and Repeat
The method, in offset platemaking, by which the same
negative can be imposed upon the press plate any desired
number of times, so that the work can be printed as many
"up" as greatest economy dictates. Serves the same purpose,
in many respects, as the use of electrotypes in letterpress
printing. (PR)   B.B.

Step Lines
Same as droplines. (P)   B.C.B.

Stereo
Short for stereotype. The printing plates from which
newspapers or other long press runs are produced. Because
stereotypes are used almost exclusively on rotary presses,
they are generally in the form of one-half a cylinder, but any
printing plate, flat or curved, cast from a paper matrix is
properly called a stereotype. Stereos are made from mats,
mats are made from electros, electros are made from type
and original engravings. These steps are necessary when
larger quantities are to be printed, because engravings wear

325

out after about fifty thousand impressions and type becomes too battered for further use after 75,000 to 100,000 impressions. (PR)

B.B.

Stereotype

See Bromide. (P)

T.E.B.

Stet

From the Latin, meaning "let it stand." Used to indicate that matter marked for correction or omission is to remain as it was originally. (P)

B.C.B.

Stick

The composing stick or type holder used by the printer who sets type by hand. A *stickful* is about two inches of type. When a copyeditor is directed to "trim a stickful" from a story it means that he is to shorten the story by about two inches. The part on linotype machines that holds the type lines is also a stick. (P)

B.C.B.

Sticker

A page that is not to be replated. (P)

B.C.B.

Stick-Up Initial

A large initial letter protruding above the normal type line. (PR)

B.C.B.

Still

An ordinary photograph of a scene from a movie taken during the filming or blown up from a frame from the film itself. (F)

G.W.

Still Etching

Etching of halftone images on copper in a tray without agitation of the ferric chloride solution; face down etching. (PR)

J.S.M.

Stinger

An arbitrary term used to describe short and intense

musical or sound effect punctuation in dramatic programs. (B)   J.C.W.

Stipple
Any arrangement of small and individual dots (or indentations on a plate) sufficiently close together to afford the effect of a tone or tint. (PR)   J.S.M.

Stock
Term applied to paper used in printing. (PR)   P.W.B.

Stock Cuts
Material that may be used by advertiser in his print advertisements. Consists of photographs or printing plates such as prepared-in-advance photographs of farm scenes that may be used by the advertiser of farm implements. (A)   P.W.B.

Stock Shots
Films of people, events, or objects that have been filed for use in motion pictures or television shows. These are filed by subject matter. (B)   P.W.B.

Stone
The imposing stone upon which the printer makes up the page; it may be of either stone or metal. (PR)   B.C.B.

Stop
Order to discontinue a newspaper subscription. (P)   T.C.M.A.

Stop
The opening of the lens diaphragm. (F)   G.W.

Stop Motion
A production technique in TV films similar to animation, but more simplified and generally less expensive (B)   H.V.G.

Stop Motion
Shooting a film by exposing only one frame at a time.
(F)   G.W.

Stopping Down
Reducing the aperture of a lens; using a smaller aperture.
(F)   J.S.M.

Stopping Out
Opaquing or blocking out negatives; staging of etched
plates. (PR)   J.S.M.

Storecasting
Point of purchase broadcasting of music, news and advertising. (B)

Story Board
A series of drawings showing the sequence of a TV film,
announcement or program. One drawing is used for each
change of scene and both pictures and script are included.
(B)   H.V.G.

Straight Line Image Reverser
Optical device attached to process lenses for lateral reversal of negatives without the necessity of turning the
camera at right angles to the original or copyboard. (PR)
                                                                J.S.M.

Straight Matter
Body matter or plain paragraph type composition. (PR)
                                                                R.R.K.

Straight News
A plain recital of news facts with no attempt at featuring
or fancy writing or embellishment of any kind. (P)   B.C.B.

Strathmore
The name of a high quality antique finish paper made
both in cover and book weights by the Strathmore Paper
Company, of Massachusetts. Some people have fallen into

the habit of using "Strathmore" as a generic term in referring to antique cover stock. That's a mistake. (PR)　　　　B.B.

Streamer
Same as "screamer" or "banner." (P)

Streamer Markings
Dark strips in a negative in which the density of some long narrow object in the image is extended to adjacent parts; generally due to lack of agitation. (F)　　　A.S.

Street Sales
Papers sold by individuals on the street as distinguished from those sold by dealers with permanent shops or by a carrier boy with a regular list of customers. (P)　　A.B.C.

Street Vendors
Sellers of newspapers on streets. (P)　　　　A.B.C.

Stress Marks
Marks on prints due to mechanical contact or pressure. (F)　　　　　　　　　　　　　　　　　A.S.

String
Clippings pasted together in a long strip or in a scrapbook. (P)　　　　　　　　　　　　　　B.C.B.

String and Button
An envelope whose flap is secured by a string that wraps around a paper button. (PR)　　　　　H.V.G.

Stringer
Correspondent, usually paid on space basis. (P)　B.C.B.

Strip Show
A radio serial, usually on the air fifteen minutes several times a week at a certain hour. Originated from daily cartoon "strip." (B)　　　　　　　　　　　H.V.G.

Stripfilm, Stripping Film
Gelatin process emulsions for line and halftone photog-

raphy coated on a temporary support, which permits stripping or removal of the negative after fixing and washing of the developed image. Modern substitute for wet collodion plates. (PR)   J.S.M.

Stripfilm Camera
Process camera specially designed for use of stripfilm in roll form, the apparatus accommodating rolls of different width and provided with a shearing device for cutting exposures from the rolls. (PR)   J.S.M.

Stripping
Used in both photoengraving and lithography, the term means the process of combining two or more negatives in the making of a single plate. The "stripper" in an offset plant corresponds somewhat to the lock-up man in letterpress operation. He assembles the component parts of each page into one form for printing; in lithography this precedes the making of press plates. (PR)   B.B.

Stripping Table
A light table; a glass-topped table, with a light source beneath the glass, on which a stripper works. (PR)   R.R.K.

Strobe
Multiple electronic flash illuminating a moving subject several times for exposure on a single piece of film. (F)
H.V.G.

Studio
A room specially built for the purpose of recording, filming or broadcasting programs. (B)   H.V.G.

Stuff
The raw material of a story. (P)   B.C.B.

Sub-Head
A secondary title or heading. A bold face caption inserted

between paragraphs to break up lengthy columns of text. (P)   H.V.G.

Sub-Head
Group of words giving additional and transitional information between a heading and the body copy. (A)   H.V.G.

Subliminal Advertising
Uncommon TV and film commercial technique which flashes a visual message on the screen for a split second, so that the viewer is not consciously aware of having seen it. (A)
H.V.G.

Subscription Agency
An individual, firm or corporation obtaining subscriptions for two or more publications. Subscriptions (except those resulting from a direct mail effort) produced for one publisher by another publisher are classed in Audit Bureau of Circulations reports along with those obtained through agencies. (P)   A.B.C.

Subscription Salesmen
One who, as a regular or temporary or part-time vocation, solicits subscriptions for a paper or periodical. He may receive his compensation on either salary or commission basis, or both. (P)   A.B.C.

Subscription Salesmen's Copies
Copies of a publication carried by a subscription salesman to aid him in obtaining subscriptions. (P)   A.B.C.

Substance Numbers of Paper
A standardized system used by all paper manufacturers for identifying paper weights. The weight of 500 sheets (one ream) of the standard size of each individual kind of paper. (PR)   R.A.F.

Sub-Substitute
Subfire means a new fire story. (P)   B.C.B.

331

Sulphate Wood Pulp
Prepared by digesting wood with mixture of sulphate of soda, caustic soda, and sulphide of soda. (PR)   R.A.F.

Sulphite
Pulp made from wood chips cooked under a solution of bisulphite of lime. (PR)   R.A.F.

Sunrise-Watch
Same as dog-watch and lobster-trick. (P)   B.C.B.

Super
Used in connection with paper, it's a contraction of S. & S. C., which stands for Sized and Super-calendered. In its manufacture this paper is run between heated calender rolls, after a sizing has been added to the pulp. The better grades of super stock will carry 120-line halftones acceptably, but it is not as good a paper for this purpose as the process coated and enamel sheets. (PR)   B.B.

Superimposition
Blending of two television pictures. (B)   P.W.B.

Superior Letter (or Numeral)
A very small letter or number, set slightly above the body of the type, and generally used as a reference to a foot-note. (PR)   B.B.

Supplementary Story
Same as "follow." (P)   T.E.B.

Surface Development
Development in which only the superficial layers of silver in the emulsion are acted upon. Characteristic of fine-grain developers. (F)   A.S.

Surface Plates
In lithography, this refers to plates made by the albumen method, as distinguished from the deep-etch method. (PR)
B.B.

Surprinting
Superimposing one negative on another in making engravings. (PR)   H.V.G.

Sustaining Program
An unsponsored program presented by the station, usually as a public service. (B)   H.V.G.

Swatch
A color sample used as a guide for matching color. (PR)
                    H.V.G.

Swatch
In direct mail; a piece of material that is attached to a mailing piece to indicate to receiver what entire product might be like. Sellers of clothing find the technique especially useful. (A)   P.W.B.

Sweating-On
Operation of firmly attaching zinc and copper etchings (as well as electrotypes) to a solid metal base by a soldering procedure involving the use of a sheet of molten tinfoil as the binding medium between the two surfaces. (PR) J.S.M.

Switcher
Television device used in control room to cut, dissolve, fade, and to superimpose. (B)   P.W.B.

Symbol
Something other than itself which is the conception of what it represents. An example of a verbalized symbol is the name for an object, which abstracts the conception of the object or the name from the physical object itself. A symbol is not a natural phenomenon. It is arbitrary. It is social, and can be both verbal and non-verbal, which implies a relationship of symbols with the signs which they represent.

A recent notion is that man has a biological need and gift to transform experience into imagery and language, which has posed new questions about what a symbol is and how it functions in human behavior and activities and its importance in the act of communicating and in individual response to communication. See discursive and non-discursive symbolism. (C)

Symbol, Unconsummated

A logical, significant form capable of conceptualizing a rational and meaningful experience in symbolic form, yet really unrealized in any fixed or generalized discursive form. Music has been defined as such a symbol which evokes connotation and various articulations, yet is not really defined (after Langer). (C)

Symbolic Transformation

The translation of experience of sense data into symbols, and the basis for such important human faculties as abstraction and imagination. (C)

Symbolism

The symbolic process by which man abbreviates gross experience into manageable symbol form. See symbol. (C)

Symbolism, Discursive

This notion is primarily associated with lexical issues and the established systems of syntax or of mathematics which treat propositions and deal with logical thinking in language. An ultimate would be "presentational symbolism" (after Langer) or the larger syntactical pattern developed serially wherein conception and meaning are widened, e.g. the language of number systems.

Words and logical thinking are consecutive, strung out one after the other in serial fashion. A mouthful of words cannot be said at once. They have to fit in a succession, following a definite order. This is the case also with mathematical symbols. (C)

Symbolism, Non-discursive

The notion that any logical form, even other than what

334

is "discursive" may symbolize factors in experience. It depends upon the content of one's perception in space-time, the object, and the transaction of the two, or what could be labeled a *gestalt*, an insight or intuition.

These are non-rational symbols, as in all the forms of symbolic expression used in painting, religion, formal rituals, daily rituals, etc., where the meaning apparently comes all at once, if it comes at all. A photograph has a certain relationship of parts, but whatever the total picture says comes across as one looks. The whole visual structure is stated in just one single glance. The meaning of the total symbol tends to come across through the simultaneous impression of the parts. (C)

Sync
Synchronization—the matching of sound and pictures. (F)   G.W.

Syndicate
An organization either inside or outside of a newspaper office that buys and sells newspaper and magazine features, such as comics, pictures, department articles, etc. (P) B.C.B.

Syntactics (a Branch of Semiotic)
The study of syntax; of the signs and rules relating to signs. (C)   C.C.

Syntax
The formal aspect of a language. (We distinguish descriptive syntax and pure syntax.) (C)   C.C.

T

T.A.B.
Traffic Audit Bureau. An organization supported by advertisers, agencies and outdoor media which audits traffic exposure of outdoor advertising.

T.
Abbreviation for "time" when used in conjunction with number of insertions, such as 1-t, 13-t, etc. (A)   H.V.G.

Table
The general term for any tabulation, as of figures. (P)

B.C.B.

Tabloid
A newspaper physical format, usually five columns wide and roughly 17 inches deep. (P)

Tack
Stickiness, as in printing ink. (PR)   R.R.K.

Tack Room
Engravings mounted on wood are generally held in place by tiny tacks; these may be placed either at the top and bottom or at the sides, but in either case a narrow margin or shoulder must be left in the metal to accommodate them. The choice of position should be governed by the way in

which the page is to be made up, as the shoulder or tack room will prevent either type or other engravings being placed flush against it. A method is now gaining acceptance among engravers by which plates are attached to the mounts by a plastic adhesive, eliminating the tacks and hence the shoulders. This may become the universal practice eventually. (PR) B.B.

Tag
The announcer's closing to the present drama, either to end the story or to encourage the listeners to tune in for the next episode. Example: "What will happen to little Mary tomorrow? Will she be rescued from the burning building? Be sure to hear tomorrow's episode." (B) N.A.B.

Take
A small portion of news manuscript or any copy given out to machine operators by the copycutter to be set in type; a small portion of a story sent by the copyeditor to the composing room. (P) B.C.B.

Take
One shot, picture or sound; also means a good shot. (F)
G.W.

Taking a Balance
Checking microphones for proper level. (B) N.A.B.

Talent Cost
The amount in addition to time charges paid for the production of the program. (A) H.V.G.

Talk Back
A microphone in the control room that enables the director to talk to the cast in the studio. (B) N.A.B.

Tank
The developing container. (F) G.W.

Tape
Perforated paper used in teletype or teletypesetter. (P)
B.C.B.

Tape Recording
The recording of sound magnetically on a strip of oxide coated tape. (B) H.V.G.

Tass
The sole agency for collecting and transmitting news within the U.S.S.R. It maintains bureaus throughout the world. It is the main source of news for national news agencies politically associated with Russia. (P) (B)

Tear Sheets
Pages upon which an advertisement appears, torn or cut out of publications, sent to the client as proofs of insertion. (A) H.V.G.

T.B.A.
Abbreviation for "To Be Announced." (A) H.V.G.

Teaser Campaign
A series of advertisements, usually in small space, designed to arouse curiosity and create interest run before and leading up to the date when an important announcement is made. (A) H.V.G.

Telecast
A broadcast, program or show on television. (B) H.V.G.

Teleflex
Rear projection that gives special effects during live telecasting. (B) P.W.B.

Telephoto
A photograph transmitted by wire. (P) B.C.B.

Teleprompter
A rolling script device used off-camera for performers who have difficulty in remembering lines. Lines are printed

large enough to be read at a distance on a revolving sheet which keeps pace with the show's action. (B)   H.V.G.

Telescopic Lens
A lens that magnifies distant or small objects. (F) G.W.

Teletype
The machine used in a radio or TV station to receive news bulletins or to send and receive messages from network headquarters. (B)   H.V.G.

Television Gray Scale
Resolution of colors in scenery, costumes, and performers' faces into corresponding gray values in black-and-white TV. Has a shorter contrast range than other photographic media. (B)   H.V.G.

Telop
Method of projecting an opaque card or slide used for titles, etc. (B)   H.V.G.

Tempera
An opaque water base pigment used mainly for illustration. Dries with a dull (mat) surface. (A)   H.V.G.

Temperature Control
Maintaining the temperature of photographic solutions at some specified degree for highest efficiency and uniformity of negatives and prints. Modern devices for the purpose include temperature controlled darkroom sinks. (PR) J.S.M.

Tempilstik
Crayon-like material for marking metal and other surfaces intended to be heated, the marking melting at a specific temperature and indicating that the required degree of heat has been obtained. (PR)   J.S.M.

Tempo
The pace and timing of a picture. (F)   G.W.

Ten Point

The "points" that are used to designate the sizes of type refer to the height of the slug on which the type is cast. As the slug must, of course, be large enough to accommodate the full height of any letter in the alphabet, both capitals and lower case, including all ascenders and descenders, the size of the body of the letters can often be deceptive. 18-point *Nicholas Cochin,* for instance, actually looks smaller than 12-point *Futura,* while in the case of *Coronet* the capitals are so much larger in proportion to the lower case letters that one can be easily fooled in estimating the size required for a given heading.

One point, by the way, is 1/72 of an inch, or 1/12 of a pica. (PR)   B.B.

Tension Lockup

The system which prevents the "breathing" or buckling in the middle as happens with ordinary compression lockup plates at high speed on presses. Hooks which hold the plate to the plate cylinder, reach underneath the plate and, by tension outward, pull the plate down firm on the cylinder. This allows more plate area or printing area on the press. (PR)

Tent Card

A small, folded card for table display. (PR)   H.V.G.

Test Campaign

Testing an advertising campaign in a local or regional area before proceeding on a large-scale basis. (A)   H.V.G.

Test Pattern

Chart transmitted by television stations before programs are telecast. Consists of lines, circles, and a gray scale. (B)
P.W.B.

Text

Straight or body matter of a book. (PR)   H.V.G.

Text Paper
Book paper that has been moderately calendered to produce a smooth printing surface without completely destroying the rough-textured appearance. Not suitable for the printing of halftones, unless they have been made especially for the purpose, in which case the screen would be much coarser than customary and unsuitable for most subjects. (PR) B.B.

T.F.
"Till Forbid." Used in insertion order, meaning to run the advertising as ordered until further notice. (A) H.V.G.

Theme
The subject or central idea of a program, or particularly apropos music that identifies a specific show. (B) H.V.G.

Thermography
The process of dusting freshly printed sheets with resinous powder; when heated, the powder fuses, forming a raised surface of the print, simulating copperplate engraving, usually used on business and calling cards, and like work. (PR) R.R.K.

Thick Stick
A direction to the printer to set type one third of a column wide—used in tabulations of various kinds, lists of names, articles, etc. (P) B.C.B.

Thin Gage Metal
Zinc and copper sheets for photoengraving rolled to either 18-gage (.049″) or 21-gage (.032″), instead of the normal 16-gage (.065″) thickness. Introduced during World War II as a metal conservation measure. (PR) J.S.M.

Think Piece
Speculative or opinion story. (P) B.C.B.

Thinner

Benzol solution used to thin the consistency of rubber cement. (A) H.V.G.

Thirty

Used in newspapers, either wire services and written copy, the symbol—30—denotes the end of the story. (P) R.A.F.

Three-Color Photography

That branch of photography in which colored originals or subjects are reproduced by making color separation negatives therefrom through proper color filters, the negatives dividing the hues of the original into the three primary colors, and from which printing plates are made to be printed in yellow, red and blue inks (more accurately, yellow, magenta and blue-green). (PR) J.S.M.

Three-Color Process Plates

Those used for three-color printing, but specifically referring to tricolor halftone etchings. (PR) J.S.M.

Three-Color Process Printing

The method of printing in which all hues of an original are considered possible of reproduction by use of three separate printing plates, each plate used for printing or recording one of the primary colors of the original. The plates usually are made by recourse to three-color photography and the employment of halftone separation negatives, though they may also include plates made from line drawings and shading sheet originals, as well as those produced by bendaying and manual separation of colors on each of the plates. (PR) J.S.M.

Three-Point Bar System

A method and device for registration of images in color composing, the device consisting of a right-angled metal bar provided with three movable points or wedges for accurately positioning any number of photographic images on a single plate or film. (PR)   J.S.M.

Throw a Cue
Visual hand signal to talent; a signal to begin action or speech. (B)   H.V.G.

Throwaways
Shopping newspapers. (A) (P)

Thumbnail Sketch
A miniature layout, usually very rough. (A)   H.V.G.

Tie-Back
A sentence or paragraph in a story that *rehashes* or reviews events of a related character. (P)   B.C.B.

Tie-In
In broadcasting, a commercial announcement given by the local announcer after a break in a network program, or at the end of the network program. Usually, the name will be given of the local retailer who sells the product advertised in the main program. (B)   P.W.B.

Tie-In
The part of a story that relates a contemporaneous event, or relevant information, to the news being reported. (P)   B.C.B.

Tight
More news than is needed for a particular issue. Hence, on days when newsworthy events are plentiful, a paper is said to be "tight." (P)   T.E.B.

Tight
Artwork ultrarealistic in detail. (See Loose.) (A) H.V.G.

Tight Paper
A paper so crowded with advertising that the news space

343

must be reduced. It is the opposite of a *wide open* paper. (P)   B.C.B.

Tight Show
A program that has been timed to fit exactly into a time period. (B)   N.A.B.

Time
Units purchased on radio and television stations such as "Station Breaks," "ID's," 10-20-30 second, 1 minute, etc. (A)   H.V.G.

Time Buyer
The "buyer" responsible for making the best selection of radio or TV coverage for the advertiser. (A)   H.V.G.

Time Charge
The rate charged by a station or network for various segments of time. (A)   H.V.G.

Time Copy
Copy set in type and held for future use. (P)   B.C.B.

Time Discount
Reduction from regular rates allowed by publisher when advertiser contracts to run advertising for a certain number of insertions. (A)   H.V.G.

Time Signal
A short commercial preceded or followed by a time check. (B)   H.V.G.

Tint
In reproduction, the effect of shade by hatching or by a series of regularly spaced lines and dots; a halftone tint. In printing, reduction of a solid color, or weakening of a color by admixture with white. (PR)   J.S.M.

Tint Block
A solid panel of color which appears under type matter

344

of pictures, used for artistic effect or emphasis. If the second color on the page is strong or deep, it is advisable to have the tint block screened, to reduce its color value. Otherwise it will be difficult to read or see the black type printed over it. (PR)   B.B.

Tint Chart
A chart or representation of halftone dot formations in various tonal strengths, or of benday or shading sheet patterns of different types, either in black or color combinations. (PR)   J.S.M.

Tintlaying
The operation of bendaying. (PR)   J.S.M.

Tint Plate
A printing plate bearing either a solid, stippled, line or dot surface, used for printing light colors, usually in conjunction with a plate in bold or heavy key. Sometimes applied to parts of an illustration requiring darkening in color. (PR)   J.S.M.

Tint Print Solution
Resinous mixture employed in double printing and work involving more than one exposure on the sensitized metal. (PR)   J.S.M.

Tint Screen
Takes its name from its origin in the photoengravers' screen. The expression, for instance, "a screen of the red" means that a solid red has been broken up into dots by being photographed through a screen, and its color value changed. Thus, if the dots were very fine indeed, a brilliant red would be made to appear light pink. The commonly used expressions "25% screen" or "60% screen" are to a certain extent misnomers; they actually mean 25% or 60% of the original color. Different shades of the same color can be

obtained in one press impression by means of the screening process. (PR) B.B.

Tintype
Ferrotype. (PR)

Tip
A bit of information which leads to a story, hence a *lead*. (P) B.C.B.

Tip In
A bindery operation by which an insert may be pasted into a publication, either by a strip of paste along one edge or, if the insert is folded, along the edge of the fold. (PR) B.B.

Title Line
Same as signature and byline. (P) B.C.B.

Titles
Announcements or credits of a program produced on film, cards, or slides. (B) H.V.G.

Titles
The footage preceding and following the actual story on which information is given about title, who made the film, and so forth; also, words which are superimposed on the film, as in silent pictures. (F) G.W.

Toenails
Parentheses. (P) B.C.B.

Token
See word-token and sign-token. (C)

Tombstone
When heads of the same sizes are placed side by side they are said to be tombstoned. (P) B.C.B.

Tonality
An art term, used to describe the effectiveness with

which the photographer has reproduced the tonal gradations of his subject, or the effectiveness with which he has
used tonal gradation to express an idea or feeling. (F)   A.S.

Tonal Key
The balance of light or dark tones of a photograph. If
light tones prevail with few or no dark tones, the photograph is said to be "high key"; If the opposite, "low key."
(F)   A.S.

Tone
In originals and illustrations, the effect due to harmonious
relation of light and shade. A photograph giving an approximately true monochrome rendition of the various colors
and atmospheric effects of nature is said to have correct tone
values. (PR)   J.S.M.

Tool
To increase the depth of a thin white line in an engraving to prevent it from filling with ink. Done by hand
with a sharp v gouge. (PR)   H.V.G.

Top
The acid resisting image on metal plates intended for
relief etching; the ink image produced by the albumen
process especially after reinforcement with topping powder.
(PR)   J.S.M.

Top Heads
Headlines intended for the tops of columns only. Generally headlines with banks or decks. (P)   B.C.B.

Top Lines
The type lines forming the top of a headline. (P) B.C.B.

Topping Powder
Any of several commercial preparations of finely ground
white resin, used for dusting ink images and increasing the
acid resistance of the print prior to etching. (PR)   J.S.M.

347

Total Net Paid

Total of all classes of a publication's circulation for which the ultimate purchasers have paid in accordance with the standards set by the rules. Includes single copy sales, mail subscriptions and specials. (P)　　　　A.B.C.

Totalux

A photoelectric device to control the duration of camera exposures. Luxometer. (PR)　　　　J.S.M.

Tr

Abbreviation of transpose, used when letters, words, sentences or paragraphs are to be changed in position. Matter is "ringed" and connected by lines to indicate changes. Also abbreviation for turn rule. (P)　　　　B.C.B.

Trade Advertising

Advertisements of consumer items directed to "the trade" —wholesalers and retailers in the distribution channel. (A)
　　　　H.V.G.

Trademark

Any mark or design affixed to a product which identifies and distinguishes it from others. (A)　　　　H.V.G.

Trade Name

A name identifying a business. Also, a brand name of a product or service. (A)　　　　H.V.G.

Trading Area

The area surrounding a city set up by the Audit Bureau of Circulations whose residents would normally be expected to use the city as their trading center. (A)　　　　H.V.G.

Traffic Count

The evaluation of outdoor poster readers by an actual count of traffic passing the poster. (A)　　　　H.V.G.

Traffic Department

The department in an advertising agency which schedules

348

work through the various departments and follows up to see that jobs are completed on time. (A)   H.V.G.

Trailer
A short film made up of excerpts from a feature film, which is shown as part of the regular film program to gain the interest of the audience in a future showing. (F)

Transfer
In lithography, the sheet or gelatine-like film containing the design that is to be transferred to a printing surface, either metal or stone. (PR)   R.A.F.

Transfer
An ink impression from an etched plate used to make a duplicate impression on another plate, and sometimes employed as a register aid in color platemaking. (PR)
J.S.M.

Transcription
A superior quality recording used for broadcast purposes, usually recorded at 33⅓ r.p.m. Also called an E.T. or "electrical transcription." (B)   H.V.G.

Transition
Broadcast term referring to the technique of moving from one scene to another in a presentation. Can be done musically, by fading out voices, by sound effects, and by other means. (B)   P.W.B.

Translucent
Permits the passage of light, but scatters it so that no image can be formed. (F)   A.S.

Transparency
Photograph in color on film. (See Kodachrome.) (F)
H.V.G.

Transparency

A photographic positive on a clear or transparent support. (PR)   J.S.M.

Transparency Holder

The carrier or arrangement for holding transparencies (and negatives) in position on process cameras so that the images may be illuminated with transmitted light during photographic reproduction. (PR)   J.S.M.

Transparent

In paper, permitting the passage of light, also called show-through. As opposed to opaque. (PR)   R.A.F.

Transparent Impression

An ink proof taken on transparent or translucent material; the impression taken by a proprietary process, in which both the front and back of the material bear the same impression in accurate register with each other. (PR)   J.S.M.

Transparentizing

Rendering the paper support of photographic images translucent by treatment with greasy or oily substances. (PR)   J.S.M.

Transportation Advertising

Car cards or other types of poster advertising appeals in street cars, subways, buses, etc. (A)   H.V.G.

Transpose

To switch the position of two words or letters. (PR)   H.V.G.

Transposition

The process of reversing the tonal character of a photographic image; chemical reversal; reverse prints. Changing the position of an image. (PR)   J.S.M.

Trap

Proper laying or confinement of ink in successive impressions during wet color printing. (PR)   J.S.M.

Travelogue

A short film which superficially describes a people or place. (F)

Treatment

The preliminary guide to the film written before shooting the script. (F)   G.W.

Trendex

A rating service, similar to Hooper and Nielsen, measuring TV shows. (A)   H.V.G.

Trial by Newspaper

Supposed threat to the administration of justice when the right of access during court trials or recesses is granted to the news media. Issues raised are the possible psychological effects on witnesses, jury, lawyers and other participants; also the effect on-the-spot coverage would have on the trial system and proceedings. (P)

Trial Subscription

Subscriptions for less than one year. (P)   A.B.C.

Trichromatic

Consisting of or using three colors. (PR)   J.S.M.

Tricolor Filters

Those employed in three-color photography for exposure of separation negatives. (PR)   J.S.M.

Trim

To reduce the length of a given story. (P)   T.E.B.

Tropical Developer

Any developer prepared especially for developing under

tropical conditions. Such developers must yield satisfactory results when working at temperatures up to 90°F or even higher. (F)   A.S.

Trucking Shot
A traveling shot, in which the camera itself is in motion. (F)   G.W.

TTS
Abbreviation for teletypesetter. (P)

Turn
A story is said to *turn* when it runs from the bottom of the last column on the first page to the top of the first column on the second page. Such stories require no jump heads, as they *read* from the one page to the other. Also, a story *turns* from one column to another, under a cut, under a box, etc. (P)   B.C.B.

Turn Rule
Meaning to invert a rule, broad side up, in the body of a story to indicate an alteration or correction is on the way. (P)   B.C.B.

Turn Story
The story that runs from the last column of the first page to the first column of the second and therefore requires no jump heads. (P)   B.C.B.

Turntable
An arrangement on the truck or stand of process cameras whereby the camera can be turned sideways or at right angle to the copyboard when using a mirror or prism for lateral reversal of negatives. (PR)   J.S.M.

Tusche
Greasy, water-soluble black liquid applied to plates with pen or brush, for repairing the image when broken or missing on offset-lithographic plates. (PR)   R.R.K.

24-Sheet

Large outdoor advertising medium. So called because of the number of sheets formerly required to make the finished poster. (A)   H.V.G.

Two-Color Process

A method of reproduction in which two plates, line or halftone, are printed in two practically complementary colors to give a full-color effect. A two-color halftone consists of two plates each made from a separate negative from the original, the latter either monochrome or colored, and the plates etched to produce the desired color effect when printed in two contrasting colors. (PR)   J.S.M.

Two-Line Initial, Two-Line Figure

Initials and figures that are two average type lines in depth. There are also three- and four-line initials. (PR)   B.C.B.

Two-Pay Agency

A subscription agency working on the two-pay plan. (P)   A.B.C.

Two-Pay Plan

Designation of sales plan under which the subscription solicitor collects from the subscriber a portion of the subscription price and the publisher or the subscription agency receives the balance direct from the subscriber. Some publishers refuse to start service until second payment is received. (P)   A.B.C.

Two-Thirder

An advanced printing apprentice (PR)   R.R.K.

Tying-In

Coming into a chain program which may already be in progress. (B)   J.C.W.

Tying-Up

The process of wrapping type forms with cord to keep them from being pied. (PR)   R.R.K.

Tympan

The paper that covers the platen or impression cylinder of a letterpress. (PR)   R.R.K.

Type

Printers' letters, in metal to sizes of 144-point and wood in larger sizes, having a character cast or cut in relief at one end. (PR)   R.R.K.

Typebook

A book showing various families and sizes of type. (P)   B.C.B.

Type Face

The design or style of a type letter. Usually named after the designer such as Bodoni, Caslon, Goudy, etc. (PR)   H.V.G.

Type Family

A group of related type faces in series, such as Garamond, Garamond Bold, *Garamond Italic, Garamond Bold Italic.* (PR)   H.V.G.

Typefounding

The manufacturing of types. (PR)   R.R.K.

Type High

In general practice, this term refers to the height of a linotype slug. Unless instructed to the contrary, engravers mount plates on wood in such a way as to exactly equal this height. In the absence of specific exceptions, type-high in the United States is .918 of an inch. (PR)   B.B.

Type Louse

A mythical bug, which naive novices search for and never find, to their chagrin, in print shops. (PR)   R.R.K.

Type Rule

Lines, of various thicknesses, which the printer can insert in making up pages of type and engravings. These lines must be perfectly straight, but with that limitation the printer can often save you the expense of having plates made of lines which are to be used for decorative purposes. Instead of including decorative lines of this kind in your artwork and sending them off to the engraver for zinc etchings, it sometimes pays to check with the printer to determine whether he can't give you the same effect by the use of type rules. (PR)   B.B.

Type Style

Usual references are: Roman, Italic, Type Script, Old English and Gothic. Condensed type is narrower than usual, Extended type is wider and Bold Face is heavier. (PR)
H.V.G.

Typographer

A master typographical designer of printed matter. (PR)
R.R.K.

Typography

The art of setting and arranging type for printing or reproduction. (PR)   H.V.G.

U. and l.c.
Upper and lower case letters—capitals and small letters. (P)

Ultraviolet
That section beyond the violet end of the visible spectrum, the rays of which exert a high degree of photochemical action. (PR)   J.S.M.

Under
A show that runs shorter than time allotted. (B) N.A.B.

Undercolors
In color photography and platemaking, those primary colors and black not sufficiently eradicated in separation negatives and prints to produce an accurate multicolor reproduction without extensive corrections and reetching of halftone printing plates. (PR)   J.S.M.

Undercut
A condition in relief etching in which the acid or mordant has penetrated beneath the printing surface, causing thinning or weakening of lines and dots, and interfering with stereotyping or electrotyping. (PR)   J.S.M.

Underexposure

Insufficient action of light on a sensitized photographic surface, resulting in thin or weak images and loss of detail. (F)   J.S.M.

Underlay

A piece of paper or built up sheets placed or pasted underneath a printing plate to increase or decrease local pressure when printing, thereby improving the quality of the impression. (PR)   J.S.M.

Underlines

Lines used beneath a cut. Synonymous with "cut lines." (P)   T.E.B.

Underscoring

Musical background behind action and dialogue. (F)
G.W.

Uni-Base

A mounting material in the form of honeycombed magnesium plates on which relief etchings are attached either with tape or with thermoplastic adhesives. (PR)   J.S.M.

Unibath

A one-bath developing and fixing process for film. It is virtually free of time and temperature restrictions (minimum room temperature is 68 degrees F.). Every grain of silver in the emulsion is either used in forming the image or discarded. A hypo neutralizing agent in the solution assures permanence. (F)

Unit Scale

Commonly used term for "The Standard Scale for Photoengravers, Form I" which became effective in 1940. Prior to that date, all engravings were priced by the square inch. The standard scale sets up a standard of unit values from which prices can be computed; it is not a price list. It consists of two parts: I. A square-rule chart by which the unit value of any engraving can be determined, and 2. A list of the various additional charges which may be assessed under specified circumstances.

All engravers quote "per unit" and the number of units in any given engraving may be determined from the chart and its side-rules. The unit measurement is a constant factor, so a direct comparison may be drawn between various prices quoted. (PR)   B.B.

United Press International (UPI)

A privately owned service, representing the merger between United Press news agency and International News Service, UPI distributes local, national and international news and has exchange agreements with the major world news agencies. (P) (B)

Unmounted Plate

A printing plate not attached to a wood block. (PR)
                                                                    R.A.F.

Unpaid Copies

Copies distributed either entirely free or at a price inadequate to qualify them as paid in accordance with the rules. (P)   A.B.C.

Upper Case

Capital letters, as opposed to small letters. The term originated from the fact that capital letters were formerly kept in a separate type case which was held in a stand above the case containing the small letters. (PR)   H.V.G.

Up Style

Style wherein the use of capitals is emphasized. Its opposite, the "down" style, naturally reduces the use of capitals to a minimum. (P)   T.E.B.

V

V.I.
Volume indicator needle on console. (B)

Vacuum Copyboard
A board or arrangement on process cameras for holding originals in place during exposure by means of atmospheric pressure. (PR)   J.S.M.

Vacuum Holder
A perforated or channeled metal plate on which films and negative papers are held in position in the focal plane of darkroom cameras by withdrawing the air between the film and support, the material then securely held by the pressure of the atmosphere. (PR)   J.S.M.

Vacuum Printing Frame
A frame in which contact between a photographic image and sensitized surface is maintained by atmospheric pressure, the air being withdrawn from the frame by an electrically driven pump. (PR)   J.S.M.

Vandercook Press
A make of proving machine used by letterpress printers and trade composition houses for pulling proofs for reading and for photographic reproduction. (PR)   R.R.K.

Van Dyke
Print of an offset job exposed on sensitized paper for approval before making the plate. (PR)   H.V.G.

Variable-Area Track
A sound track in which sound is recorded in black peaks and valleys. (F)   G.W.

Variable-Density Track
A sound track in which sound is recorded in varying exposure densities. (F)   G.W.

Variable-Opacity Screen
Halftone screen of photographic nature, showing line or dot formations of graded density. (PR)   J.S.M.

Varitype
Trade name for an elaboration of the old familiar typewriter, having a device by which words and letters can be spaced so that all lines are of equal length (justified). It also has interchangeable type faces. It is not a typesetting machine, or a method of printing; plates must be made from the work it produces, just as they would be from ordinary typewriting. (PR)   B.B.

Varnish
There is, of course, at least a small percentage of varnish in most printing inks, but it is possible to run a sheet that has already been printed through the press again for an impression of clear, colorless varnish, giving the completed work a shiny, glossy, appearance. Occasionally used on the covers of publications. (PR)   B.B.

Vellum Finish
Paper or cardboard made with a surface that looks and feels like real vellum. (PR)   R.A.F.

Velox
A photographic print or artwork screened into halftone dots for use as line copy. (PR)   H.V.G.

Verse Print Process

A proprietary method of making reverse prints on zinc with cold enamel. (PR)   J.S.M.

Verse Style

A direction to the printer, meaning set type after the fashion of poetry. (P)   B.C.B.

Vertical Publication

A business publication aimed at a specific group of readers, as opposed to a horizontal publication that is designed for a cross section of industries. (A)   P.W.B,

Vertical Recording

A recording system where the needle vibrates up and down, or vertically in the groove. (B)   H.V.G.

VHF

Very high frequency, 30 to 300 megacycles. (B)

Video

A term commonly used as a synonym for television broadcast. Also used to denote the visual portion of a television program. It is derived from the Latin word videre, meaning "to see." (B)   H.V.G.

Video-Scene Process

Two cameras locked together electronically so that performer and background are synchronized. The actor performs on a set specially prepared to reflect light back toward the camera. This produces a sharp cut-out of the performer's image which is then inserted into a selected background. (B)

Videotape Recorder

The videotape recorder is a device which records on a strip of magnetic tape the electrical signals which emerge from a television camera system, very much as the audio tape recorder records on a narrow strip of magnetic tape the electrical system which emerges from a microphone system. The machine will record both picture and sound, as it is being picked up in the studio, and immediately replay both picture and sound. Like an audio tape, a television tape recording can be erased, and a new recording placed on the same tape many times. Like an audio tape, a television tape recording can be recorded on one machine and played back on another, or copies of the original tape can be made and played back on many other machines.

The videotape recorder may accurately be regarded as the television counterpart of the professional high-fidelity sound tape recorder. It is not an electrical counterpart of the moving-picture camera. Just as the recording of sound requires one or more microphones, properly placed for best pickup, so videotape recording requires one or more television cameras and microphones properly placed for best picture and sound pickup.

The videotape recorder stores every detail which is fed to it, and will replay, in electrical form, the information it has received through cables as often as is required.

Videotape recording is essentially a new way of storing moving pictorial information, a memory for the television camera, which does not depend upon chemicals, which is capable of immediate replay, and whose medium can be erased and re-used. It can be viewed as a supplement to motion picture photography, and a replacement for photography, particularly in television. (B)

Viewing Cabinet
An illuminated desk, table or cabinet whereon colorfilm transparencies and photographic images can be viewed and examined by transmitted light, the illuminant usually having a color temperature slightly above 3,200° K to show the images to best advantage. (PR)   J.S.M.

Vignette
A photograph, halftone plate or impression showing the

362

background or a portion of the illustration gradually shaded off toward the edges. Halftones of this character blend gradually from full tones through succeeding lighter tones until they appear to merge with the paper on which they are printed, the effect due to the gradual reduction of dot size as the edges of the plate are approached. (PR)   J.S.M.

Vignette
The process of regulating the distribution of light in such a way that the image obtained fades out toward the edges, leaving no sharp boundaries. (F)   A.S.

Visual
A preliminary rough sketch showing variety of ways in which various elements in an advertisement can be arranged. (A)   H.V.G.

Voice Over
Narration that accompanies the action on the TV screen, meaning voice "over" action. (B)   H.V.G.

Voice-Over
Narration recorded after the photography has been made. (F)   G.W.

Volume Indicator
A meter located in the station control room indicating the volume intensity coming through the system. (B) H.V.G.

W

Wait Order

Instructions to a publication to set and hold advertisement for insertion on a date to be specified later. (A)

H.V.G.

Wale Process

A method of rotary letterpress printing based on the employment of a printing surface in which text matter and illustrations are etched in relief as an integral unit on a thin sheet of metal, this curved and attached to the impression cylinder of the press to furnish the complete printing element. (PR)

J.S.M.

Wall Banner

A paper, cloth or cardboard sign of large dimensions used on walls to advertise a product or service. Sometimes hung over a high wire stretched across store. (PR)   H.V.G.

Warning Lights

A system of signaling studio performers when TV camera is on-the-air. Red and green lights, usually mounted under the lens turret, indicate whether the camera is preparing for pick-up (green light) or actually transmitting the image (red light). (B)

H.V.G.

Wash Drawing
Drawing done in varying shades of gray, black and white, usually in transparent water color. (A)   H.V.G.

Washington Press
An old type of proof press requiring pulling of a hand lever for application of pressure to the printing surface. (PR)   J.S.M.

Water Color
Transparent water base pigment. Also used to designate a drawing made with water soluble paints. (A)   H.V.G.

Waterhouse Stop
A lens diaphragm in the shape of a thin sheet of metal or paper bearing circular or irregular apertures of definite size, the stop inserted into the slot cut in the barrel of process lens; the flash stop in halftone photography. (PR)   J.S.M.

Watermark
A faint design or lettering pressed into paper while it is still in pulp form. (PR)   H.V.G.

Wax Engraving
Method of reproducing ruled forms and maps by cutting lines into a wax case, by a thin sheet of copper, molding or stamping type and then electroplating. (PR)   R.A.F.

Web Press
Large, high-speed presses such as are used for newspaper printing or other long run work. They are fed from rolls of paper instead of sheets, and the paper is festooned in and over and under the cylinders—hence the "web." (PR) B.B.

Weight
A term used to define the thickness of printing papers by so many pounds per 500 sheets of a certain size, i.e.,

20 lb. bond means that 500 sheets of such paper weigh 20 lbs. (PR)   H.V.G.

Western
An American film drama or TV drama which glorifies or exaggerates the cowboy and early American frontier life.

Wet Color Printing
Procedure of color printing in which colors are successively and rapidly applied before the previous impression has had opportunity to dry. (PR)   J.S.M.

Wet Collodion Process
A method of photography in which glass plates are coated with salted (iodized) negative collodion, then sensitized by immersal in an acidified silver nitrate solution, and exposed in a moist condition. (PR)   J.S.M.

Wetplate
A photographic plate produced by the wet collodion process. (PR)   J.S.M.

Wet Printing
Printing whereby successive colors are laid down before the preceding colors are dry. (PR)   H.V.G.

Wetting Agent
Any of various chemical substances which reduce the surface tension of a liquid, thereby promoting smoother and more uniform results when added to photographic solutions. (PR)   J.S.M.

Whatman
High grade English water color paper and board. (A)
                                                                      H.V.G.

Whirler
An apparatus for coating metal and glass plates with light-sensitive solutions by revolving the plate horizontally under the influence of heat. (PR)   J.S.M.

White Space
The blank area of a piece of printing not covered with type matter or illustration. (PR)　　　　H.V.G.

Whodunit
Mystery or detective program on radio or TV. (B)
H.V.G.

Whorfian Hypothesis
The controversial doctrine advanced by Benjamin Lee Whorf, a self-tutored linguist, that every language has culturally ordained structure by which the users not only communicate, but which influences their formation of ideas, as well as perceptual and evaluative habits.

Widow
Short last line of a paragraph or block of copy. (PR)
H.V.G.

Wild
Shooting without the sound, which is recorded separately. (F)　　　　G.W.

Window
A transparent panel on the face of an envelope that permits the address on the insert to show through. (PR)
H.V.G.

Window Streamer
An advertising medium—usually a strip of paper posted on a store window, carrying the advertising message in one or more colors. (A)　　　　H.V.G.

Wipe
One scene disappears from the screen, while another replaces it as though one were being wiped off during the replacement. (F)　　　　G.W.

Wipe
Transition between scenes in television, where one scene

replaces another in geometric fashion, i.e. expanding circle, a fan, a roll, etc. (B) H.V.G.

Wire-O Binding
A continuous double series of wire loops run through punched slots along the bindery side of the book. (PR) R.A.F.

Wirephoto
A syndicated process of transmitting photographic images by telephone, telegraph or wireless waves; phototelegraphy. (P) J.S.M.

Wire Recording
Recording by a magnetic process on a thin wire. (B) H.V.G.

Wire Side
The under side of a sheet of paper as it comes off paper-making machine. (PR) R.A.F.

With the Grain
A term applied to folding paper parallel to the grain of the paper. (PR) R.A.F.

Woodcut
A wood engraving; an illustration engraved on wood. (PR) H.V.G.

Wooden Head
Term applied to dull, meaningless headlines that tell nothing. (P) B.C.B.

Word Space
The space between words. Usually, to justify a line of type by increasing the normal amount of space between words. (PR) H.V.G.

Word-Token
A physical utterance; the physical embodiment of a word-type. See sign-token. (C) C.C.

Word-Type

(A universal, a linguistic concept.) A word of the language. A word as listed in a dictionary. (C)   C.C.

Work and Flop

A variation of the more frequently used "Work and Turn," in which the same procedure is used, but after printing one side of the sheet the lift of paper is "flopped" instead of being turned on its horizontal axis. (PR)   B.B.

Work and Turn

This is one of those expressions that most printers use every day of their lives and thoroughly understand, but that most of them find very hard to explain. It refers only to printing on both sides of the paper, as in publications. Visualize the front and reverse sides of a page, the "heads" and "tails" sides, printed side by side on a large sheet of paper, instead of back to back. If you print one-half of the total quantity required in that position, then turn the paper over, turn it so that the front side is back to back with the reverse side, and print that side of the sheet, you'll have a completed job. The same operation can be applied, of course, regardless of the number of pages being printed at once. Thus a sixteen-page work and turn form would carry the "heads" sides of eight pages and the "tails" sides of eight. "Worked" and "turned" to the correct position, when the other side of the paper was printed all sixteen pages would be complete. (PR)   B.B.

Work Print

An assembly of scenes used during the editing, from which the final negative is made after the work print has been completely cut and assembled. (F)   G.W.

Work Up

Occasionally, under the great pressure applied by the press, a piece of the "furniture" used to fill in a form will work up to the level of the type and cause a blemish in printing. Careful pressmen are always on the lookout for such an accident and if it occurs they immediately correct it and discard the sheets on which the blemish appears. (PR)   B.B.

Working Drawing

A perfected drawing of a crudely executed design or preliminary sketch made for reproduction purposes from originals unsuitable in their actual condition. (PR)   J.S.M.

Wove Paper

Paper having the appearance of a piece of cloth, having fine lines running each way of the sheet. (PR)   R.R.K.

Wow-Wows

Abnormal vibrations in sound, usually resulting from faulty projection. (F)   G.W.

Wrap Up

Complete story, distinguished from a story in takes. (P)   B.C.B.

Wrong Face, Wrong Font

Type of different style or size than that specified, occurring in midst of text. (PR)   B.C.B.

XYZ

Xerography

A duplicating process in which an image is printed on paper through a series of electrical charges. (PR)   H.V.G.

Yellow Journalism

Journalism which emphasizes the obscene, the risqué, the gory, the sensational. (P)   T.E.B.

Zinc Etching (or Zinc)

Used for the reproduction of line drawings, type matter, or other copy without shaded or tinted effects—in other words, just lines and solids. Zincs can be made from such copy as steel engravings, fine script, shorthand, mechanical tracings, proofs from wood engravings, drybrush or crayon drawings, but in cases where the copy is "difficult" it involves an extra charge of about 25% over the zinc etching scale. Zinc etchings, as such, have no screen or halftone dots, and are not to be confused with zinc halftones. (PR)   B.B.

Zinc Halftone

Form of halftone made in a coarse screen on zinc. (PR)
H.V.G.

Zipatone

Cellophane shading sheet upon which a black or white design has been printed. Acts as a benday substitute. (A)
P.W.B.

Zomag

Special lightweight alloy for relief etching in photoengraving; electron metal; magnesium metal. (PR)   J.S.M.

Zonal Error

A defect in photographic lenses which causes the size of the image to change with use of apertures or stops of different sizes. (F)   J.S.M.

Zone Plan

Method of concentrating advertising in a limited area instead of covering the entire country at once. Used for new products, limited appropriations, sampling, etc. (A)   H.V.G.

Zoom

The camera moves (or appears to move) sharply toward the subject being photographed. (F)   G.W.

Zoom or Zoom In

An optical trick, accomplished either with Zoomar lenses or by dollying the camera toward or away from the subject. The effect is a quick enlargement or reduction of the image on the TV screen. (B)   H.V.G.

NOTES

1. B. Jowett, trans., Plato: *The Republic*, New York: Modern Library, n.d., Book X, 378 ff.

2. Karl Marx and Friedrich Engels, *Literature and Art*, New York: International Publishers, 1947, p. 1; Cf. Louis Harap, *Social Roots of the Arts*, New York: International Publishers, 1946, p. 16, *et. passim*.

3. Thorstein Veblen, *The Theory of the Leisure Class*, New York: B. W. Huebsch, 1924, pp. 126-166; Christopher Caldwell, *Illusion and Reality*, New York: International Publishers, 1947; Ralph Fox, *The Novel and the People*, New York: International Publishers, 1945; Vernon Parrington, *Main Currents in American Thought*, New York: Harcourt, Brace, 1930; V. F. Calverton, *The Newer Spirit*, New York: Boni and Liveright, 1925; *The Liberation of American Literature*, New York: Charles Scribners, 1932; Granville Hicks, *The Great Tradition*, New York: Macmillan, 1939.

4. For detailed examples of the kinds of literary research published during the last 20 years, see the journals: *Sociology and Social Research, Social Forces, American Journal of Sociology, American Sociological Review*, et al.

5. Milton C. Albrecht, "The Relationship of Literature and Society," *American Journal of Sociology*, LIX, 5 (March, 1954), pp. 425-436.

6. Raymond F. Bellamy, "Art and Literature," *Social*

Control, Princeton: D. Van Nostrand Co., 1956, p. 247; see also Hugh Duncan, *Language and Literature in Society: A Sociological Essay on Theory and Method in the Interpretation of Linguistic Symbols with a Bibliographical Guide to the Society of Literature,* Chicago: University of Chicago Press, 1953.

7. Leo Lowenthal, *Literature and the Image of Man: Sociological Studies of the European Drama and Novel, 1600-1900,* Boston: Beacon Press, 1957, p. 257.

8. Hornell Hart, "Changing Social Attitudes and Interests," *Recent Social Trends in the United States,* New York: McGraw-Hill, 1933, Vol. 1, pp. 342-382.

9. James H. Barnett, *Divorce and the American Novel, 1858-1937: A Study in the Literary Reflections of Social Influences (Ph.D. dissertation), University of Pennsylvania,* 1939.

10. Martha Wolfenstein and Nathan C. Leites, "An Analysis of Themes and Plots," *Annals of the American Academy of Political and Social Science,* 254 (1947), pp. 41-48.

11. C. Wright Mills, *White Collar: The American Middle Class,* New York: Oxford University Press, 1951.

12. Ruth A. Inglis, "An Objective Approach to the Relation Between Fiction and Society," *American Sociological Review,* 3 (1938), 530-532.

13. Bernard Berelson, *Content Analysis in Communications Research,* Glencoe, Ill.: The Free Press, 1952, p. 95.

14. *Ibid.,* p. 98.

15. Plato's *The Republic, loc. cit.*

16. Havelock Ellis, *From Rousseau to Proust,* Boston: Houghton Mifflin, 1935, Vol. V; J.L. Hughes, *Dickens as an Educator,* New York: D. Appleton Co., 1903; Forest Wilson, "The Book that Brewed a War," *Readers Digest,* XXXVII (May, 1941), pp. 103-107.

17. Albert Guerard, *Literature and Society,* Boston: Lothrop, Lee and Shepard, 1935, p. 337.

18. Robert B. Downs, *The Books That Changed the World,* New York: Mentor Books, 1956, Vol. 7.

19. Herbert Blumer and Philip M. Hauser, *Movies, Delinquency and Crime,* New York: Macmillan, 1933.

20. "Juvenile Delinquency" (Motion Pictures), cited in U.S. Congress, Senate Committee on the Judiciary, *Hearings Before the Subcommittee to Investigate Juvenile Delinquency,* April 6 and 7, 1955, 84th Congress, 2nd Session, (Washington: Government Printing Office, 1956).

21. Mortimer J. Adler, *Art and Prudence,* New York: Longmans, Green and Co., 1937.

22. Ruth C. Peterson and L.L. Thurstone, *Motion Pictures and the Social Attitudes of Children,* New York: Macmillan, 1938.

23. Frederick Wertham, *Seduction of the Innocent,* New York: Rinehart and Co., 1956.

24. David J. Pittman, "Mass Media and Juvenile Delinquency," *Juvenile Delinquency,* New York: Philosophical Library, 1958, p. 238.

25. *Ibid.,* p. 242.

26. *Ibid.,* pp. 245-46; John W. Riley and Mathilda Riley, "A Sociological Approach to Communications Research," *Public Opinion Quarterly,* 15 (1951), pp. 445-460; see also Hilde Himmelweit, *Television and the Child,* London: Nuffield Foundation, 1958; *Children and Television Programmes,* London: British Broadcasting Corporation, 1960; Paul A. Witty, *School Children and Television,* New York: Television Information Office, 1960.

27. Elihu Katz and Paul F. Lazarsfeld, *Personal Influence: The Part Played by People in the Flow of Mass Communications,* Glencoe, Ill.: The Free Press, 1955, p. 49, *et. passim.*

28. Paul F. Lazarsfeld and Robert K. Merton, "Mass

Communications, Popular Taste and Organized Social Action," *Mass Communications,* Urbana: University of Illinois Press, 1949, p. 469.

29. Bernard Berelson, "Communications and Public Opinion," *op. cit.,* p. 500.

30. C. Hovland, A. Lumsdaine, and F. Sheffield, *Experiments on Mass Communication: Studies in Social Psychology in World War II,* Vol. III, Princeton: Princeton University Press, 1949; see also Edward Shils and Morris Janowitz, "Cohesion and Disintegration in the Wehrmacht in World War II," *Reader in Public Opinion and Communication,* Glencoe, Ill.: The Free Press, 1950, pp. 407-422; see also Kurt Lewin, "Group Decision and Social Change," *Readings in Social Psychology,* third edition, New York: Henry Holt, 1958, pp. 197-211.

31. Bryce Ryan and Neal Gross, "The Diffusion of Hybrid Seed Corn in Two Iowa Communities," *Rural Sociology,* 8, (1942), pp. 15-24; George M. Beal and Joe M. Bohlen, *The Diffusion Process,* Special Report No. 18, Ames, Iowa: Agricultural Extension Service, Iowa State College (March, 1957); H.G. Barnett, *Innovation,* New York: McGraw-Hill, 1953.

32. Pierre Martineau, *Motivation in Advertising,* New York: McGraw-Hill, 1957.

33. Hortense Powdermaker, Ed., "Dynamics of Response to Mass Communications," *Mass Communications Seminar,* New York: Wenner-Gren Foundation, 1953, pp. 83-85.

34. Lazarsfeld, *op. cit.,* p. 466.

35. Betty Wang, "Folk Songs as a Means of Social Control," *Sociology and Social Research,* XIX (September-October, 1934), pp. 64-69; "Folk Songs as Regulators of Politics," *Ibid.,* XX (November-December, 1935), pp. 161-166.

36. W. Lloyd Warner and William E. Henry, "The Radio Daytime Serial: A Symbolic Analysis," *Reader in Public Opinion and Communication,* Glencoe, Ill.: The Free Press, 1950, pp. 423-437.

37. Hovland, Lumsdaine and Sheffield, *op. cit.*

38. Leon Festinger, Henry W. Riecken and Stanley Schachter, "When Prophecy Fails," *Reading in Social Psychology*, third edition, New York: Henry Holt, 1958, p. 162.

39. Inglis, *op. cit.*, p. 532.

40. The most recent works which imply that the mass media constitute a force for social control include: A. Inkeles, *Public Opinion in Soviet Russia: A Study in Mass Persuasion*, Cambridge: Harvard University Press, 1950; E. Hunter, *Brain Washing in Red China: The Calculated Destruction of Men's Minds*, New York: Vanguard, 1951; L. Lowenthal and N. Guterman, *Prophets of Deceit: A Study of the Techniques of the American Agitator*, New York: Harper, 1949; Siegfried Kracauer, *From Caligari to Hitler: A Psychological History of the German Film*, Princeton: Princeton University Press, 1947.

41. Richard T. LaPiere, *A Theory of Social Control*, New York: McGraw-Hill, 1954, p. 519.

42. *Loc. cit.*

43. LaPiere, *op. cit.*, p. 266.

44. *Ibid.*, p. 522.

45. Wilbur Schramm, "The Effects of Mass Communications," *Kappa Tau Alpha Yearbook*, Vol. 12 (1957-58), pp. 24-25; see also Joseph T. Klapper, *The Effects of Mass Communication*, Glencoe, Ill.: The Free Press, 1960.

46. Ibid., p. 26.

47. Elihu Katz, "Mass Communications Research and the Study of Popular Culture: An Editorial Note on a Possible Future For This Journal," *Studies in Public Communication*, No. 2, Summer, 1959, p. 3, Chicago: University of Chicago Press, 1959.